C000129231

'This thorough critique of recent thinking abou
Wales is apposite and timely. Barnes' analysis
would expect of a trained philosopher, but also engagea, pa………

He pays close attention to assumptions, argument and evidence in confronting what are often insufficiently self-critical – although very widely accepted – claims about what should constitute an educationally and ethically justified approach to RE in schools today. His criticisms are always interesting and often hit their targets.

No one should attempt to enter the debate over the "crisis in RE" without first facing the challenges posed in this well written, lively and thought-provoking book.'
– **Jeff Astley**, Honorary Professor in the Department of
Theology and Religion, and Professorial Fellow of St Chad's College,
Durham University, UK; Visiting Professor of Religious and
Spiritual Experience, Bishop Grosseteste University, Lincoln, UK;
Visiting Professor, York St John University, UK

'Barnes presents us with a timely, coherent and comprehensive critique of the present state of religious education. His book identifies the gaps to be addressed and is a very welcome contribution from a significant scholar in the field.'
– **James Arthur**, Deputy Pro-Vice-Chancellor for Staffing and
Professor of Education and Civic Engagement at the
University of Birmingham, UK; Director of the
Jubilee Centre for Character and Virtues

'In the context of current radical challenges to religious education in public schools, Barnes reflects on the fundamental issues involved. He does so with such profundity and wide horizon that his analyses yield valuable insights and stimulations far beyond the UK situation.'
– **Manfred L. Pirner**, holder of the chair of religious
education and director of the Research Unit for Public Religion and
Education (RUPRE) at the Friedrich-Alexander University
Erlangen-Nürnberg (FAU), Germany

CRISIS, CONTROVERSY AND THE FUTURE OF RELIGIOUS EDUCATION

Crisis, Controversy and the Future of Religious Education sets out to provide a much-needed critical examination of recent writings that consider and respond to the crisis in religious education and more widely to a crisis in non-confessional forms of religious education, wherever practised.

The book is critical, wide-ranging and provocative, giving attention to a range of responses, some limited to the particular situation of religious education in England and some of wider application, for example, that of the role and significance of human rights and that of the relevance of religious studies and theology to religious education. It engages with a variety of positions and with recent influential reports that make recommendations on the future direction of religious education. Constructively, it defends both confessional and non-confessional religious education and endorses the existing right of parental withdrawal. Controversially, it concludes that the case for including non-religious worldviews in religious education, and for the introduction of a statutory, 'objective' national religious education curriculum for all schools, are both unconvincing on educational, philosophical and evidential grounds.

Timely and captivating, this book is a must-read for religious and theological educators, RE advisers, classroom teachers, student teachers and those interested in the field of religious education.

L. Philip Barnes is Emeritus Reader in Religious and Theological Education, King's College London. He is the author of *Education, Religion and Diversity: Developing a New Model of Religious Education* (2014), also published by Routledge.

CRISIS, CONTROVERSY AND THE FUTURE OF RELIGIOUS EDUCATION

L. Philip Barnes

Routledge
Taylor & Francis Group

LONDON AND NEW YORK

First published 2020
by Routledge
2 Park Square, Milton Park, Abingdon, Oxon OX14 4RN

and by Routledge
52 Vanderbilt Avenue, New York, NY 10017

Routledge is an imprint of the Taylor & Francis Group, an informa business

© 2020 L. Philip Barnes

The right of L. Philip Barnes to be identified as author of this work has been asserted by him in accordance with sections 77 and 78 of the Copyright, Designs and Patents Act 1988.

All rights reserved. No part of this book may be reprinted or reproduced or utilised in any form or by any electronic, mechanical, or other means, now known or hereafter invented, including photocopying and recording, or in any information storage or retrieval system, without permission in writing from the publishers.

Trademark notice: Product or corporate names may be trademarks or registered trademarks, and are used only for identification and explanation without intent to infringe.

British Library Cataloguing in Publication Data
A catalogue record for this book is available from the British Library

Library of Congress Cataloging-in-Publication Data
A catalog record has been requested for this book

ISBN: 978-0-367-37337-5 (hbk)
ISBN: 978-0-367-37338-2 (pbk)
ISBN: 978-0-429-35318-5 (ebk)

Typeset in Bembo
by Taylor & Francis Books

Printed in the United Kingdom
by Henry Ling Limited

This book is dedicated to

Prof. Dr med. Salah-Eddin Al-Batran, Prof. Dr med. Elke Jäger, Prof. Dr med. Eckhart Weidmann, Dr med. Mohammad-Reza Rafiyan and the staff at Level 9, Krankenhaus Nordwest Hospital, Frankfurt,

to

Dr Suzanne McPherson, Dr Scott McCluskey and the staff in Ward C7, Antrim Area Hospital, Antrim,

to

Mr Barry McAree, Antrim Area Hospital, Antrim,

and to

Dr Sarah Lawless, Belfast City Hospital, Belfast.

CONTENTS

ACKNOWLEDGEMENTS

This book draws on previously published articles and essays:

Barnes, L. P. (1994) 'Rudolf Otto and the limits of religious description,' *Religious Studies, 30(2)*: 219–230.

Barnes, L. P. (2015) 'Humanism, non-religious worldviews and the future of religious education,' *Journal of Beliefs and Values, 36(1)*: 79–91.

Barnes, L. P. (2015) 'Religious studies, religious education and the aims of education,' *British Journal of Religious Education, 37(2)*: 195–206.

Barnes, L. P. (2016) 'Humanism, religious education and the former Archbishop of Canterbury,' *Theology, 19(1)*: 18–25.

Barnes, L. P. (2017) 'Democracy, political salvation and the future of religious education,' in M. Shanahan (ed.) *Does Religious Education Matter?* London: Routledge.

Barnes, L. P. (2018) 'Values, human rights and religious education: A critical analysis,' in J. Astley, L. J. Francis and D. W. Lankshear (eds) *Values, Human Rights and Religious Education: Contested grounds*. Oxford: Peter Lang.

Barnes, L. P. (2018) 'Public theology or religious studies? Deliberations on the basis of multifaith religious education,' in M. L. Pirner, J. Lähnemann, W. Haussmann, and S. Schwarz (eds) *Public Theology, Religious Diversity and Interreligious Learning*. London: Routledge.

ABOUT THE AUTHOR

Dr L. Philip Barnes is Emeritus Reader in Religious and Theological Education at King's College London. He has published widely on the theory and philosophy of religious education and in the related fields of theology and religious studies. He is author of *Education, Religion and Diversity: Developing a new model of religious education* (2014); co-author of *Religious Education: Educating for diversity* (2015) and one of the authors of the multi-authored work, *Does Religious Education Work? A multi-dimensional investigation* (2013); editor of *Learning to Teach Religious Education in the Secondary School: A companion to school experience* (2017) and of *Debates in Religious Education* (2011), and co-editor of *Education and Religion (Major Themes in Education)* (2016).

PREFACE

This book is occasioned by increasing recognition that religious education in England is in crisis, albeit its nature is interpreted in different ways. The writings and positions reviewed in what follows can all be regarded as responses to this crisis. In some respects my own contribution to this is opportunistic, as in my earlier book, *Education, Religion and Diversity: Developing a new model of religious education* (2014), I argued that current models ('paradigms') of British religious education were significantly flawed and were theoretically and practically incapable of contributing successfully to the aims appropriate to education in a pluralist, liberal, democratic state. If my analysis was correct it would only be a matter of time before the continuing failure of religious education in certain regards would become apparent and the term crisis appropriately used, though only if honesty prevailed. Some degree of honesty is now apparent, but a greater degree of candour and self-criticism (and perhaps even a deepening crisis) may still be needed to encourage religious educators to reassess some of their commitments and beliefs and from holding to deficient theories and ineffective practices.

Some of the material has been shared at conferences and presented in talks and lectures to various audiences. I am particularly grateful to Professor Manfred Pirner, of the University of Erlangen-Nuremberg, Germany, for opportunities to present material at the 11th (2013) and 12th (2016) International Nuremberg Forums on Religious Education and to Professor Abdulkader Tayob for inviting me to present the plenary address at a conference on religious education in Cape Town, South Africa, and giving me the opportunity to deliver a lecture at the University of Cape Town to students and staff of the Department of Religious Studies in 2018.

Finally, I would like to thank my family—my wife Sandra, and our children Andrew, Rachel and Christopher—for their support and encouragement over the past year, which as a result of (my) illness has been at times challenging, at times depressing and at times hopeful. I have been blessed in so many ways by their company and prayers. Companionship with my wife over 35 years of marriage has been the greatest gift and the greatest source of fulfilment in my life. Finally, I am grateful to Rachel for reading over and commenting on the final draft of this material: the sense of embarrassment over my mistakes and limitations in knowledge is tempered somewhat by the fact that a member of my own family has brought these to my attention first and allowed some remedial action to be taken before publication.

Easter Day, 2019

INTRODUCTION

Early in 2012 the Religious Education Council of England and Wales announced that it intended to conduct a review of religious education to complement the Government's review of the National Curriculum, which was initially planned in 2010—religious education is a statutory subject but not part of the National Curriculum, and consequently would not be included in the government's review. The subsequent report, entitled *Review of Religious Education in England*, published in October 2013, acknowledged there was a 'crisis' in the subject: 'The RE community has felt a sense of crisis despite government assurance' (7). Use of the term 'crisis' was already on the lips of religious educators. In December 2012, Mark Chater, then Director of Culham St Gabriel's Trust, which is an endowed charity dedicated to educational work in support of religious education, had earlier stated that 'RE has been hit by a crisis so profound that we are now fighting for ... the continued existence of our subject, ... the recognisable form in which it has evolved since 1944, is under threat.' Strong words indeed. He goes on to use the term crisis six times in a short web article of three and a half thousand words.[1] The language of crisis was quickly taken up and used by other organisations that represent religious education and by the media, and has continued to be used to describe the situation facing statutory religious education. In 2015 (1), an editorial in the *Journal of Beliefs and Values*, written by Stephen G. Parker, Rob Freathy and David Aldridge was headed: 'The future of Religious Education: *Crisis*, reform and iconoclasm' (my emphasis). It began: 'Against a backdrop of threat to the position and future of Religious Education in schools ...' and then went on to refer to two conferences that were intended to respond to the crisis and chart a future direction for the subject.

Until now, the language of crisis, when used of religious education, has been reserved and applied retrospectively to describe the shift from confessional to non-confessional religious education in the 1960s and 1970s. Historians see it as a corollary of the religious crisis of the 1960s, which represented a period of decisive change in British religious history when, among other things, church membership declined rapidly and there was a weakening of the processes by which Christian identity and knowledge of Christianity was passed on to the younger generation. For example, Hugh McLeod (2005: 205 and 220), in his influential article, 'The Religious Crisis of the 1960s', identified religious education as part of the larger religious crisis (as does Field 2017: 17). The historians of religious education, R. J. K. Freathy and S. G. Parker (2015: 6) have also asked recently whether the current state of crisis is a new phenomenon, and again draw a parallel between it and 'the alleged transitions that took place in the nature and purpose of RE in the late 1960s and early 1970s' (I am unsure why they refer to *alleged* transitions, as their subsequent review and argument is predicated on the assumption that transitions *did* occur and that 'crisis' is an appropriate designation). I conclude this opening flourish by quoting from a letter sent by the Very Reverend Dr John Hall (dated 20 December, 2018), Chairperson of the 'Commission on Religion Education' to the then Secretary of State for Education, Damian Hinds MP, upon receiving the news that the recommendations of the Commission's *Final Report: Religious Education and Worldviews: The way forward: A national plan for RE*, would not be acted upon by government. The term crisis is not used in this extract; though this may be because Dr Hall felt it has been overused and other equally negative terms are needed to underline the seriousness of the situation facing religious education.

> Thank you for your letter of 6th December responding to the Commission on Religious Education's final report 'Religion and Worldviews: the way forward.'
>
> While I am disappointed with your conclusion that now is not the time to begin the reforms of Religious Education (RE) that the Commission recommended, I take seriously your commitment not to legislate on the matter in this Parliament. Nonetheless, over the course of the two years of our work, *it was clear to me and my fellow commissioners that the situation for RE was extremely precarious and that without positive action from the Government the subject risked collapse in many schools. The current situation is in our view not sustainable and we would regard refusal to act at all as an abdication of responsibility* (my emphasis).

'[T]he situation for RE … [is] extremely precarious'; 'refusal to act at all … [is] an abdication of responsibility'; other terms used are 'collapse'; 'not sustainable.' These are certainly intemperate words; and possibly simply angry words.[2]

In *The Structure of Scientific Revolutions* Thomas Kuhn (1970) introduced the concept of a paradigm or model to refer to a set of beliefs, commitments and practices that gives overarching theoretical unity and coherence to the scientific enterprise and provides a rationale for its practice and the resources to achieve its aims. Kuhn also referred to a '*crisis*-state' in scientific practice (1970: 66–76). This is where there is an appreciation by those operating within a particular (scientific) paradigm that it is beset by challenges and problems. The crisis can be resolved in two contrasting ways: the first is to attempt to revise the original paradigm in the face of recalcitrant evidence or anomalies and seek its preservation in some form; the second is to admit that the problems are insurmountable within the terms of the current ruling paradigm and be open to the possibility that there may be a new disciplinary model that can accommodate the recalcitrant evidence and anomalies that the original paradigm cannot fully explain or resolve satisfactorily. In *Education, Religion and Diversity: Developing a new model of religious education* (2014), I took up Kuhn's concept of a paradigm and used it to illustrate the ways in which post-confessional religious education has been conformed to two different sets of theo-retical and practical commitments and beliefs: liberal and postmodern models of religious education. Both models were viewed as deficient. Both generate internal contradictions as well as being incapable of realising liberal educational aims. The inevitable result, I argued, in Kuhnian terms, is that modern religious education is in a state of crisis. That this is the case, is increasingly obvious, as is illustrated by the representative quotations used above. Naturally, recognition of a crisis has exercised the minds of religious educators and elicited a range of responses; it is with these that this book is concerned. Whether any of the options considered in subsequent chapters are capable of surmounting current weaknesses while offering resources to better serve the future direction of religious education is another matter. In other words, do they truly enable the subject to strike out in a new radical direction, or are they merely adding epicycles to existing models and attempting to keep alive frameworks that are ultimately incapable of meeting cur-rent educational needs?

The structure of the argument

Chapter 1 aims to identify the weaknesses in theory and practice that account for the contemporary crisis in English religious education. A focus on these is essential, for it is in terms of these that any suggested 'solutions' are to be judged as credible and realistic. Evidence is cited from a broad range of sources, from inspection reports to the findings of empirical research.

The following chapters deal with what can be regarded as responses to the cur-rent crisis. Some responses take this as their point of departure, whereas some do not, though all responses whether explicitly orientated to the current crisis and its resolution or not assume that there are weaknesses in religious education of a ser-ious sort that can be overcome. Chapter 2 reviews *Does Religious Education Have a Future?* (2013), by Mark Chater and Clive Erricker. This work pursues a bold and innovative political agenda for religious education that aspires to achieve a demo-cratic, anti-capitalist transformation of society that is both child-centred and liberative. Chapter 3 interacts closely with Cush and Robinson's (2014) call for a new dialogue between developments in religious studies and religious education. This is used as a springboard to a wider discussion of the historical influence of religious studies on religious education, which in turn leads to a more critical account of this influence than that appreciated by them. The chapter concludes with a positive account of how theology can contribute to the practice of non-confessional religious education. Chapter 4 explores a further broad theme that has been increasingly prominent in the writing of religious educators, namely that rights or a human rights framework ought to set the agenda in the future.

The next four chapters focus on explicit responses to the contemporary crisis in religious education. Chapters 5 and 6 discuss different justifications and considerations that are adduced in favour of broadening the subject of religious education to include non-religious, secular worldviews, a view commonly voiced but rarely defended with any thoroughness or rigour: attention focuses on Humanism but not to the exclusion of other worldviews. There is much to review and to assess, as broadening the subject in this way raises a range of issues. Chapter 5 considers the Humanist case for the inclusion of Humanism in the curriculum, appeals to justice and to inclusion and toleration. Chapter 6 considers David Aldridge's case for the inclusion of worldviews in religious education, as well as his critique of an earlier statement of my opposition to broadening the subject in this way. Attention is also given to the issue of hermeneutics and its relevance to determining the proper role and place for worldviews in religious education. This is followed by a short discussion of the difference between religions and worldviews. The chapter concludes with a summary account of an interesting, recent, cautionary contribution on the place of worldviews in religious education by one of Germany's foremost religious educators, Friedrich Schweitzer.

Chapter 7 attends to 'a reforming pamphlet', *A New Settlement: Religion and belief in schools*, (both in its original and revised form) produced by the former Labour Education Secretary Charles Clarke and Professor Linda Woodhead of Lancaster University. Its argument is too wide ranging to consider in its entirety, so discussion centres around its call for a new *statutory national* Framework, for the most part modelled on the currently existing and influential 2004 (non-statutory) Framework. Attention shifts in Chapter 8 to discussion of the parental right of withdrawal of their children from religious education. This chapter covers more topics than one might have anticipated, as it provides an historical account of the emergence of the original right, takes account of and assesses two relevant empirical studies, and then after identifying other sources that call for relinquishing the right of withdrawal, focuses on the argument as developed in Baroness Butler-Sloss's report *Living with Difference: Community, diversity and the common good* (2015). Although Butler-Sloss's 'argument' is terse and under-developed, she does raise important issues relating to faith schools, indoctrination, inclusion, religious freedom and the nature of what she assumes to be an objective curriculum.

The discussion broadens out again in Chapter 9 to consider the more philosophical and intellectual portrait of religious education and its current travail provided by Liam Gearon. His analysis provides a longer historical and critical perspective on religious education that problematises the challenge of religion to education, which essentially, he believes, has to do with commitment to God, a commitment that was once widely shared in society and accorded importance, but which is now often 'culturally despised' and relegated to the periphery of life. At the periphery, what role can religion command in public institutions such as schools? Although the focus in this book has been on responses to identified weaknesses in English religious education, the material covered in Chapter 10 conceptualises the material covered in earlier chapters in a different way, that is, as providing an overview of recent contributions and writings within the field of religious education by some of its most prominent advocates. The question that then arises is: What does this overview reveal about the research priorities and interests of religious educators and about the assumptions and the values that guide their research and theorising? The answer does not make for 'comfortable' reading.

The material covered and the positions considered may be of wider interest. The travail of non-confessional religious education is not confined to Britain. Systems of religious education in other countries have their own distinctive forms, but there are similarities and shared convictions and commitments among non-confessional versions of religious education, wherever practised. Strategies and policies proposed in Britain have analogues elsewhere; and common weaknesses are not impossible. Some of the strategies and some of the responses to identified weaknesses in British religious education have been influential elsewhere and a consideration of them in an English context may bring a different perspective to their assessment and eva-luation. For example, the appeal to increase the role and significance of human rights in religious education is widely canvassed on the international stage, as is the relevance of religious studies to religious education.

Assumptions, evidence and argument

From what I have said it ought to be clear that close attention is given to assumptions, evidence and arguments in what follows, and this in turn necessitates the extensive use of quotations and quite 'close-grained' discussion of ideas and positions. There needs to be sensitivity to nuances of meaning and inflection in arguments and a desire to do justice to the positions of others, so that what others say is fairly and honestly represented. Some, no doubt, will find this focus tedious and not in keeping with the less argumentative style of many religious educators. It is important, however, not to misrepresent the positions of those analysed and criticised, and to achieve this, one must be attentive to what is said and this, in turn, requires the extensive use of quotations. All of us are properly concerned when our arguments and conclusions are summarily dismissed without discussion, perhaps on the basis that the critic knows better and does not need to justify his or her criticism. An observation to emerge from my review of recent publications, particularly those that focus most explicitly on what is termed the 'current crisis', is that the same arguments and 'moves' keep reappearing. There is not much originality: a set of assumptions is often used to frame and control debates and outcomes, which is never questioned or interrogated.

It is precisely because there is such an overlap of arguments and positions between sources that it is sometimes difficult to demarcate the contents of one chapter from another. The same considerations and the same criticisms could be advanced on a serial basis in a number of chapters. To try to alleviate this criticism an attempt is made within a chapter to address a definite subject or confine discussion to a small group of subjects or themes, and to the extent to which this is possible, to consider these in isolation from other subjects that receive attention in other chapters. Overlapping content in chapters, nevertheless remains to some extent. This means that in some cases, certain positions, the contents of some sources or their supporting arguments are referenced and discussed in different chapters. It may be necessary to bring these different discussions together to gain a full interpretation and assessment of some particular source, theme or group of themes. Interacting with the ideas of others can be a 'messy' business, particularly if what is argued is not easily dissected or divorced from other considerations.

The author's voice is not absent in all writing, including academic writing. There is no Archimedean point to view the world of religious education. For the most part, however, I have resisted reinterpreting responses to the current crisis in terms of my earlier analysis of the travail of English post-confessional religious education and to trying to show that where we are now is not the result of a few hasty policy decisions made in the last 10 or so years (a popular response) but is the result of historically extended educational, ideological and religious influences. Nevertheless, those who read or have read my *Education, Religion and Diversity: Developing a new model of religious education* (2014) will know the nature of the critical perspective that is brought to bear on things. Some limited attention is given to my earlier argument in Chapter 1 and then it drops out of the picture in favour of a more dispassionate analytical approach with wider appeal.

Finally, this current book is intended as the second study of a planned trilogy on religious education. In *Education, Religion and Diversity: Developing a new model of religious education* (2014) I developed a theoretical framework to interpret and explain the vicissitudes, developments and weaknesses of post-confessional religious education (from the 1970s onwards) in England chiefly—and, in part, in Britain more widely. This current book considers more recent developments from the increasingly acknowledged perception that (non-confessional) religious education is experiencing a crisis of identity and is uncertain about which future direction and which theoretical commitments to pursue in order to secure entirely proper liberal educational aims. The subject has failed to realise these aims; and this is beginning to be recognised by all but the most uncritical party member of the 'religious education establishment'—by which is meant those associations and representative bodies that mediate the 'positive contribution' of religious education to the public, the media, the churches, the religious communities and to the political establishment. *Education, Religion and Diversity: Developing a new model of religious education* (2014) argued that religious education's weaknesses are historically deep rooted and systemic and that these will inevitably become more manifest (as I believe they are now). In a final book I hope to 'close the circle' and consider the role and place of religious education in 'schools with a religious character' (to adopt the terminology used in legislation as a more neutral designation of 'faith schools'); thus I will have considered the nature and character of religious education in schools that are 'secular' in orientation, i.e. in the sense of eschewing any form of religious nurture, and those that are religious in orientation and/or pursue some form of religious nurture. It will address such questions as: Is religious nurture appropriate in schools that are entirely or almost entirely funded by the modern liberal democratic state? If so, what form ought religious nurture to take and what compromises may be necessary to secure its educational legitimacy?

Conventions

It has recently become fashionable in educational literature to refer to those who attend schools as students. My initial reaction was to adopt this usage and follow the dictates of fashion and political correctness, least by not doing so my arguments may not get a fair hearing on account of their presumed offence. Increasing reflection, however, has convinced me otherwise, for the reason that use of the term pupils rather than students has an advantage in relation to religious education, as it more naturally denotes those of school age rather than those who are older and attend university. At certain points in my argument it is important to be reminded that the subjects of religious education in schools are not fully developed cognitively and psychologically; a point that may be overlooked when the term students is used because of its association with older tertiary level students.

I use the term religious education to denote the curriculum subject that is devoted to the study of religion. Other titles for the subject are proposed by some of the contributions considered—the Commission on Religious Education proposes 'Religion and worldviews' (2018: 1) and Clarke and Woodhead prefer 'Religion, beliefs and values' (2018: 4). Neither of which in my view commands strong support, for both practical and theoretical reasons. In any case the title religious education has the advantage of economy of expression and of directing readers to a fairly stable tradition of reflection upon the educational role of religion in schools.

The term 'British' religious education is used on occasions to draw attention to ideas and influences that are common across religious education in the three nations of England, Scotland and Wales. At no stage is credence given to the idea that religious education is uniform across Britain: it is acknowledged that there are differences as well as similarities between religious education in England, Scotland and Wales.

Finally, there are different types of state funded schools in England, which are distinguished legally from each other. The type of school in some cases dictates the form of religious education that is offered, for example, 'community' schools must follow the local Agreed Syllabus; other types of school, depending on their foundation status, may or may not have to follow the locally agreed, non-confessional syllabus. It is not necessary for our purposes to list and explain all the different types of schools and the factors that are relevant to the form of religious education practised. In the interest of relevance a straightforward distinction is drawn between confessional religious education and non-confessional religious education; this distinction correlates in turn to the distinction between faith schools (legally defined as 'schools of a religious character') and (what I refer to as) non-religious schools or on occasions as 'secular schools.'[3]

Notes

1 See http://www.reonline.org.uk/news/whats-worth-fighting-for-in-re (accessed 1 March 2019).
2 A copy of the full letter is available at https://www.commissiononre.org.uk/comm ission-chair-responds-to-secretary-of-state/ (accessed 1 March 2019).
3 See https://humanism.org.uk/wp-content/uploads/schools-with-a-religious-character.pdf (accessed 22 May 2019) for a clear account of the different forms of religious education that are appropriate to different types of school.

1

WHAT IS WRONG WITH RELIGIOUS EDUCATION?

In a recently published retrospective review of religious education policy, Barbara Wintersgill and Ian Brine, both former Her Majesty's Inspectors (HMIs) of religious education nationally, claimed that 1993–2010 was a 'golden age for RE' (2016: 264), characterised by a partnership between local and national bodies. They lament, however, that its 'confusion of purpose and statutory oddness were not resolved in these good years'. In their view the closure of the Qualifications and Curriculum Development Authority (QCDA), announced in 2010 (following the formation of a Conservative-Liberal Democratic Coalition Government) brought about the demise of one of the main agencies that gave 'life support' (2016: 272) to religious education, and according to them, contributed significantly to the current crisis.[1] This, together with other 'reforms' (considered below) initiated by a newly elected majority Conservative Government in 2015, under David Cameron, convince Wintersgill and Brine (2016: 275) that '[m]any RE teachers, lecturers and consultants fear that the changes in education and the loss of government support... have left RE irrevocably weakened'.

At this stage I am less interested in the reasons for the current crisis than the idea that the period between 1993 and 2010 constituted a 'golden age' for religious education, as affirmed by Wintersgill and Brine. The image of a 'golden age' is indebted to Greek mythology and symbolises a perfect, early period of humanity when laws were unnecessary as justice and fraternity among all prevailed, including relationships between humanity and the gods. That there was no golden age in reality, hardly needs stating. It is a myth that endures (Garden of Eden is a variation on the same theme); one that was useful when first written and one that continues to be useful when adopted in other contexts for a variety of social, religious, and political purposes. Interestingly, Barbara Wintersgill held a senior position (1993–1997) in religious education at the School Curriculum and Assessment Authority (SCAA), during the period at the beginning of the golden age (SCAA later became the

Qualification and Curriculum Authority and latterly, before disbandment, the Qualifications and Curriculum Development Authority). In 1997, she was appointed by the Office for Standards in Education (Ofsted) as HMI and Specialist Subject Adviser for RE, a position from which she retired in 2005. Alan Brine became an Ofsted HMI in 2001 and he was a National Adviser for RE up to 2012. This means that the golden age of which Wintersgill and Brine speak, for the most part, coincided with the period when both were in highly important national positions that initiated and influenced policy and practice in religious education. All golden ages come to an end, just as in Greek mythology, Hesiod's golden age gave way to a silver age: the Book of Genesis recounts how Adam and Eve were ejected from the Garden of Eden after 'the Fall'. This is the narrative of Wintersgill and Brine: golden age—fall. On their interpretation the crisis in religious education is recent and chiefly political, due to clumsy reforms initiated by the Conservative Party in government. There is a common interpretation. The Religious Education Council of England and Wales has also lent support to it. Like Wintersgill and Brine, it has a vested interest in accrediting the end of the existence of a golden age in religious education to 2010, because up to this point it was extolling the strengths of the subject and commending an English model of religious education to religious educators in other national contexts (see Barnes 2014: 10–11).

There may be some plausibility to the idea that the current crisis relates to recent events and decisions, though it is more probable on the basis of the evidence (see below) that recent events have exacerbated an already serious situation, or revealed something that was the case for a very long time but for 'political' (ideological) reasons was expediently overlooked. The problem with the recent golden age/fall narrative is that it is too convenient. It is not sufficiently penetrating intellectually, and it consigns weaknesses in religious education to recent decisions and developments and effectively closes off critical enquiries and debate about long term systemic weaknesses and any discussion of what or who was responsible historically.

This chapter aims to take a longer, more penetrating view and attempts to identify the current weaknesses in religious education and ascertain something of their cause and location. It begins with a short review of the weaknesses identified by those who hold to (what I have termed) the golden age/fall interpretation—consistent with what is said above, this will focus on recent events and decisions that are felt to detract significantly from the success and effectiveness of religious education. There is plausibility here, however limited it is as an adequately framed and overall convincing position to hold. Three further sources of information are then drawn upon. First, attention is given to Office for Standards in Education (Ofsted) Reports, which can be regarded as reliable guides to practice in the classroom, complemented by professional and accurate analysis. Second, attention is given to the findings of a 3-year research project, entitled *Does Religious Education Work?*, funded jointly by the Arts and Humanities Research Council and the Economic and Social Research Council. Finally, some limited attention is given to correlating what is said in this context to what is argued in my earlier analysis and interpretation, *Education, Religion and Diversity: Developing a new model of religious education* (2014).

Weaknesses as recently perceived

In 2013 the Religious Education Council of England and Wales conducted 'A Review of Religious Education in England', in part to complement the new Lib-Dem, Conservative government's review of the national curriculum for schools in England, undertaken by the Department for Education (DfE) from January 2011 to July 2013. As stated in the Introduction to the Review document (RECEW 2013: 7–8):

> Beyond the need for parity, a wider set of challenges for RE has arisen in the past three years, mainly as the result of large-scale changes in education made by the Coalition government. These include the introduction of the English Baccalaureate, towards whose achievement GCSE Religious Studies cannot be counted, significant reforms of GCSE and A Level qualifications, the extension of the academies programme and introduction of free schools, all of which have implications for the way in which RE and its curriculum are decided and supported. Local authority cuts have also led to the reduction of local support for RE, and the number of new trainee teachers has been slashed. The total number of GCSE Religious Studies entries has started to decline after many years of growth.
>
> The RE community has felt a sense of crisis despite government assurance. This assurance has been challenged by many stakeholders in RE and the threats to RE confirmed in a report of the RE All Party Parliamentary Group (APPG), *RE: The Truth Unmasked* in 2013.
>
> [...] Furthermore, successive triennial Ofsted reports for RE have argued, and the APPG inquiry has confirmed, that there are significant and well-founded concerns about the uneven quality of learning and teaching in RE across the country.

A few sentences are necessary to clarify the meaning of the reference to the APPG inquiry. APPG stands for All Party Parliamentary Group (on religious education), which in 2013 conducted its own inquiry into the 'Supply of and Support for Religious Education Teachers'. It found that too many religious education lessons are taught by non-specialists. The Inquiry also revealed, among other things, that there was often inadequate access by teachers to Continuing Professional Development (APPG Inquiry 2013: 26–36). It concluded (2013: 4) that 'many teachers struggle to reach the levels of subject competence expected in the DfE's own teaching standards'.

It would be unwise to underestimate the importance of this evidence, yet it is difficult to assign some of the weaknesses identified to recent influences and decisions, i.e. post-2010 influences, and those that can be assigned to recent times do not seem nearly as serious as those that are ongoing and whose presence have, for the most part, accompanied the subject from the 1970s or 1980s onwards. For example, that too many religious education lessons in schools are taught by non-specialists has been a constant refrain of the Religious Education Council for decades, and rightly so; its position, moreover, has been backed up with evidence and statistics (see NATRE 2017: 29–36). In doing this it has performed an invaluable service to religious education, even if little seems to change. Equally the complaint that religious education teachers are often those most deprived of support for Continuing Professional Development is also a perennial criticism. The observation (APPG Inquiry 2013: 4) that 'many teachers struggle to reach the levels of subject competence expected in the DfE's own teaching standards' is obviously extremely serious, though the major implications here may be for those engaged in the training of religious education teachers, which has not changed significantly over recent years. The most serious weakness to which the Religious Education Review (RECEW 2013: 8) refers is that of the 'uneven quality of learning and teaching in RE across the country', yet even this is not a recent complaint but one that goes back decades. In 1991 Stephen Orchard, General Secretary of the Christian Education Movement, conducted an analysis of HMI from Reports 1985–1988 on religious education. Here are some of his findings (Orchard 1991: 16):

> There were 91 schools where it is possible to categorize the HMI report as critical or commendatory towards the religious education provision. Of these only 38 are commendatory and 53 critical.

After commenting on the high degree of non-provision revealed in the reports, he continues (1991:19–20):

> Where religious education is included in the curriculum for all pupils the standard may be poor. Pupils are given unimaginative and repetitive lessons, with no attempt at development of the subject or to differentiate content and method according to the ability of the pupils. This amounted to a further 60 schools.
>
> On this analysis more than half of the schools attempting to provide religious education across the curriculum are failing at the point of professional competence in teaching.
>
> [...] more rigorous planning and schemes of work for religious education were needed in most schools.

Orchard conducted the same exercise some years later, this time looking at reports from 1989–1991. Little had changed; again significant evidence (Orchard 1993: 27 and 24) of 'poor teaching and unbalanced content' and 'half the teenagers at school will have no RE or RE of a very poor quality'. In other words, the 'uneven quality of learning and teaching in RE across the country' to which the RE Council Review refers is nothing new. There are no further reviews of inspection reports of this nature available from the 1990s from which to draw a more complete picture. Perhaps there ought to have been talk of a crisis all those years ago, but there wasn't! 1994, however, did see the publication of *Religious Education in the Secondary School: Prospects for religious literacy*, by Andrew Wright. This was one of the first books both to identify serious weaknesses in post-confessional religious education in England and to begin to develop a theoretical framework to explain how and why these were occurring. In his view liberal theological beliefs that looked to a common, undogmatic spirituality lay behind much that was 'wrong' with religious education theorising and practice. The book covers a wide range of topics within a relatively small number of pages, and as it was intended for students and teachers alike, it is highly accessible. Nevertheless, it does provide evidence that religious education was not nearly as successful or effective in the 1990s as many now presume it to have been (a theme developed in Wright 2000, 2004 and 2007).

What is regarded as having brought about the post-2010 crisis in religious education? The RE Council Review (2013: 7 and quoted above) refers to the introduction of the English Baccalaureate, from which achievement in GCSE Religious Studies is excluded, significant reforms of GCSE and A Level qualifications (reforms that few religious educators question), and the extension of the academies programme and introduction of free schools, (both of which are required to teach religious education)—academies and free schools 'without a religious designation' are free within certain limits to construct their own religious education syllabus, though they may choose to follow the local agreed syllabus and it may be this freedom that some more 'centrally minded' religious educators dislike. The Religious Education Council Review also refers to the reduction of local support for religious education (this may be true for other subjects as well), and to reductions in the number of new trainee religious education teachers (by all accounts now bursaries for religious education have been reinstated, this is no longer the case). Finally, the Review records that the total number of GCSE Religious Studies entries has started to decline after many years of growth. The introduction of the English Baccalaureate probably accounts for this as religious education/studies is not included in the list of subjects that contribute to it: religious education remains compulsory for all students, nevertheless. What the Review does not record, in this time of 'crisis', is that in 2016 religious studies in England and Wales had the highest number of entries since 2002; 284,057,[2] although there was a drop in 2017 (England and Wales) and in England in 2018 (to 229,189)[3]: when one compares the entries in GCSE religious studies with the entries for the English Baccalaureate (2018), religious studies had more entries in 2018 than nine of the 15 EBacc subjects.[4]

Where am I going with these observations? I am not arguing that there is no crisis. There is. Yet the significant 'markers' of crisis and underperformance, that is, the extent to which the subject has failed to provide religious knowledge at any great depth and a sophisticated understanding of religions, while relating religious content to the interests and *Lebenswelt* of students and contributing to their personal development, have been well known and documented over a long period of time. What our discussion reveals is that what has prompted talk of a crisis by professional groups representing religious education and religious educators *at this time* has probably more to do with what is perceived as a recent loss of status, rather than the enduring and uneven quality of learning and teaching, which has long existed.

Loss of status has resulted from the exclusion of religious education from the English Baccalaureate, from schools failing to provide religious education at different key stages, from the possibility of reduced numbers pursuing the subject at GCSE, which some argue will mean there will be even less need in the future for qualified specialist teachers, and from the removal of GCSE Short Courses from school performance measures (see Commission on Religious Education 2018: 10). Certainly, those schools that do not fulfil the law in their provision ought to be compelled to do so (see NATRE 2017: 8): the law is in place and what is needed is effective monitoring and enforcement.

The features listed above are concerned with the formal and not material aspects of religious education. This is my point. That fewer pupils pursue the subject to (external) examination level, that the EBacc continues without giving recognition to religious education/studies, and that the GCSE Short Course no longer contributes to school performance statistics—these reduce the status of religious education but not its educational value. Too many spokespersons for religious education seem to equate any loss of formal status for the subject with its educational relevance and effectiveness. What ought to be focusing the minds of reviews and commissions is the quality of teaching and learning, i.e. the material aspects of religious education. Presumably, the contributors to these various documents will voice the opinion that their recommendations, while for the most part framing their talk of crisis in formal terms, do consider material issues and make recommendations about the material content of religious education. This is the case, but what is necessary is that attention and justification is given to the ways in which new material proposals, such as enlarging the curriculum to a range of non-religious worldviews, will actually overcome current weakness in teaching and learning. There must be a correlation between proposed new content and identified weaknesses and some rationale given for why current weaknesses cannot be overcome within the terms of existing content and why an enlarged or revised content base is required. This is an issue to which we shall return.

Why is there *currently* talk of a crisis in religious education? Part of the inspiration for use of the language of crisis owes something to the way in which the main associations that represent religious education, the Religious Education Council and other associations, have felt marginalised politically since 2010 and the defeat of New Labour, with the subsequent closure of the Qualifications and Curriculum Development Authority. Prior to 2010 religious education associations enjoyed privileged access to government and to curriculum bodies such as the QCDA and earlier to the National Curriculum Council. Cordial relationships of influence and power sharing had been established and these were lost upon the formation of a Liberal-Conservative Coalition government. The fact that it is these associations that are in the vanguard of speaking of a crisis in religious education lends support to the contention that it is their loss of influence that has moved them to speak in these terms, though other factors and influences are relevant.

Ofsted reports

Between 2007 and 2013 The Office for Standards in Education (Ofsted) produced three reports that evaluated the strengths and weaknesses of religious education in primary and secondary schools and discussed the key issues at the centre of religious education. The reports are based principally on evidence from visits to both primary and secondary schools in England. The sample of schools typically represented a cross-section, including voluntary controlled schools, but did not include voluntary aided schools, for which there are separate inspection arrangements. Such reports ought to be regarded as informative and authoritative, based as they are on what is observed by HMIs in classrooms and in detailed consideration of teaching and learning support materials. The reports are reasonably comprehensive and on occasions state similar things about the same issues: they are also accessible on the web, which means we can be selective in this context and confine what is said to the main points, which is that weaknesses in religious education of a serious nature have long been recognised, even if talk of a crisis is of recent usage. Extensive use will be made of quotations to allow the findings of the reports to speak for themselves.

Making Sense of Religion *(2007)*

The first report to be considered is *Making Sense of Religion: A report on religious education in schools and the impact of locally agreed syllabuses* (2007), which draws on evidence about religious education from whole-school inspections over the period 2001 to 2006, that is, from the golden age of religious education, according to Wintersgill and Brine.

The following statements are drawn from the Executive Summary (2007: quoting extracts from 5–7).

> The past few years have seen an overall improvement in RE. Much greater consensus exists about the nature and purpose of the subject, reflected in the publication of the Framework in 2004. Fewer schools fail to meet the statutory requirement to teach RE and in many schools the profile of RE is positive. Although there is some very good practice, including high quality teaching, standards overall are not high enough and there are wide variations in the quality of provision. Achievement by pupils in RE has improved over the past five years but remains very inconsistent.
>
> At its best, RE equips pupils very well to consider issues of community cohesion, diversity and religious understanding.
>
> Despite these improvements, important weaknesses remain. Many locally agreed syllabuses for RE still do not define progression in the subject clearly enough and therefore do not provide a secure basis for effective teaching and learning, curriculum planning and assessment. Because assessment is often weak, subject leaders do not have enough reliable evidence about pupils' progress and are not able to analyse strengths and identify priorities for improvement.

There are fifteen 'Key findings', of which two only need be quoted:

Pupils' achievement at Key Stage 3 is very inconsistent. In 2004/05 it was good or better in 61% of schools and satisfactory in 31% of schools. More recent survey visits have found achievements in RE to be good or better in only four out of 10 schools and satisfactory in about half of schools.
Aspects of teaching, assessment, curriculum and leadership and management are not good enough in many secondary schools. Too much teaching at Key Stage 3 is unchallenging. Serious weaknesses remain widespread in the way that levels of attainment are used in planning and assessment.

The report also refers to improvements both in pupils' achievement in RE in primary schools over the period between 2001/02 and 2005/06 and in the 'leadership and management of RE' and to the fact that national strategies on religious education in primary schools have been largely positive.

Transforming Religious Education *(2010)*

The 2010 report, *Transforming Religious Education*, is based on evidence from visits to 94 primary and 89 secondary schools in England between 2006 and 2009. Here are a few extracts from the Executive Summary (2010: 4–6):

There is an urgent need to review the way in which the subject is supported at a number of levels. Among the questions to be considered are: whether the current statutory arrangements for the local determination of the RE curriculum are effective; whether there is sufficient clarity about what constitutes learning in RE and how pupil progress can be measured; and whether the provision for professional development in RE is adequate.

The quality of RE in the sample of primary schools was broadly the same as that reported in 2007 and not enough was of good quality. In schools where achievement was satisfactory, several key weaknesses were common which inhibited pupils' learning. Most notably, the pattern of curriculum delivery of the subject often limited the opportunities for sustained learning in RE. Schools visited took the subject seriously but, in too many cases, teachers lacked the knowledge and confidence to plan and teach high quality RE lessons.

The quality of RE in the secondary schools visited was worse than in the schools involved in the 2007 survey. The proportion of schools where RE was inadequate was considerably higher than previously. Among the factors which detracted from the quality of the provision were the impact on RE of the recent changes to the wider curriculum, particularly at Key Stage 3, and weaknesses in the quality of learning in much of the provision for the short course GCSE in religious studies.

As in 2007 there are 15 'Key findings': three of which are:

There is uncertainty among many teachers of RE about what they are trying to achieve in the subject resulting in a lack of well-structured and sequenced teaching and learning, substantial weaknesses in the quality of assessment and a limited use of higher order thinking skills to promote greater challenge.

Where RE was most effective, it used a range of enquiry skills such as investigation, interpretation, analysis, evaluation and reflection. However, this use is not yet defined clearly enough or integrated effectively within guidance to schools and, as a result, is not embedded sufficiently into classroom practice.

There were a number of specific weaknesses in the teaching about Christianity. Many primary and secondary schools visited did not pay sufficient attention to the progressive and systematic investigation of the core beliefs of Christianity.

Religious Education: Realising the potential *(2013)*

This report draws on a wide sample of evidence from 185 schools visited between September 2009 and July 2012. It also draws on evidence from a telephone survey of a further 30 schools, examination results, other reports published by Ofsted, extended discussions with teachers, members of standing advisory councils on religious education and other religious education professionals, and wider surveys carried out by professional associations for religious education. It begins (2013: 4–7) on a positive note and then returns to familiar negative themes.

> At its best, it [religious education] is intellectually challenging and personally enriching. It helps young people develop beliefs and values, and promotes the virtues of respect and empathy, which are important in our diverse society. It fosters civilised debate and reasoned argument, and helps pupils to understand the place of religion and belief in the modern world.
>
> [...] evidence from the majority of schools visited for this survey shows that the subject's potential is still not being realised fully. Many pupils leave school with scant subject knowledge and understanding. Moreover, RE teaching often fails to challenge and extend pupils' ability to explore fundamental questions about human life, religion and belief.
>
> The structures that underpin the local determination of the RE curriculum have failed to keep pace with changes in the wider educational world. As a result, many local authorities are struggling to fulfil their responsibility to promote high-quality religious education. In addition, other changes to education policy, such as the introduction in 2010 of the English Baccalaureate (the EBacc), have led to a decline in RE provision in some schools.

The report then helpfully identifies 'eight major areas of concern' (2013: 40): low standards, weak teaching, problems in developing a curriculum for religious education, confusion about the purpose of religious education, weak leadership and management, weaknesses in examination provision at Key Stage 4, gaps in training, and finally the impact of recent changes in education policy. In relation to low standards, the report (2013: 9) has this to say about the teaching of Christianity:

> The 2010 report highlighted the concern that too many pupils were leaving school with a very limited understanding of Christianity. Many of the schools visited for the previous report 'did not pay sufficient attention to the progressive and systematic investigation of the core beliefs of Christianity'. The development of this understanding remains one of the weakest aspects of achievement. The current survey included a specific focus on the teaching of Christianity in 30 of the primary schools inspected, and the evidence suggests this is still a major concern. Inspectors judged pupils' knowledge and understanding of Christianity to be good or outstanding in only five of the schools. It was judged to be inadequate in 10 of them, making teaching about Christianity one of the weakest aspects of RE provision.

In light of these reports it is difficult to maintain that there ever was a golden age of religious education. One limitation of the reports is that they represent a certain inspectorial way of looking at religious education. There is no attempt to consider the importance and effect of historically extended influences over religious education or to ascertain the role that different theoretical understandings play in conditioning/determining the success of learning and teaching and to the extent to which they facilitate or frustrate the fulfilment of the stated aims of the subject.

The *Does Religious Education Work?* research project

This section summarises the findings of a 3-year research project, to which I contributed, entitled *Does Religious Education Work?* The main findings were published as a book with the same title as the original research project. It constitutes one of the most (if not the most) extensive and sustained research project to investigate the 'workings' of religious education. The overall aim was to understand the particular and peculiar nature of religious education in different part of the United Kingdom, to diagnose the challenges facing contemporary religious education and to offer suggestions for future planning and policy. The research generated a wealth of data and results, which drew on a combination of policy work, ethnography, Delphi methods, Actor Network Theory, questionnaires, textual analysis, as well as theological and philosophical insights. What is summarised here provides an inadequate and selective account of the findings that seem (to me) most relevant to current concerns. For ease of comprehension and economy of space the findings will be set out as bullet points: the relevant page references in the book will direct those who desire greater detail about the points summarised.

- At the initiatory two-day Delphic Seminar the invited experts, who represented a wide cross-section of religious educators, engaged in different capacities in schools, support agencies, teacher training and organisations, were more preoccupied by policy matters than research findings (2013: 5).
- Quite a number of teachers observed in classroom situations felt uneasy talking about the transcendent aspects or 'other-worldly' aspects of religions: 'Steeped as many appear to be in the discourse of secular relativism' (2013: 37–39; quoting from 39).
- There was a strong tendency for teachers to stress the ethical aspects of religions over their religious aspects (2013: 40).
- Too many expectations of what religious education can achieve and to the 'concerns and anxieties' to which it can contribute (2013: 41–45).
- Teacher's interpretations of the theological and doctrinal claims of a particular religion or tradition appear sometimes to have little connection to official explanations or to the interpretations and explanations upheld by those communities themselves. 'Equally, some treatments of religion offered formulaic, superficial and anodyne accounts of a tradition' (2013: 46–47; quoting from 47).
- Despite claims to the contrary there was little evidence of a critical element in religious education (2013: 48–49).
- Many of the current attempts to justify religious education at national levels serve to facilitate 'civil religion' imprinted with non-religious values (2013: 87–95).
- 'The tendency of government guidance, and justifications from professional RE organizations themselves, [is] to promote instrumental rationales for the study of RE, they [a number of those that participated in the Delphi discussions] contended, [this has] led to misrepresentations of religion and a bland curriculum for tolerance' (2013: 119).
- There was a desire in many cases to avoid (in the name of 'respect') comparisons between religions (2013: 121).
- '[O]ften in classrooms across quite different schools, serving quite distinctive community ecologies, students are introduced to concepts and ideas, practices and claims, that are superficially descriptive and offer no particular insight into the theological, philosophical or ethical claims of particular religious traditions' (2013: 123).
- Perhaps the most powerful influence on the teachers in our study was the increasing demand on religious education to act as the 'catch all' for interventions, ranging from community cohesion to healthy eating (2013: 177).
- The impression is often given that there is nothing to 'learn in the subject since everyone is entitled to his or her opinion' (2013: 184–185).
- Responses by students to the question, 'Do you believe your school has helped you get along better with members of other religious groups?' showed that students in denominational schools were 'significantly more likely' to respond positively than students in 'diverse schools' (2013: 208).
- 20 per cent of students believe themselves to spend quite a lot of time 'watching videos' (2013: 214).
- Minimal evidence of the use of primary religious texts (2013: 221).

- Much religious education fails to locate to religious ideas in their religious and discursive context (2013: 224).
- Students seem to be invited to construct their own version of religion that embraces their spirituality while little attention is paid 'to the linguistic and conceptual demands of the geneaologically (*sic*) rich traditions of religious systems, and the otherness that they embody' (2013: 226).

The strength of those observations and identified weaknesses is that they are almost exclusively focused on classroom practice, i.e. the material and not the formal aspects of religious education. They are not concerned with how religious education teachers and associations that represent the subject view their status on the basis of external criteria, say whether religious education receives sufficient funding or whether it is excluded from the EBacc and then chiefly on these observations speak of a crisis. The evidence adduced by the *Does Religious Education Work?* project shows that the crisis is real enough and real for internal reasons that focus on teaching and learning.

Education, religion and diversity

In *Education, Religion and Diversity: Developing a new model of religious education* (2014), I drew on and extended Thomas Kuhn's account of how one conceptual paradigm or model in science succeeds another to illustrate the nature and character of post-confessional religious education. Kuhn's ideas were used to support the view that the post-confessional history of religious education in Britain is best characterised as dominated by two contrasting and competing disciplinary models that have determined its nature and practice: a liberal paradigm or model that was educationally dominant until the 1990s and a postmodern model that emerged in the late 1990s. To confuse matters, both still exert influence: the former is associated with the older generation of religious educators, many of whom have now passed into retirement, and the latter is associated with a younger generation of religious educators whose university education and training were pursued at the same time as postmodern ideas became academically influential. It was also argued that religious education is subject to an on-going profound crisis that neither of these two models can resolve because both generate 'a concatenation of nagging problems' (Stackhouse 2014: 177) or anomalies that are in part generated by each particular model and which each does not have the theoretical resources to resolve. My solution was to urge the adoption of a new post-liberal model of religious education, which I believe does have the theoretical resources to overcome the present crisis. This is not the place to repeat what I have said elsewhere and about the ways in which a post-liberal model overcomes existing anomalies. What I do want to do is to illustrate how the weaknesses identified by the team of researchers that participated in the *Does Religious Education Work?*

project relate to our two deficient but influential liberal and postmodern models of religious education.

In highly ramified and abstract terms the liberal model of religious education overlooks differences between religions and posits a deeper unity in complementary religious experiences—the resonances of this with modern, post-Schleiermacher liberal theology should be obvious. This orientation has bequeathed a range of weaknesses to religious education and some of the weaknesses identified in the *Does Religious Education Work?* project reflect this: stress on the ethical aspect of religions; formulaic and superficial accounts of a tradition (for ultimately differences don't much matter); emphasis on authentic spirituality that lies at the heart of all religions; comparisons between religions are odious because deep down they differ little; the lack of a critical element, and so on. By contrast, and again in highly ramified, abstract terms, the postmodern model of religious education accentuates difference and diversity and expresses a strong degree of incredulity towards religions, often thinking of them as totalising discourses. Acceptance of 'the Other' is predicated either on the assumption of agnosticism (in its original sense of lack of knowledge), for no-one truly knows the truth about religion or on the assumption that religious difference is extensive and admits of no adjudication, for religious truth is always personally constructed (though not this assumption presumably!). Neither assumption provides a foundation for challenging intolerance and bigotry and for developing more positive relationships between different communities and societies. This model also lends itself to a range of weaknesses (quoting examples from the *Does Religious Education Work?* project): disparagement of the transcendent aspects or 'other-worldly' aspects of religions; preference given to relativistic and secular interpretations of religion; instrumental rationales for the study of religious education; toleration as the deepest value but one which is based on the deconstruction of religious truth-claims; 'reverent' agnosticism is preferable as religions can be oppressive; religious education is concerned with opinions, of which most are equal except those that are accused of producing intolerance; the credibility of constructing your own version of religion, for who is to say it is not *personally* authentic, and so on.

Educational responses to identified weaknesses

What is a proper educational response to identified weaknesses? The answer to this initially seems straightforward: one addresses the identified weaknesses and frames responses to meet the weaknesses. There needs to be a correlation between weakness and response. The response must be relevant to the weakness and attention needs to be given to its justification or rationale and the reasons why it is believed that the response, typically as some form of intervention, is adequate and will do what is intended. On a longer timeframe, one needs to test whether the response has worked and overcome the weakness. There is no suggestion that conducting 'research' of this kind is uncontroversial:

there may be different measures of success and different ways to test outcomes, and so on. Personal convictions and beliefs enter in at every stage and controversy or uncertainty may remain after testing. Research and testing can take different forms: from rigorous quantitative to less statistical qualitative research, or perhaps a cycle of action research, or even less formal and indeterminate assessments. The basic premise remains, that of identified weakness and a response. For example, both the 2010 Ofsted report, *Transforming Religious Education*, and the 2013 Ofsted report *Religious Education: Realising the potential*, identified that too many pupils were leaving school with a very limited understanding of Christianity, particularly of its central beliefs; 'this understanding remains one of the weakest aspects of achievement' (2013: 9) in religious education. Given the importance of Christianity, historically, culturally, socially and religiously in Britain, and in the legislation on religious education, this a serious issue. It certainly constitutes one of the issues to which any identification of a crisis in religious education needs to develop an adequate response. The same applies to other identified weaknesses. Not to address major weaknesses that are identified in a range of relevant sources is to raise the question whether talk of a crisis by religious educators and representative bodies and organisations is being used to further their own ideological agendas and not to further the genuine educational aims of the subject.

This chapter has been concerned with identifying weakness in religious education. The identification of these weaknesses is based on a range of measures and drawn from a range of sources that can claim high levels of credibility and objectivity. It is those identified in this chapter that need to be overcome if religious education is to fulfil its potential. Is this not stating the obvious? One might think so, but what our subsequent discussion will show is that most writers either simply overlook the weaknesses, after a perfunctory and selective reference to them, and state their own vision of what religious education should be or construct their own 'imagined' catalogue of weaknesses to serve their own purpose and agenda. Many seem to have a fixed view of the future direction religious education ought to take and weaknesses are then fabricated to support this direction or are regarded as irrelevant. The current crisis becomes a coat hanger upon which any preferred garment may be hung.

Notes

1 It ought to be pointed out that the closure of the QCDA was not universally criticised and there were those who welcomed its demise on the grounds that its expense, centralising tendencies, unaccountability, the bureaucratic burden imposed on schools and stifling of curriculum initiative and freedom at the local level did not sufficiently serve the interests of schools and education; see Burkard and Rice (2009: 6–15).
2 See https://www.religiouseducationcouncil.org.uk/news/falling-numbers-of-religious-stu dies-gcse-entries-suggests-schools-struggling-to-meet-legal-obligations/ (accessed 23 March 2019).

3 See https://www.religiouseducationcouncil.org.uk/news/falling-numbers-of-religious-stu
   dies-gcse-entries-suggests-schools-struggling-to-meet-legal-obligations/ (accessed 23 March
   2019).
4 See https://assets.publishing.service.gov.uk/government/uploads/system/uploads/attachm
   ent_data/file/712450/Report_-_summer_2018_exam_entries_GCSEs_Level_1_2_AS_a
   nd_A_levels.pdf (accessed 23 March 2019).

2

DEMOCRACY, IDEOLOGY AND A NEW WORLD ORDER

In *Does Religious Education Have a Future?* (2013) Mark Chater and Clive Erricker argue for a radical reform of the subject based on, what they describe as 'principles of pedagogy set free from religious concerns'.[1] Their study comprises nine short chapters, divided into three parts: different representations of religion and of education; the politics, pedagogy and discourse of religious education; and finally, (2013: 6 and 105–146) their case for a 'radical transformation of religious education', a transformation they believe is needed for RE 'to survive' (2013: 6). The chapters in the first two parts are written separately, with a brief response to each chapter by the other author; whereas both co-author the final part. Responses are invariably short, commendatory and positive, with each endorsing the other's argument and position; consequently, each chapter is here regarded as expressing the views of both authors and for this reason there will be no differentiation made between them; both will be regarded and referred to as authors of all chapters.

Both Chater and Erricker have written extensively on religious education, and as Geoff Teece (2014: 108–109) has commented, in a review in the *British Journal of Religious Education*, their collaboration 'is the result of two lives lived at the heart of its subject matter and reflects the authors' experience in the forefront of academic and political/policy aspects of their subject'. Teece (2014: 109) is unrestrained in his admiration:

> Chater demonstrates at times brilliant insight into the political and policy dimensions of the educational context. His chapter on the politics of RE should be compulsory reading for all of [*sic*] the subject's stakeholders. Erricker provides, perhaps, the most provocative offerings. His outstanding grasp of and insight into pedagogy is clear, whilst his problematising of the study of religion which urges religious educators to engage with the realities of the global context of religion and belief is extremely challenging.

Theirs is a radical agenda that conceives pupils and students as 'manufacturers of knowledge', 'makers of Morality', 'makers of insight' and 'makers of change' (2013: 140): 'religious education is unambiguously for the sake of the world, not for the religions; it offers the chance to make knowledge and change' (2013: 145). The liberationist accent sounded here is present throughout.

Perhaps because of their involvement in religious education over the years, Chater and Erricker are more attentive to the historical, political, religious and social context of contemporary religious education than many of the contributors considered in this book. This is a clear strength of their work, as is also the fact that they move from general considerations about the nature of religion and of education before reviewing policy and pedagogy in con- temporary religious education; only after this do they rehearse their own posi- tive proposals for the renewal of the subject. There is refreshing honesty about their admission of serious weaknesses in 'the English model of RE', 'which… has been failing to fulfil its potential' (2013: 2). They even conceive their work as a warning to religious educators elsewhere, who might be tempted to emu- late English religious education, given historically its much trumpeted 'success' by some representative bodies and practitioners (2013: 2). They state candidly (2013: 3):

> This book… could serve as a warning to national jurisdictions of education as to where their interest in English RE might lead them. Some of the most characteristic features of English RE up to this moment, for example its compromises between the interests of communities and those of educators, or its balancing act between 'learning about' and 'learning from' religion, should come with a health warning for other national systems.

Whether one agrees with these examples of weaknesses or not, it is patently clear that they have engaged at first hand with the issues that a critical reading of post- confessional history of British religious education raises and reached their own distinctive, albeit controversial, conclusions. This is a welcome and long overdue admission, and contrasts with the rhetorical claims, vocal until recently, of the Religious Education Council of England and Wales, that British religious educa- tion was the envy of the world and was in a position to help other countries develop both successful policies and pedagogies (see Barnes 2014: 10–24).

Much of our discussion of Erricker and Chater will be structured around the two themes of what, according to them, is wrong with contemporary religious education in England and how they believe the situation can be rectified; the latter will incorporate their vision of the form religious education should take in the future. Discussion will also focus on two related subjects, namely capitalism and democracy and the relationship between them, both of which figure prominently in their overall argument and both of which rarely come within the purview of religious educators.

Global religion

One noteworthy feature of their account of contemporary religious education is the importance they attach to 'the global context of religion and belief' (which is the actual title of their first chapter) and with economic and geo-political movements in particular. Most of their attention is concentrated on the role of religions as ideological forces that seek to further their own 'specific and exclusive aims' (2013: 12). Their discussion of this, however, is strangely idiosyncratic, in that their treatment focuses chiefly on the baleful effects of religions in different societies, which is believed by them to be inspired by efforts 'to evade regulation in order to undermine the jurisdiction of nation states' (2013: 12) at points where their interests coincide. Moreover, their criticism is almost exclusively confined to Christianity, and to 'Vatican Roman Catholicism', in particular: paedophile priests, the Church's opposition to homosexuality (the Episcopal churches are criticised as well), the role of the Church in ignoring human rights abuses and of failing to support legislation to prevent rights abuses, the opposition of the Church to subjecting its priests to secular law, and so on. Some negative comments are included on other religious traditions, for example, Shia Islam is, like Vatican Christianity, accused of being 'genuinely hierarchical and autocratic', as is 'the Russian Church' (2013: 13). What is disconcerting about these remarks is that there does not seem to be any appreciation of how authority is negotiated and exercised within different religious traditions or any acknowledgement of diversity within the traditions criticised. Each religious tradition is regarded as monolithic and historically unchanging, and assumed to be largely incapable of reform. In the West, as elsewhere, the forms of religions are enormously varied and contingent on local conditions and contexts, something of which they do not take cognizance. In addition, no account is taken of the way many religious traditions have attempted to be faithful to their foundation documents, in the form of sacred scriptures, alongside familiar interpretations, hallowed by tradition, while at the same time responding to the challenges of modernity and post-Enlightenment traditions of critical thought.

A degree of understanding, however, is expressed for the 'resurgence of militant religious movements across the world' as they are 'partly… a response to the rapacious activity of some Western interests' (2013: 13). There is truth in this interpretation, though it clearly needs to be complemented by other interpretations that take account of a wider range of factors, not least the specific influence of both local culture and fundamentalist (often Wahabi) versions of Islam. This minor correction illustrates what is wrong with their interpretation of the global influence of religion and belief: it is one-sided, tendentious and incomplete. The positive influence of religion on society is overlooked, say religion's capacity to generate social capital (Putnam 2000; Smidt 2003; Hollenbach 2008), or to contribute to personal well-being (Francis 2010; Diener et al. 1999; Green & Elliott 2010),[2] or to act as a force for political reform and as an agent of reconciliation in divided societies (Johnston & Sampson 1995; Gallagher & Worrall 1982; Brewer 2011), and finally, how religion improves educational attainment, social mobility and lowers engagement in risky behaviours. There is also virtually no discussion of non-religious ideologies and beliefs (despite the chapter title) and consequently no discussion of their baleful effects—that some of the worst evils perpetuated on humankind in the twentieth century were pursued in the name of and under the direction of rational science; that nation states maintain exclusive rights to the use of force/violence and can act belligerently toward other countries, occasionally on the pretext of spreading democracy and human rights; and more narrowly in relation to religion, that secular states often restrict religious freedom and impose their authority and values over religious communities in the name of inclusion and equality.

Recent news reports confirm that secular organisations and groups are just as liable as religious organisations to (in the words of Chater and Erricker) further their own 'specific and exclusive aims' and 'to evade regulation' at the expense of honesty, transparency and justice. A case in point are revelations that representatives of British non-governmental organisations (NGOs, what colloquially are called 'charities', though many of these now receive generous state funding, i.e. they are supported by public money raised through taxation),[3] whose express aim is to offer 'overseas' aid and support in times of economic emergency, exploited and demanded sexual favours from the very people they were there to help. It has emerged that after the earthquake of 2010 in Haita, which left the country decimated, Mr Van Hauwermeiren, the head of Oxfam's mission, along with numerous other 'aid workers', including those from other NGOs, regularly paid for sex (which is illegal) and on occasions made sexual activity the precondition or payment for receiving aid (see Carolei 2018). When subjected to an investigation, some of the accused also physically threatened witnesses. To compound matters, Oxfam and other NGOs, while initially failing to investigate complaints, when required to do so, dismissed staff but failed to pass on evidence of wrongdoing, with the result that those guilty of sexual offences and exploitation acquired prominent new positions in other NGOs. Stories of this nature are truly alarming. The point of drawing attention to them is not to exonerate or diminish the actions and policies of religious traditions, it is to record that secular, non-religious organisations are as capable of compromising justice and truth as readily as the religious traditions to which Chater and Erricker refer and to underline their rather one-sided treatment of religion and belief. Religions have positive and negative effects, for individuals and for communities and societies, as do secular worldviews and beliefs. This is not to say that there is an equal amount of good and evil consequences between religions and secular worldviews or even between religions. One fashionable and understandable (given the bigotry often expressed toward Muslims in the West) academic option in response to accusations of the inherently violent nature of Islam, often illustrated by reference to the concept of jihad and to the distinction between Dar al-Islam—the 'abode of peace', where God's law is implemented, and Dar al-Harb—the abode of war, which awaits the forceful implementation of God's law, is to refer to the Crusades and Christian anti-Semitism and to assume an historical equality of good and evil effects between Islam and Christianity (see Barnes 2013). Such may or may not be the case but only a detailed, extensive and dispassionate study that takes account of all the evidence can confirm or deny equal culpability. Thankfully on such matters we do not have to make a judgement. The matter is introduced to make the incidental point that the current ruling political principle of equality need not necessarily receive support from and enjoy application to historically extended traditions of religion and unbelief. If it is the case that the good and bad consequences of different religions are evenly matched or similarly with regard to the religions and secular worldviews, such as Humanism and Marxism, it is a contingent matter, not one written into the nature of the universe by an invisible hand that ensures liberal equality has a metaphysical foundation across all religions and worldviews.

A sense of balance, proportion and a more wide-ranging consideration of evidence would have corrected Chater and Erricker's image of religion as almost exclusively 'a reactionary [ideological] force' (2013: 12). All too easily they construct a binary distinction between repressive religion and liberating secular beliefs. This, as we shall see, serves their purposes well as they endeavour to evacuate religious education of 'religious concerns' and seek to develop a fully secular form of religious education.

Ideology

The negative portrayal of the global influence of religion in the first part of their book, however, is deliberate, as it prepares the way (in subsequent chapters) for the unveiling of a new form of religious education that is free of 'religious facts', 'religious knowledge' and 'religious truth', because they are forms of 'pedagogical fundamentalism' (2013: 123–124). Instead, religious education must embrace 'the most creatively discursive, democratic and dynamic aspects of constructivist educational theory and practice' (2013: 132). There is a problem, however, one that they themselves note but fail to appreciate fully: in their view,

> all curricula are forms of selection, elevating certain kinds of knowledge and repressing others, and… all forms of officially approved speech or literature are ideological.
> *(2013: 133)*

But if all curricula are ideological, the charge of ideology loses its force, for how can there be unofficial curricula, unless Chater and Erricker mean that schooling should be free from all legal, legislative and government influence? An analogous point can be made in relation to liberal and wide-ranging applications of the term 'miraculous' by some religious believers to (what may properly be regarded as) natural phenomena or coincidences that have the effect of deconstructing the distinction between natural and supernatural causation; consequently the category of the 'miraculous' is evacuated of meaning. Similarly, if every belief and value in the curriculum is ideological, then presumably Chater and Erricker's proposals for religious education, should they be instantiated in a curriculum, are also ideological. If every curriculum is ideological, then to label some belief or value or curriculum as ideology does not carry any negative or critical force. At some level Chater and Erricker may have anticipated the relevance of this objection and the susceptibility of their position to criticism, for they acknowledge that 'some forms of organized control of the educational processes is (*sic*) inescapable' (also note that they equate curriculum 'knowledge' with 'control'); and then add, 'But this does not render all forms of control equal in their influence' (2013: 133). This, however, misconstrues the issue. The critical point is not that forms of control differ in their influence, to say this is uncontroversial, for who disputes that influences may not be evenly felt or distributed: it is that some influences or degrees of influence are appropriate and some inappropriate; some uses of power and authority are warranted and legitimate, some are not. For Chater and Erricker to label the current curriculum in education, and religious education in particular, as ideology carries no negative associations whatsoever, if all curriculums, including their own, are equally ideological. To advance their position in the terms in which they have chosen to debate the curriculum, they either need to distinguish between good and bad ideology and provide the reasons for so doing, or show how the authority and power structures that provide the foundations for their proposals represent benign and morally defensible control over the curriculum rather than despotic and morally inappropriate control. In a strict sense they do neither, if by this is meant that they develop self-critical, rational arguments. Nevertheless, they are not without a response. There are two appeals that figure prominently and rhetorically throughout the book; both of which seem intended to offer some kind of broad justification for their critique of current provision and supportive of the direction they believe religious education should take, that of a positive appeal to democracy and democratic practices and that of a negative stance towards capitalism. Neither is developed systematically, but they are worth considering, given the role they play in their overall position: one would be warranted in summarising their position as advocating what they regard as *democratic, anti-capitalist* transformative religious education.

Democracy and democratic schooling

Chater and Erricker regard democracy as a positive value: it and its cognates occur over 100 times in fewer than 150 pages and the Index of the book records 73 pages in which the term democracy is used. Here are some examples of their usage: religious organisations and traditions such as Vatican Catholicism and Iranian Shia Islam are *anti*-democratic 'by virtue of their truth being universally valid, [they] are also necessarily imperialist' (2013: 13); they allege that the epistemologies of some religious traditions 'are at odds with democratic principles' (2013: 17); they speak of 'contradictions' between the interests of the religious authorities (in a church school, in their example) 'and the educational processes paid for by a democratic state' (2013: 18); that religious groups and some specific ideologies, 'such as free-market capitalism... seek "offshore" status within which they are not subject to democratic regulation' (2013: 23); and that compulsory universal schooling (2013: 29) and centralised power in education should be viewed as 'anti-democratic' (2013: 32). These examples, which could easily be multiplied, illustrate the ways in which appeals to democracy are used by Chater and Erricker to condemn different positions and commitments.

The problem is that overuse by them of this appeal, without any development or supporting argument, creates uncertainty about what democracy actually means or entails. In one of the examples above, a democratic education is presented as opposed to compulsory universal schooling and centralised power in education. This is surely questionable. Irrespective of the strengths and weaknesses of both centralisation and compulsion in education and schooling it is difficult to know how a straightforward appeal to democracy clinches the argument against both. Ironically, in the year following the publication of *Does Religious Education Have a Future?*, Chater (2014: 256) wrote in support of a centrally imposed national curriculum for religious education 'to address the... weaknesses in RE': how does his endorsement of this policy relate to his earlier opposition to centralisation and compulsion in education? Are there principles to account for his 'change of heart' or is this an example of political expediency? It is also difficult to know what to make of the claim that the epistemologies of some religious traditions (somewhat predictably they refer again to 'Vatican Roman Christianity, certain versions of Islam and Fundamentalist and Literalist Christian movements' and others; 2013: 17) are undemocratic. How are democracy and epistemology related? What is a *democratic* epistemology of religion? Is it one that appeals to reason alone, after the manner of some eighteenth-century deists, or is the appeal not to reason but to natural revelation? By use of the term democratic is it meant that all must have equal access to truth about God. (Is it undemocratic to specify one particular religious object as epistemically privileged?) An extension of this point might be that religions that claim special revelation through sacred books or events in history are undemocratic because everyone may not be in the requisite place or position to have access to special revelation. Could they simply mean that the truth of a religion, such as Christianity or Islam, should be decided by public vote? Their call for a democratic epistemology of religion is at best ambiguous, and at worst a claim that most philosophers would dismiss as ridiculous and absurd. By contrast, in some cases what they mean by democracy in education is more straightforward: that attention should be given to 'the voice of pupils', that lessons should engage with their questions about religion, and so on. Most of what they say on these and related issues, however, could be more clearly and unambiguously stated without appealing to democracy. It simply is good pedagogy and practice to encourage pupils to express their views and to engage with critical issues about religion and religious life; an appeal to democracy is not required, and historically has not been used to justify a critical element in English religious education, where this has been introduced.

The continual use of the term and its antonyms (and their cognates) by Chater and Erricker in contexts where their meaning is not obvious or is unnecessary creates the impression that any process, institution, pedagogy, curriculum, epistemology, religion, or any position in relation to education and schooling with which they disagree is simply labelled anti-democratic, and to say this is sufficient of itself for them not to have to develop an argument. In philosophical terms democracy and its cognates often seem to assume the role of place-holders that carry little or no semantic information beyond the simple fact that their use expresses a positive attitude: the use of the terms denote that Chater and Erricker view some particular thing or process positively. On some occasions the appeal to democracy by them has some force, as when it is used as a shorthand for democratic values, say that of equality or inclusion, though their temptation is again to think that appeals of this nature 'trump' all other considerations. What they overlook is that there is a range of democratic values—freedom/liberty, justice, the common good, the pursuit of truth, for example. The simple point is that these values can conflict, and in the case of a practical field of study and enquiry like education where other values and aims are also relevant, it is naïve to think that an appeal to an indeterminate concept of democracy can exclusively guide policy and practice.

There is both contradiction and irony in Chater and Erricker's appeal to democracy; first the contradiction. They have already been quoted as deploring any compromise between representatives of religions and religious educators because, in their view, educators should wholly determine the curriculum. Let us retreat from this discussion for now to set things in context. Agreed syllabuses, to be used by voluntary controlled schools and local authority schools within the local areas and produced under the aegis of local education authorities, have long been a feature of English religious education. Their legal role was reiterated and extended under the 1988 Education (Reform) Act, which alongside requiring the Agreed Syllabus Conference (which draws up the syllabus) to review the locally agreed syllabus for voluntary controlled schools at least every 5 years, also requires it (for the first time) to include representatives from the principal non-Christian religions in the local area, alongside teacher and council representatives and representatives from the Church of England. The inclusion of representatives from the principal non-Christian religions in the drawing up and resourcing of agreed syllabus constitutes a case of local democracy, in which individuals from different religious communities are required to work together with others and through dialogue and debate agree on policy and content for the local area. Local community agreement on religious education of this form, however, is heavily criticised by Chater and Erricker and consequently they look forward to its 'demise' (2013: 103). They reuse and apply the metaphor of 'moving offshore', which was originally used to describe the ways in which religions seek to bypass and evade democratic regulation by the state, to refer to the potential that local syllabus committees have of structuring religious education according to 'a different rationale and pedagogical rules from any other subject' (2013: 103). But surely a national syllabus committee is just as liable to (re)structure religious education and distinguish it from other subjects according to a different rationale and pedagogical rules. Moreover, they fail to note that local syllabus committees, in constructing syllabuses, are acting in order to conform to the democratic regulation of the state.

The irony in Chater and Erricker's use of democracy and its cognates is that on other occasions in their book they challenge the use of binary distinctions in educational debates and arguments, that of a content/skills dichotomy, for example, yet never question their own extended use and appeal to the binary distinction between democratic/undemocratic beliefs and practices. First, as already pointed out, not every educational debate is susceptible to or even illuminated by an appeal to democratic values and procedures (however construed): an educational policy may be impracticable, inappropriate, unnecessary, ineffective or even illegal and its theoretical underpinning inadequate, unjustified or evidentially weak. None of these concerns need have any relevance to the democratic/undemocratic distinction. Second, there is not an absolute distinction between democratic and undemocratic policies, practices, values and commitments. There are different accounts of democracy and of democratic values, and of their relevance and application. A democratic state may be contrasted with a totalitarian state, say 1930s Britain with Stalin's Soviet Union, or a democratic practice may be contrasted with an undemocratic practice, say taking account of the opinions of those who require some particular social service, as opposed to not taking account of their needs and opinions. These are reasonably straightforward examples, but there are countless other examples where the distinction is less clear or is ambiguous in its application. For example, are Islamic states that follow Sharia law undemocratic, if the majority of the population want to live under Sharia law? What about a government policy that enjoys little support from teachers' unions, yet enjoys support from parents and the population at large (if that is determinable)? Chater and Erricker believe that compulsion in schooling is undemocratic, yet the effect of allowing teachers and schools to construct their own curriculums may be to deprive pupils of requisite skills and knowledge to participate reflectively and critically in democratic politics and debates. Third, in many cases the uses of democracy and its cognates (and their antonyms), denote a *range* of values (or meanings) and it is simplistic to believe that the values comprising both sets—democratic and undemocratic—necessarily relate in an appositional way throughout. Finally, democratic positions, if by this is meant the views of the majority of citizens, can be in opposition to the rights of individuals. For example, if the majority of citizens disagree with gay marriage then there should not be legal provision for gay marriage, or if the majority wish to reinstate capital punishment then it should be reinstated. These may not be good examples, but they illustrate the point that there are important and influential accounts of democracy that can be brought into opposition with some interpretations of human rights. The binary democratic/undemocratic distinction fails to take account of this.

Since the publication of *Does Religious Education Have a Future?* debate about the nature and meaning of democracy has deepened. In 2016 one of the world's largest democracies elected Donald Trump to become the 45th President of the United States of America and in a referendum on 23 June 2016, 51.9 per cent of the participating UK electorate voted to leave the European Union; the turnout was 72.2 per cent (which is a higher percentage than any participation in a General Election since 1997). Both results confounded experts and went against the political views of most of the professional and political elites in both nations. The term populism has been taken up and used to describe such processes whereby popular, anti-establishment political movements have become vocal and campaigned against what is perceived by them as the policies and self-serving interests of the cultural, social, political and intellectual groups that dominate and control society (see Hayward 1996, where elitism and populism are contrasted as the opposite poles between which political leaders need to steer). Current usage fits well with Cas Mudde and Cristóbal Rovira Kaltwasser's (2017: 6) academic account of populism as a 'thin-centered ideology' that postulates a 'pure people' and a 'corrupt elite', which can be appropriated by different political perspectives and 'thicker' ideologies. Another characteristic of populism that has been identified is criticism of the complicated, representative democratic systems of modern government and, by contrast, expressed preference for direct democracy (see Moffitt 2017: 142–150, for discussion), as in referendums—the United Kingdom's European Union membership referendum of 2016 and the political system in Switzerland may be cited as examples. Direct democracy finds inspiration in the classical city state republics of Greece, such as Athens, and (in part) from Jean-Jacques Rousseau's *The Social Contract* (1997 [1762]). How does this relate to Chater and Erricker's call for greater democracy in religious education? It is to remind them that democracy is a two-edged sword: 'the people' may or may not support your policies. It may be presumptuous of Chater and Erricker to think that their form of religious education would win popular democratic support from the various interested constituencies or from the wider public, or even from pupils.

Capitalism

If advancing democracy is the chief virtue of education systems and the 'engine' of the reform of religious education for Chater and Erricker, 'free-market capitalism' is viewed as ultimately the recalcitrant force that opposes positive reform. Free-market capitalism, for them, encompasses a range of values, but unlike democracy these impede and frustrate educational reform and progress. Like some religious traditions, free market capitalism seeks 'offshore' status to be free of 'democratic regulation' (2013: 23). They endorse Ivan Illich's view that societies are encouraged (by vested interests) to believe that they 'need' education and schools on the basis of an 'assumption of scarcity' (2013: 28); and it is this assumption that is the premise of capitalism and of all 'capitalist' activity, which for them is not merely economic but extends to all aspects of life. This way of framing things, however, is problematical for it clearly overlooks the fact that scarcity is an environmental and social reality (the earth's resources are not infinite and most social advantages cannot be equally distributed, for example, top grade examination results). There is the problem of the depletion of natural resources: declining freshwater resources and crude oil, loss of soil fertility, and shortages of crucial minerals like zinc, copper, and phosphorus which are used in the production of a range of 'products' that are essential to industry, well-being and life. If one of the primary causes and determinants of capitalism is acknowledgement of the reality of scarcity or, at a social level, the reality of 'burdens' as well as 'benefits' (Rawls 1971), it is difficult not to concede that it ought to enjoy a degree of credibility and relevance.

Beyond their idea that capitalism is predicated on scarcity, Chater and Erricker never attend to the nature of capitalism, let alone consider the view that there are varieties of capitalism, for capitalist economies can differ in fundamental ways. The term is never defined by them, rather it is used to denote the forces that oppose authentic education. Let us attempt a broad definition of capitalism and at least clarify what it is they oppose. Capitalism is an economic system in which capital goods are owned by private individuals or businesses. The production of goods and services is based on supply and demand in the general market (market economy), rather than through central planning (planned economy or command economy). There are well known criticisms of capitalism, of which Marx's critique in *Das Kapital* in terms of exploitation, domination, and alienation is the best known. Marx, for example, opposed the concept of private property, which, in his view, denies the benefits of ownership to others and thereby creates conflict and produces competition over objects and resources. By contrast, he supported the idea that 'the people' ought to own the land, resources, labour, the means of production and make all economic decisions. Overlooking criticism of capitalism as a particular economic system, Chater and Erricker have set themselves an ambitious intellectual challenge if they are to show how the ills of contemporary schooling in Britain and of religious education in particular are related to capitalism. To give credence to their position they are required to show that there is a necessary connection between capitalism and the weaknesses of the English system of education, and then show how this extends to include religious education. The whole thesis sounds not only difficult to substantiate but counter-intuitive, in that the education systems (including tertiary education) of those countries that have espoused capitalism are widely regarded as the most successful in the world —South Korea, Japan, Finland, and we may even include the United Kingdom. In his Reith Lectures of 2012, *The Great Degeneration How institutions decay and economies die* (2014), the historian Niall Ferguson amasses evidence and argues that 'meaningful competition [between schools accredited with a degree of autonomy] favours excellence', whereas a state monopoly system almost invariably produces 'mediocre quality' education (2014: 127 and 128). What is it about capitalism that casts a dark shadow over schooling and curriculum religious education? Evidence is needed by Chater and Erricker, not assertion.

Chater and Erricker also fail to take account of the historical genealogy of capitalism, which is closely related to the emergence of democracy. One thinks here of John Locke's (1632–1704) defence of natural rights of ownership and of private property in Chapter V of *The Second Treatise of Government* (2016 [1689]) as necessary limitations on the authority and reach of the state and the arbitrary actions of the monarch, and of Max Weber's (1864–1920) account of the origins of capitalism in *The Protestant Ethic and the Spirit of Protestantism* (2001 [1904–1905]), which links it to (chiefly) Calvinist and Puritan forms of religion that (*mutatis mutandis*) emphasised personal freedom, thrift and the (moral) right to benefit from and to dispose of one's assets, financial and otherwise. In simple terms, capitalism is one (complicated) consequence of the emergence of natural rights, the rise of individualism and of the modern state, which on this interpretation functions to protect individual rights and to enforce the rules necessary for the free exchange of goods and services. Liberal economic policies are related to liberal values and a liberal state. These complex relationships are overlooked by Chater and Erricker. They are committed to some form of anti-capitalist economics that operates in an enlarged public realm, yet (in contradistinction to socialist and Marxist models) can dispense with central planning and control and the curtailments on personal liberty that most economic commentators believe are required by such an economy. While there are problems with capitalism, their uncompromising anti-capitalist stance reveals a naïve understanding of the nature of modern economies where finance (money) and value are related in order to ensure distribution in efficient and effective ways. They never raise the question of how their vision of state collectivism is consistent with personal freedom and the economic rights of individuals. What also evades their attention is the range of contradictions that they espouse in supporting democracy while criticising capitalism and the competitive environment it (for them) necessarily creates: for example, they are critical of centralised planning and authority in education (2013: 12), yet espouse a centrally planned economy, which is the implication of their rejection of free-market capitalism; they argue for greater freedom in education, yet are critical of publicly funded faith schools, which extend the principle of diversity in educational provision, and of deregulation in education. Contradictions abound.

A much wiser starting point to think about the relationship of economics to politics and social justice, is, unlike Chater and Erricker, to begin with recognition of the reality of scarcity, and the competition between self-interested individuals that inevitably follows from this. Once this is admitted one can seek to reflect upon the notion of fair distribution and how benefits and burdens are appropriately (justly) distributed to the greatest advantage of the greatest number, or to the greatest benefit to the least-advantaged members that is consistent with others having the freedom to accrue whatever advantages and benefits they can. John Rawls's (1921–2002) account of 'justice as fairness' (1971) is one such influential attempt to relate self-interest and freedom in a way that is believed by him to be consistent with moral and political principles which can be reflectively endorsed by all individuals autonomously. Much work would need to be done to relate any position on economics and social justice to education. In fact, the real weakness in Chater and Erricker's discussion of these issues, which conveniently summarises all that has been said in this section, is that the line of reasoning from their commitment to democratic values and their criticism of capitalism to religious education and its theory and practice is both tenuous and inconsistent.

What is wrong with current provision in English religious education?

Clearly, as is acknowledged by most commentators, and by Chater and Erricker, there is much that is wrong with religious education. For them, political, economic and cultural influences 'determine' the curriculum: the movement is downward, from global political, economic and cultural forces to the national level, and then these same forces, through a series of steps, determine education and religious education at the local level. These forces coalesce around the issue of power and control, and in their opinion this exercise of power and control is anti-democratic and should be reversed.

In their Introduction they note that 'British RE – and particularly its largest element, the English model – attracts admiring interest from some other national systems' (2013: 2), and list examples of the assumptions that 'sit behind this admiring interest':

> that offering young people information about diversity serves to promote harmony and cohesion; that agreed syllabuses and teaching approaches give young people free rein to ask questions and express views; that the localized world of RE protects the subject from undue influence by religious communities or political, economic or cultural forces; that the quality of RE, the rigour of its demand and the relevance of its content has been successful; that the distinctive construction of RE as 'learning about religion' and 'learning from religion' has helped teachers to plan with educational integrity and coherence.
>
> *(2013: 2)*

They reject these assumptions: some of the above quotations recast in negative terms express their position, for example, that offering young people information about diversity *does not* serve to promote harmony and cohesion; that agreed syllabuses and teaching approaches *do not* give young people free rein to ask questions and express views, and so on. Some of the points they make in criticism of English religious education are convincing, though hardly novel. It was clear at least from the late 1980s that phenomenological approaches to religious education that aim to provide 'objective' information about religion, inspired by Ninian Smart (1927–2001) and *Working Paper 36* (Schools Council 1971), were achieving little in terms of effectively challenging religious prejudice and bigotry or in developing respect for those from 'minority' religions and cultures. Moreover, by bracketing out critical issues, ostensibly to foster an unbiased understanding of religion, pupils failed to acquire the skills to assess and evaluate religious phenomena and religious truth claims, even though many of them were culturally exposed to a diverse range of beliefs and values to which they had (as pupils now have also) to relate and, on occasions, from which they had to choose. Equally influential in depriving pupils of the skills and abilities to evaluate religion was the assumption, common to most phenomenological approaches of the period, that each of the different religions mediated spirituality and genuine encounters with the divine. 'Toleration' of others and respect for them were believed (uncritically and without evidential support) to be achieved either by an 'empathetic' study of 'other' religions or by mutual acknowledgement of the essential spiritual orientation of the different faiths. Often associated with phenomenological religious education (and its multi-faith successors, the experiential approach, for example) is the view, properly criticised by Chater and Erricker, that religion is always something positive and good (to off-set obvious criticism this is usually qualified by speaking of *authentic* religion). For them this is related to a wider criticism, which is that modern religious education is heavily indebted to Western post-Enlightenment values, 'human rights and rational assumptions' (2013: 73) and has allowed itself to be shaped uncritically by these assumptions. One would have appreciated a more detailed and fine-grained discussion of this, but the point, if not overstated, does have substance.

Other criticisms made by Chater and Erricker are less persuasive; one of which only, given its importance, will be considered. They are critical of distinguishing between 'learning about religion' and 'learning from religion' as attainment targets, and this '[i]n spite of the testimony of many teachers and consultants' (2013: 53). For them there should be one target, though (frustratingly) they do not specify what this should be. They claim that the two targets 'will inevitably divide and dilute efforts, and set up – or perpetuate – tensions in the pedagogy of RE' (2013: 53). The critical question is why should there be a tension or if there is, and both sides of the tension expresses important aspects of religious education, why a satisfactory pedagogy that retains both is not possible. It is difficult initially to appreciate how knowing about a religion and coming to understand its beliefs, practices and ethos could obstruct or come into conflict with learning something about oneself on the basis of one's encounter. It could be contended that knowing more about religions and religious phenomena actually creates more opportunities for self-discovery and self-reflection, for as one's knowledge of religion grows, so potentially do the occasions in which learning from religion can occur. There may be tensions, perhaps when the significance of one of the two targets is exaggerated over the other; yet not to distinguish between learning about religion and learning from religion and to treat both as important creates the likelihood either that religious education becomes concerned exclusively with religious content to the neglect of its relevance and challenge to pupils, or that religion becomes instrumental and configured to serve some nebulous concept of self-development. One can only learn from religion, if one knows about religion.

Religious education, while being historically concerned with providing an understanding of religion (which is central to learning about religion), also aims to engage pupils in the challenge of reflecting upon religion and religious phenomena and of seeing the relevance of different aspects of religion to their lives and experiences and to the lives and experiences of others. The content of religion and the processes that enable an understanding of religion can also contribute both to the self-development of individuals—as they ask questions about the kind of persons they want to become and the values, commitments and purposes they want to endorse—and to the kind of society and communities to which they want to belong, and the values and beliefs that should characterise social and political life. It is this that the two assessment targets aim to conceptualise and facilitate (whether they achieve this is another matter). There may be tensions between them, but the solution to abandon one or the other or both, as Chater and Erricker propose, is unwise, for not to recognise either of the two targets means that they will be neglected and overlooked by teachers. The content of religious education must relate to the life-world of pupils, not only to communicate successfully the meaning of religion and religious phenomena, but also to ensure that they reflect upon and engage with the resources within religion to develop positively as persons. We develop as persons and acquire self-knowledge through interaction with others and through our learning experiences. The study of religion can contribute to this. This defence of the relevance of both learning about and learning from religion need not be tied to this particular form of words. There are other ways of expressing the distinction, say that of meaning and significance or that of exposition and application. The important point is that attention is given to religion and to the relevance of religion both to the lives of individuals and to communities.

Constructing a brave new world

Chater and Erricker advocate a new form of religious education where power and control are, according to them, returned to pupils in the classroom and then 'from the classroom to the movements of thought and national structures, and up to the global level of cultural, economic and political' (2013: 1). 'It should be the purpose of RE in our time to begin a counter-chain upwards' (2013: 1). They envisage religious education as revolutionary and 'transformative', with the potential to change the world:

> Young people learning RE would be engaged in a single process of becoming the co-designers and co-constructors of ideological and cultural products that address their own, their community's and humanity's most pressing problems.
>
> *(2013: 140)*

Whether young people in school possess the necessary knowledge, understanding, critical skills and experience of life both to determine their own curriculum and to prescribe solutions to the challenges faced by modern, pluralist societies is debateable. Most educators view schooling as the means by which young people acquire the knowledge and skills to become full citizens and to participate in social and political debates, whereas Chater and Erricker view pupils in schools as well placed to develop solutions to meet 'humanity's most pressing problems'. There is also the issue whether 'young people's agency' (2013: 140), in which they place so much faith, will take the form and express the values that Chater and Erricker endorse.

Positively, transformative religious education will spread the 'good news' of their version of democracy and banish free-market capitalism. This is a bold new agenda for religious education. How it relates to religion is not entirely clear. Perhaps this is where their earlier, chiefly negative, account of the global influence of religion becomes relevant: religious education could equip pupils to identify and reflect upon the negative influence of religion in the modern world, and where religion has had influence in the ways in which Chater and Erricker approve, it may be transformed into more positive educational applications. In fact, they entertain the wider hope that the religions, their theologies and religious institutions, by entering into the spirit of transformative education, may also be reformed in ways consistent with their interpretation of democracy, equality and rights. Religious education is 'unambiguously for the sake of the world, not for the religions; it offers the chance to make knowledge and change' (2013: 145).

Chater and Erricker (2013: 144) are aware that their theory of transformative religious education is only contingently related to religion and to religious education as currently practised; they admit that '[i]t might be dismissed as a blend of RE, citizenship and some parts of PSHE [Personal, Social, Health Education][4] together with some politics and philosophy'. Indeed, this is a real possibility. Unfortunately, they identify the reason behind such dismissal as the objection that their revised form of religious education does not qualify as a disciple because it draws on a range of different subjects and disciplines. Their response, predictably, is to point out that religious education is and never has never been a discipline but has always drawn on a range of disciplines. It may be noted in passing that Ninian Smart (1968) always referred to religious studies as a field of study, and similarly with religious education. The real force of the objection, however, is not that religious education, as they construe it, fails to encompass a single discipline, rather that it embraces a range of disciplines and themes that by their own admission may not have any relationship whatsoever to religion—after all religion is not now the object of study. The 'new subject' that they envisage, 'will be a disciplined set of enquiries into questions of power and truth' (2013: 144), from which it seems religions could potentially be excluded completely. They acknowledge that these enquiries are no longer appropriately designated as '*religious* education' (2013: 146). The designation that does seem appropriate for what they propose is 'politics' or 'citizenship education'. In which case their position is perhaps best construed as a call for the replacement of religious education in schools by a new form of political education that aims to inculcate anti-capitalist values through progressive child-centred pedagogies. Given their commitment to democracy, however, one may ask whether there is a democratic mandate for this?

According to Chater and Erricker's transformative religious education will enable young people to 'become manufactures of knowledge' and 'makers of morality' (2013: 140). They will 'plan and articulate their enquiries', albeit with the support of teachers, who need no longer be 'preoccupied with subject knowledge' (2013: 140). How true, for there is no longer a subject concerned with religion and there is no longer knowledge or truth or facts to be imparted, at least in the traditional sense, for they discount all objective claims to knowledge or truth. All claims to knowledge are disguised means of gaining control and power over others. But wait, what ought we to make of Chater and Erricker's proposals for religious education? Let us take them at their word and discount that they are advancing claims to truth or knowledge and interpret them as attempting by fine words and rhetoric to gain power and control over others and to convince them to espouse their ideological, transformative version of religious education and have it enforced on pupils. Together, they tell us, we could 'manufacture' and 'make' a liberationist curriculum a reality (to use their own metaphors). But what are the raw materials from which we construct meaning? Manufacturing and making presuppose the existence of resources. Manufacturing knowledge and making morality require resources—actions, behaviour, ideas, concepts, experiences, beliefs, truth claims, and however circuitous the connection, many of these 'resources' claim to connect to, and to reflect, the way things are in the world external to ourselves. In a sense Chater and Erricker admit as much when they express their support for democracy and denounce free market capitalism. Some ideas and concepts correctly reflect the nature of the world and the way things are; some theories explain the data or the facts better than others; some behaviour is correctly described as morally wrong and some morally right, and so on. We learn through interacting with ideas and assessing for ourselves how faithfully they track the truth. We construct meaning and make sense of reality, but our constructions are limited by the nature of reality. Interpretations of the world are constrained by the nature of what is to be explained; some meanings are warranted, and some are not; some interpretations are plausible, some are not. It is the challenge of education to introduce pupils to the diversity of human thought and ideas in a way that enables them to understand the world and in religious education, in part, to provide them with the skills and abilities to reach their own conclusions about controversial matters, religion and religious commitment being obvious examples. Such is a liberal curriculum, whereas, by contrast, Chater and Erricker's liberationist curriculum is deeply conservative in the sense that they want their own political ideals and commitments to be privileged through education.

What Chater and Erricker fail to realise is that it is a focus on religion and the subject matter of religion that gives coherence to the subject of religious education in schools, and it is this focus that determines the disciplines and themes that are relevant to classroom theory and practice. In addition, it is the focus of religious education on religion that provides the strongest educational justification for the inclusion of the subject in the curriculum. It is the religious, cultural, historical, political and social importance of religion in its various forms that justifies the study of religion in schools.

Religious education and the new world order

In a number of books, the political philosopher John Gray (2004 and 2008) alerts us to the dangers and self-contradictory nature of grand utopian, political schemes that aim to create a new world order. His historical judgment (on the basis of the evidence of history) is that all such schemes end in failure: 'the dream of the utopia never comes about. What eventually emerges is something different—not the utopia but a reversion to something more like normal life, but only after terrible and pointless suffering'.[5] Chater and Erricker want a new political form of religious education that will change the world, establish democracy, and banish capitalism. They hope to inspire a movement that begins in the classroom and eventually ends in a transformed global political, economic and cultural order. As a first step they require a new form of religious education: one that dispenses with any intrinsic connection to religion. They denounce faith schools and faith institutions; dispense with religious knowledge, while affirming their own socialist creed; conclude that parents should be deprived of the right to withdraw their children from religious education; relegate Standing Advisory Councils on Religious Education to the role of 'voluntary panels for resourcing the subject' (2013: 146), and so on. The contradictions with true democracy and democratic values are already mounting; yet ironically all these policies are recommended by Chater and Erricker as aspects of their educational programme, which is the first step to the creation of a new democratic world order. How strange that support for Gray's thesis should come from so unlikely a place as religious education. What remains for those of us religious educators that are less politically ambitious is to work for small incremental changes that in time could transform the subject.

Notes

1 This quotation is taken from the unnumbered page that follows the title page and presents a summary of the content of the book.
2 See Cohen and Johnson (no date) for a judicious and generally positive analysis of evidence and research.
3 In 2017 Oxfam received £31.7 million in UK government funding.
4 Now Personal, Social, Health and Economic Education (PSHEE).
5 Quoting from John Gray, 'Critiques of Utopia and Apocalypse' http://fivebooks.com/interview/john-gray-on-critiques-of-utopia-and-apocalypse/ (accessed on 2 March 2016).

3

RELIGIOUS STUDIES, RELIGIOUS EDUCATION AND THE RETURN OF THEOLOGY

In a recent article in the *British Journal of Religious Education*, Denise Cush and Catherine Robinson (2014: 14–15) have argued that 'a dialogue needs to be re-established between religious studies in universities and religious education in schools and teacher education in the spirit of the pioneers of non-confessional multi-faith religious education'. Such a call is welcome, as there is much that both parties to this dialogue can learn from each other that will contribute to enhancing the quality of teaching and learning in the respective educational contexts. The discussion by Cush and Robinson is almost entirely one sided: the main sections of their article are devoted to short overviews of some trends and approaches in religious studies. The focus is on what religious educators can learn from religious studies, an orientation conveyed by the title of the article—'Developments in religious studies'. In the final sentence, however, it is stated that 'religious studies could certainly learn from religious education in respect of the latter's attention to pedagogy and awareness of the potential for academic study to contribute towards students' personal development' (2014: 15). This shows that Cush and Robinson recognise the importance of pedagogy and the personal development of pupils in religious education; no doubt by personal development here they do not mean to exclude their social development or indeed the social development of communities and how this could contribute to social cohesion. The ways in which attention to both pedagogy and the personal development of university students can be enhanced by attention to developments in religious education in schools is left unstated. At one point only in the article is reference made to the influence of religious education over religious studies, in this instance to the way in which the popularity of philosophy and ethics (conducted under the title of religious education/studies) in schools has encouraged some universities to offer degree courses that combine religious studies with philosophy and ethics (2014: 5). This is clearly evidence of formal, rather than material influence. In fairness to Cush and

Robinson their focus is on what religious educators can learn from acquaintance with developments in religious studies or as it may also be called the academic study of religion. This is an entirely defensible position and this orientation is assumed here.

Cush and Robinson's call for a more meaningful dialogue between religious studies and religious education ought to be endorsed, but unlike them I believe that a more critical, discerning and discriminating approach is needed than they exhibit and has been exhibited by some religious educators in the past. This qualification, in part, reflects recognition of both the positive and negative historical influence that religious studies has exerted over post-confessional religious education in England. One might think intuitively that the influence of one area of study over another typically produces both positive and negative effects, yet this common assumption is often rejected, albeit implicitly, by many religious educators. The common narrative, and that endorsed by Cush and Robinson, is that the influence of religious studies over religious education has been invariably positive and that the negative features of post-confessional religious education can be accredited to periods when this influence has waned or has been punctuated and interrupted by other influences, perhaps by government interference through statue and regulation, or by the influence of unqualified teachers who are unfamiliar with the sophisticated discussions of religious matters by scholars of religion, which qualified, specialist teachers are assumed to exercise.

This chapter will interact closely with what Cush and Robinson have to say about their proposed dialogue with developments in religious studies. This is used as a springboard to a wider discussion of the historical influence of religious studies on religious education, which in turn leads to a more critical account of this influence than that demonstrated by them. Emerging out of this is the need to consider the aims of both religious studies and religious education and how these are relevant to any discussion about their relationship. The chapter concludes with a positive account of how theology (yes, theology) can contribute to the practice of non-confessional religious education.

Some preliminary observations

Cush and Robinson (2014: 8) review a number of developments in religious studies that they believe 'have something to offer religious education'. They provide short accounts of feminist theory, queer theory, postcolonial theory, religion and belief, both in contemporary Britain and in a 'globalised world', and they review the debate within religious studies on the use of the concepts of 'religion' and 'religions'. Their presentation and application of this material to religious education is not uncontroversial. For example, they quote approvingly from feminist theory that:

> the objectivity of the scholar... is neither possible or desirable.... Further, from a feminist perspective, were objectivity to be possible, it would still be unethical because religions sometimes advocate or defend teachings that are

damaging and to pretend otherwise would amount to an abstention from judgement that fails to acknowledge suffering.

(2014: 9)

It would have been helpful if Cush and Robinson had explained what they mean by objectivity, as it can mean different things—a reasoned position, one free from subjective bias, a judgement that commands universal assent (we may think of this as a Kantian view), or a judgement that appeals to public evidence and discounts private emotions and commitments. The most likely interpretation of the usage by Cush and Robinson is that they equate objectivity solely with neutrality; hence their acknowledgement that feminists are not neutral about their commitments: feminists hold certain values—mutuality, equality of the sexes, democratic use of power, non-violence, etc. Perhaps equating objectivity with neutrality and opposing it to moral valuations, however, as Cush and Robinson do, is not the best way to further the aims of feminism in education or to commend the commitments of feminism to religious educators. There are meanings of objectivity that are relevant and applicable to religious education; meanings that are possible and not 'undesirable'. Objectivity can be a positive epistemic virtue, in any of the other senses referred to above: it is good to be objective and listen to both sides of an argument and to consider evidence fairly and impartially. Without a claim to moral objectivity (which takes up a different meaning of objectivity) it is difficult to appreciate the force of legitimate feminist criticism of patriarchal aspects of society, otherwise moral criticism may be dismissed as subjective and relative. Typically when we, along with feminists, criticise child marriage or clitoridectomy or forbid education to females it is not meant solely that such actions are wrong for those who live in *our* society, or even Western society more generally, it is meant that they are morally wrong in every society, objectively wrong.

One of the chief weaknesses in the review by Cush and Robinson is that they provide few classroom examples of the implications for religious education of developments in religious studies, and in some instances they overlook examples where ideas and insights from religious studies have already been appropriated and applied. For instance, in their discussion of postcolonial theory they speak of the need for religious educators to 'attend to indigenous voices and engage with indigenous concepts' (2014: 11). This suggests that this has not happened in religious education, which may be disputed. Robert Jackson and his development of an interpretive approach (1995 and 1997) did much to bring this issue to the attention of religious educators in the later 1990s by drawing on the ethnographic anthropologist Clifford Geertz's distinction between 'experience near' and 'experience distant' concepts. Jackson also took account of Geertz's notion of translation and the associated hermeneutical processes whereby 'insider accounts' of religious speech and practices are translated into 'locutions of ours' (Jackson 1997: 37). It is also worth noting that in the same writings Jackson gave attention to the challenge of defining religion and to questioning the categories of meaning and interpretation that historically have determined the names of the different religions and the posited distinctions between them (though not entirely satisfactorily in my view). These insights from religious studies have already been appropriated by religious educators, for the most part in quite constructive ways. One of the strengths of interpretive religious education is that it attends to debates in religious studies (see Barnes 2014: 180–217 for an extended discussion of the strengths and weakness of an interpretive approach).

Cush and Robinson (2014: 11) also speak of 'revitalising indigenous norms and values', which suggests a campaigning role for religious educators towards elements of other cultures and religions. Which indigenous norms and values and whose values and commitments should teachers seek to revitalise, and how does this relate to their espousal of individualist, secular Western values, which contrast with the more communitarian, traditional norms of most 'indigenous' groups? A campaigning note is sounded in their discussion of feminism, and in other places as well. They seem to be unaware that some of their recommendations, which are rooted in feminism or queer theory, for example, are politically and religiously controversial. Subjects and viewpoints that are appropriate to adult university students, who often elect to study potentially controversial subjects, cannot be assumed to be equally appropriate to schools that aim to be inclusive of pupils from communities with different values, whose critical faculties are in the process of development.[1] The negative point is that they do not take account of the different context of religious education in school and of religious studies in university, and the bearing these contexts have in determining educational aims, purposes and practices; a subject to which we shall return.

Interpreting religious education

The aim of acquainting teachers with developments within the academic study of religion is part of a wider (largely unstated) perspective that Cush and Robinson hold about the history and current state of religious education (chiefly in England). They would not be advocating new ideas and influences if they do not think there are deficiencies or weaknesses in current provision, yet they never tell us what these are; at the very least they are committed to the idea that religious education can be further improved by consideration and adoption of their recommendations. There is, for them, something to be gained by initiating a dialogue between religious education and religious studies; and they have identified the areas where they believe teachers should revise their practice or incorporate new ideas into their teaching in the light of developments in religious studies. Furthermore, talk by them of re-establishing dialogue suggests not only that current provision in religious education is wanting or can be improved in certain respects but that the original influence of religious studies on religious education was positive and heralded a period of progress for the subject. The subject is not now progressing and once again steps are needed to renew it. They do not speak of a crisis in religious education, but they do believe that there are current weaknesses that need to be overcome, which in their view can be accomplished only by reference to religious studies.

That this narrative about the history and development of post-confessional religious education is implicit in Cush and Robinson is not because it is deemed by them to be controversial and that recognition of it might reduce support for their argument. It is rather that this narrative is assumed by them to be true and uncontroversial: it does not need to be stated explicitly because it is the accepted story, endorsed by most religious educators. The 'received' narrative of post-confessional religious education in England is of an auspicious beginning, initiated by Ninian Smart and others, in response to developments in religious studies. This broad, popular narrative (held explicitly or implicitly) can be refined and revised in different ways. One may think of original inspiration from religious studies to religious education, gradual decline until the present and now the hope of renewal by reference to religious studies, or perhaps original inspiration and punctuated periods of renewal under the influence of developments in religious studies. An example of the latter is to argue that Robert Jackson's appropriation of the interpretive anthropology of Geertz in the 1990s acted to renew religious education, and that a new stimulus for renewal is now needed, and according to Cush and Robinson available, from religious studies. This narrative can accommodate any number of periods of renewal, as it can also accommodate different interpretations of the reasons for renewal. Supporters of the status quo may want to interpret the need for renewal in undramatic language that suggests natural and rational progress, whereas others may want to interpret the need for renewal in more dramatic language, using terms such as 'malaise', 'serious challenges' or even 'crisis', the term used recently by the Religious Education Council's *Review of Religious Education in England* (2013: 8).

The next section of this chapter is devoted to refining this narrative. It might be imagined that the matters to be discussed are theoretical and remote from the classroom, of academic interest only. This is not the case. Refining the prevailing narrative about the historical influence of religious studies over religious education has far reaching implications for contemporary practice and for the future direction of religious education. It might also be imagined that the preceding discussion of Cush and Robinson is irrelevant to this refining process. It is not, for what will be shown is that implicit in their appeal (and that of others) to religious studies to reinvigorate religious education, and the wider narrative of which this is part, is an alternative, deeper narrative about the history and 'progress' of religious education, which makes better sense of its history and current state. An appreciation of the relevance and appropriateness of this alternative narrative illustrates the need both for the subject to strike out in a slightly different direction from that envisaged by Cush and Robinson, and for a more self-critical, reflexive attitude to be shown by religious educators toward developments in religious studies. In simple terms, the type of religious education that Cush and Robinson want, will not be achieved *solely* by copying developments in religious studies but also by the subject of religious education re-orientating itself to the moral and social aims of education and developing policies and practices consistent with this.

Religious studies and the transition from confessional to non-confessional religious education

The broad outlines of the story that I am about to retell is familiar to many (Copley 2008a; Jackson 1990; Thompson 2004; it is also told more fully in Barnes 2014).[2] What is important for our purposes is to identify the terms and nature of the debate in which the transition from confessionalism to non-confessionalism occurred in its historical context in England and how this has been perceived retrospectively. Attention is given to Ninian Smart, whose work is widely portrayed as providing the catalyst for change as well as determining the future direction of religious education. To appreciate the nature of the transition and why Smart's contribution came to be so influential, some background knowledge is needed.

Up until the late 1950s it was commonly and uncontroversially assumed that Britain was a Christian country and that the school had an important role to play in the promotion and continuation of Christian faith and culture. Some maintained that it was Britain's Christian culture and its democratic system of government, which was widely believed to be derived from Christianity, that enabled it both to reject the fascism movement in pre-war Britain and to provide the moral resolve to oppose Hitler and not capitulate. Acquaintance with locally produced Agreed Syllabuses of the immediate post-war period, underline the confessional nature of the subject (see Loosemore 1993). Pupils were expected to adopt Christian beliefs and values and, in this way, lay down a firm moral foundation for work and for service to the community.

Traditional attitudes to the nature, role and importance of religious education in the 1960s, however, came to be challenged, chiefly as a response to wider social, economic and intellectual changes. The major influence, which can be regarded as an organising theme that gives coherence and unity to these other changes, was that of the process of secularisation. The traditional interpretation is that the Industrial Revolution initiated the process of secularisation in Britain and that it proceeded gradually, yet ineluctably, in the succeeding centuries, until in the late 1950s and early 60s its advance reached a point, with the questioning of traditional authorities such as the state, the church and inherited systems of deference and patronage, including the monarchy, that its consequences became more apparent to social commentators. The process crossed a threshold that brought a new awareness of its significance. More recently the historian Callum Brown (2009) has argued that, rather than being a gradual process, concomitant with the rise of modernity and industrial society, secularisation was a sudden affair initiated largely by the abandonment by women of their traditionally assigned roles of 'home makers' and models of virtue. In response to the sexual revolution, which separated sex from marriage, which in turn took advantage of available contraception that separated sex from pregnancy, and to changing economic conditions that encouraged (required even) women to join the work force (a development initiated during the war) and participate in society, women gained greater autonomy to determine their own lives and values. Brown's argument, as summarised by Carole M. Cusack

(2011: 269), is that 'the discourse of female virtue and domesticity was intimately connected with Christianity, and when it collapsed Christianity did too'. It is women in the home who had been the guardians of Christian belief and values and once their guardianship was relinquished, Christianity lost its affect over the young. It is not necessary to choose between these two interpretations of the process of secularisation. Whichever is preferred, in the 1960s many religious educators concluded that the stable diet of biblical history and of biblical study were no longer appropriate to an increasingly disinterested and even sceptical audience in schools, which no doubt reflected the attitudes of many parents.

Throughout the sixties religious educators responded in different ways, with many attempting to rescue Christian confessionalism by taking more account of the interests of pupils, reducing the amount of biblical content to be covered or taking advantage of liberal initiatives in theology that encouraged less dogmatic but more experientially focused accounts of Christianity. A few advocated replacing religious education with moral education. Ninian Smart entered this debate in 1968 with the publication of *Secular Education and the Logic of Religion*. He identified a tension (1968: 90), which he referred to as 'the schizophrenia' lying at the heart of contemporary British religious education, between Christian confessionalism, 'entrenched in our school system,' and the secular and neutral institution of higher education: 'Neutralism is in part a reflection of the plural society in which we live'. The twin themes of the need for neutrality in public institutions and recognition of the pluralist nature of modern British society undermined the educational basis for confessional religious education. The schizophrenia of modern religious education can be resolved by its rejection and the adoption of (what he believed to be) an open and religiously neutral approach that aims to provide an understanding of religion.

The following year Smart was appointed to the directorship of the Schools Council Secondary Project on Religious Education. The *Working Paper*, Number 36 in the series (entitled *Religious Education in Secondary Schools*), produced under his direction in 1971, unsurprisingly draws upon his earlier arguments and endorses his earlier conclusions, though they are extended somewhat. Negatively, confessional religious education (now called 'dogmatic') religious education is interpreted as subversive of educational values and equated with indoctrination. Positively, in its place an 'undogmatic or phenomenological approach' is proposed, one that finds its rationale and commitments in the continental tradition of the phenomenology of religion and aims at religious understanding. According to Smart this means both that a range of religions should be studied and that they should be studied 'objectively.'

The stimulus Smart gave to phenomenological approaches to religious education was soon taken up and explored more fully by others who drew on the work and writings of Gerardus van der Leeuw (1964), Rudolf Otto (1958[1917]), Friedrich Heiler (1961), W. B. Kristensen (1960) and Mircea Eliade (1958). The epistemic and ontological commitments of the phenomenology of religion, and even its specialist vocabulary—terms such as *epoché* and *eidetic vision*—became the currency of British religious education (see Sharpe 1975). Pupils were encouraged to bracket out their critical presuppositions, the act of *epoché*, and 'enter into' and intuit the essence of religious phenomena, i.e. through an *eidetic vision*. Empathy for others is achieved through imaginatively entering into their experience and 'walking in their shoes.' Michael Grimmitt (1973/1978), for example, did much to popularise the work and ideas of van der Leeuw among religious educators and Robin Minney (1975) and John Marvell (1976) popularised the ideas and interpretation of Otto.

The standard commitments and emphases of phenomenological approaches to religious are widely evidenced in the writings of British religious educators throughout the 1970s and 1980s (see Barnes 2014: 94–112): religion is an essential element of human nature; the different religions reveal 'our primal destiny and our relation to God' (Eliade 1959); the essence of religion is religious encounter with the Holy (*das Heilige*, or the Sacred), and so on. Also appropriated from the phenomenology of religion was the divorce of religious education from moral education, for as *Working Paper 36* (1971: 67) states, 'the study of ethics and the study of religion are separate and distinct... areas of study'. Equally influential was the idea of setting aside one's initial presuppositions and critical rational faculties and being open to the experiential reality of religion. Whether intended or not the effect of this was for the most part to exclude critical discussions of religion or its truth claims from religious education.

Revising the narrative of Cush and Robinson

What this short account of the emergence of non-confessional religious education shows, under the influence of Smart and others and their advocacy of a phenomenological approach, is that while providing a positive rationale for multi-faith religious education and a rejection of Christian confessionalism, it also bequeathed a set of commitments that have contributed significantly to systemic weaknesses within post-confessional religious education, which in turn have contributed to the current crises about which many religious educators now speak. The problem is that they do not look to the possibility that the phenomenology of religion exerted both a positive and a negative influence over religious education and that the current crisis, which is typically regarded as recent, is the product of historically extended systemic weaknesses.

Anyone familiar with debates in religious studies will know that in the last few decades proponents and practitioners of the phenomenology of religion have been heavily criticised from within religious studies. Smart, Eliade and van der Leeuw are now referred to disparagingly by some as 'religionists' or as 'crypto-theologians' (Fitzgerald 2000; McCutcheon 1997). The methodology of bracketing, which is presented as intended to achieve objectivity, is also accused of serving to protect religion from criticism, while simultaneously aiming to initiate, through professed neutrality, an awareness of the underlying spiritual reality that comes to expression in religious phenomena. Religious studies, at this period in its history, had its own substantive normative position and normative knowledge; it, like theology, had certain commitments and values that were constitutive of its theory and practice. The myth that religious studies is neutral and objective, however, remains among some religious educators; particularly the myth that the direction charted by Smart and phenomenology inspired religious education was not only neutral and objective but also positive in almost all regards (see the debate between O'Grady 2005, 2009 and Barnes 2007, 2009). For example, in 1989, Brian Netto identified continuing 'theocentric assumptions' (1989: 163) in British religious education, as evidenced by the fact that Christianity was (in law) accorded greater curriculum time than other religions (a feature which arguably is justified by its historical significance in Britain and which strictly has nothing to do with theology) and then went on to argue that the phenomenology of religion provides the model for religious education to emulate, in the mistaken belief that it enshrines neutrality and objectivity of the kind contradicted by theology! British religious education while eschewing Christian confessionalism, under the influence of one important stream of the academic study of religion, nevertheless espoused confessionalism of a sort, more liberal, ecumenical and religiously inclusive, but still a form of confessionalism.

A convincing case can also be made that religious education's divorce from moral education can be traced back to *Working Paper 36* (1971) and the then popular thesis among philosophers and phenomenologists of religion (following Schleiermacher and Otto) that morality and religion are discrete areas of experience. For analytical philosophers of this period morality was confidently presumed to be self-justifying and did not need religion for (epistemic) support—a not uncommon view was that religion cannot provide such support, whereas phenomenologists regarded religious experience as the essence of religion and moral matters only of secondary concern. The effect of this, what Stephen Parker and Rob Freathy (2011: 258) refer to as the 'dissociation' of religious education from moral education, limited any contribution religious education might make to the moral development of pupils. The demotion of moral issues to a peripheral position within religious education also alienated the subject from the 'life-world' of many pupils, whose moral idealism aspired to be sharpened and refined through a consideration of morally contentious subjects that impinged on their experience—animal rights, issues of crime and punishment, sexual morality, and so on.

A situation was created where some of the major weaknesses in British religious education resulted from its dependence upon an influential stream of twentieth century religious studies, that of the phenomenology of religion. It, in turn, is one expression of post-Enlightenment religious thought, an expression which under the influence of Schleiermacher (1928 and 1958) distinguished religion sharply from rational knowledge and morality. Normative commitments acquired from religious studies have resulted in misrepresentations of the nature of religion, compromised its contribution to the spiritual, moral and social aims of education and frustrated a clear rationale for critical discussions of religion and of religious truth claims based on the belief that this would undermine phenomenological processes of intuiting religious truth. What is clear is that religious educators need to become more reflexive and self-critical in their reading of the post-confessional history of religious education in Britain and more critical in their reading and appropriation of developments in religious studies. Many of the pioneers of non-confessional religious education, in their rejection of Christianity as a normative basis for religious education in an increasingly pluralist society, naively assumed that religious studies was objective, neutral and apolitical (see McCutcheon 1997). As a consequence, ideas and commitments were appropriated that were equally normative, only in more disguised and subtle ways, and, as it turned out, ideas and commitments that were inadequate to providing a sophisticated understanding of the nature of religion and in contributing to the moral and social development of pupils.

It has already been pointed out that there are weaknesses in the appeal to developments in religious studies by Cush and Robinson. They seem unaware of the controversial nature of some of their proposals and they refer to ideas and 'insights' that have already been appropriated by religious educators. They also show partiality in the movements to which they refer and the issues they raise. The focus of their discussion is on developments in religious studies that are responses to campaigning (liberationist) movements whose origins lie outside religious studies and whose interests extend far beyond religion, for example, the identification and critique of 'naturalised heterosexuality' (2014: 9) by feminists and proponents of queer theory is not confined to the subject of religion, but is directed to the range of institutions in society, for all institutions and societies in one way or another assume and perpetuate particular gender roles and sexual identities. What Cush and Robinson fail to consider are developments within religious studies that relate directly to the aim of understanding religion and interpreting the beliefs, practices and values of the principal religions, which is an important aim (though not the only aim) of religious education as required by the Education Reform Act of 1988. Examples include new approaches to reading and interpreting sacred texts (Griffiths 1999; Schaper 2009), new understandings of the role of ritual in religions, often inspired by the work of Catherine Bell (1992 and 1997), and post-Wittgensteinian appreciations of the importance of belief in the religions, which take account of the linguistic and conceptual nature of religious 'texts' (see Anttonen 2000; Penner 2000). There are resources within religious studies that can profitably be appropriated by religious educators, provided they are self-critical and discerning in their appropriation.

Why do Cush and Robinson confine their discussion to the issues they do? They state (2014: 4) that they will concentrate on 'theoretical and methodological perspectives', yet give no justification for their narrowness of vision. The perspectives they consider, however, are revealing and confirm our analysis and interpretation that under the influence of religious studies, religious education became detached from moral education. Interestingly, the developments in religious studies they review relate in some way or other to what may be called the issue of equality; in broad terms they relate to morality, for clearly equality is a moral or ethical principle, even if its relevance and its application are often contested. Cush and Robinson want religious education to become effective in challenging discrimination, prejudice and intolerance in society; they want to re-moralise religious education. Their stress upon the need for religious education to 'destabilise stereo-typical portrayals' (2014: 9) of religions, and their emphasis upon diversity within religions is intended to contribute to the creation of a more inclusive society, characterised by respectful relationships between individuals and between communities. They explicitly link their curriculum proposals with their ethical vision for religious education when they speak of the subject making 'space for smaller traditions' because 'many newer or minority religious groups face discrimination and marginalisation in religious education as elsewhere' (2014: 13). The problem for them, as already noted, is that they look for inspiration from examples within religious studies whose origins lie outside it. What they also fail to appreciate is that there is material internal to the religions that is relevant to their agenda. They equally fail to appreciate that the aims of religious studies differ from religious education, and this difference limits the resources that can be appropriated by religious educators to contribute to the moral and social development of pupils in schools. What is not being claimed is that religious studies provides no resources that are relevant to religious education, rather that the resources are limited to content that is far from central to the academic study of religion, and that the content appropriated from the study of religions requires creative application by teachers for it to be an effective vehicle of moral education. In what ways do the aims of religious studies differ from the aims of religious education?

The aims of religious education and those of religious studies

What are the aims of religious studies at tertiary level education? Here are a few representative answers:

> Religious Studies is the exploration of the expression of religion in human culture. It explores human ideas about the divine, as well as the way religious concepts are expressed in texts, rituals, and belief systems. It studies the history of religion as well as important religious figures.
>
> (Memorial University of Newfoundland)[3]

> Religion is a vital aspect of human history and culture. To understand the modern world, it is necessary to understand religion. It is relevant to choices, identity and practices in everyday life, and is implicated in decision-making in everything from human rights, to the environment, to security.
>
> (Open University)[4]

> Religious beliefs, behaviours and institutions are powerful components in human societies. Understanding their motivations and structures can help the search for solutions to major challenges in the contemporary world.

This programme allows a deepening engagement with theory and method in religious studies.

(University of Edinburgh)[5]

In broad terms the aim of the academic study of religion is to understand religion, its nature, diversity and role in history and in contemporary societies. It is an intellectual humanistic discipline. It does not presuppose personal commitment, nor does it aim to undermine personal commitment. As such, it is sometimes equated with a scientific approach to religion (though see above)—neutral, impartial, rational (not rationalistic). On Continental Europe the study of religion is often referred to as *Religionswissenschaft*—'the science of religion'. Religious studies makes few moral demands of students (not to engage in plagiarism, for example) and does not regard furthering their moral or social development an important concern; it is for the most part almost exclusively academically orientated.

Interpreting the different religions and understanding the nature of religion are central to religious studies, as is how religions are to be explained and represented. These aims are also shared with religious education, and for this reason religious educators can profit from new ideas and developments in religious studies, though there is the challenge of translating new academic insights into forms of thought and language that pupils in schools can appropriate on the basis of their evolving and more limited conceptual abilities. Certainly the aims of religious education overlap with those of religious studies, for education about religion necessarily involves knowing about the different religions and understanding the nature of religion, and availing of the tools of analysis and insights from religious studies are relevant to this. But understanding and interpreting religion is not the sole aim of religious education, there are other aims that relate more explicitly to the educational, social and developmental purposes of education.

The moral purpose of education is a common and constant theme in modern British educational legislation. Section 7 of the 1944 Education Act required Local Education Authority schools 'to contribute towards the spiritual, moral, mental and physical development of the community' (1944); and Section 1(2) of the Education Reform Act (1988) requires the curriculum in a maintained school to promote 'the spiritual, moral, cultural, mental and physical development of pupils at the school and of the society'. More recent legislation confirms the continuing connection between the moral and social development of pupils and education and schooling. Non-statutory guidance (endorsed by prominent religious educators) makes it clear that the subject of religious education is particularly relevant to the realisation of the moral and social aims of education. Even while the subject officially distances itself from moral education, it also advances the claim that post-confessional multi-faith religious education challenges prejudice and intolerance (see Barnes 2014: 218–231). The aims of religious education have always extended beyond that of facilitating an understanding of religion to include contributing to the social and moral aims of education—to prepare pupils to live amidst moral and religious diversity; to help them to develop self-respect, to make wise moral choices and to equip them to contribute positively to society. These aims and aspirations are shared with families and communities. The natural and obvious place for religious educators to look to 're-moralise' religious education is to the moral content of the different religions, and although this is not a prominent aspect of the academic study of religion there is material that is relevant: each of the religions has a vision of the good both for the individual and for society; each of the religions has a historically evolving body of moral teachings; and each of the religions has made important responses to contemporary moral issues. There is the challenge of conceptualising and incorporating this material into classroom teaching for the purpose of furthering liberal educational (social) aims and for relating it to pupils in schools at different stages of their cognitive and emotional development.

The 2007 Birmingham Agreed Syllabus provides one interesting, stimulating and educationally and philosophically sophisticated way of doing this (Felderhof & Thompson 2014). Yet even syllabuses have their limitations and often it is up to the individual teacher to make creative connections between what is to be appropriated from religions in terms of content and the best pedagogy to use to further the religious, moral and social aims of education in a school context. The statement 'it is up to the teacher' may not be the best expression of what is meant, for it could convey the idea of a perfunctory duty that is performed by teachers, whereas it is precisely in the delivery of religious content through an appropriate pedagogy, complemented by the communicative skills and expertise of the teacher, that the excellence of so many teachers of religious education is shown. This is not to demean the skills of university teachers or to suggest that pedagogy is not important to them, though it is fair to say that whereas they can normally assume common intellectual aptitudes and positive interest by students, this is not the case for school teachers who are required to relate religious material to a wide range of pupils with different aptitudes and interests. In addition, the challenge is to relate the material not only in terms of conveying religious knowledge and understanding but in a way that contributes to the personal and moral development of those taught. Religious education can appropriate much from religious studies, yet the latter is not the whole of religious education; there is little awareness of this in the discussion of Cush and Robinson.

Theology, religious studies and religious education

Once it is appreciated that religious studies has presuppositions, commitments and 'prejudices' of its own (see Lewis 2011 for a particularly clear defence of this view), it invites and creates the possibility for a new dialogue between the various schools of theology and religious education, not just in faith schools but in non-religious schools (see Roebben 2016). Neither religious studies nor theology is neutral; consequently, if religious studies can be a conversation partner with religious education, why not theology? Showing that religious studies includes normative commitments and makes normative claims and yet can provide worthwhile resources for religious education opens the door to a new creative dialogue between religious education and theology, and not just Christian theology. Is a new dialogue between religious education and theology so easily effected? The matter is more complicated than one might think however, for there remains a distinction of sorts between theology and religious studies in regard to their respective normative claims, at least as theology has been historically practised and as religious studies is currently practised.

The discipline of theology in the West is usually taken to denote Christian theology (and its many sub-varieties thereof), the term can also denote and include Islamic or Jewish theology, and even Hindu theology, which relates to the theistic traditions within Hinduism; there are also wider uses of the term to denote beliefs about the 'divine' or the 'Ultimate' (Hick 1989), where the concept of God is absent (as in Theravada Buddhism) or is indeterminate in meaning. My belief is that theology in these different varieties is relevant to religious education, to the extent that the religions of which their theologies are an expression are relevant to religious education (and the examples of religions I have given are clearly relevant). This is not a position that can be adequately defended or illustrated here. Theology is never in the abstract but is some particular theology, and for the purpose of illustration, discussion will be confined to Christian theology, mainly because it is the tradition which historically has had the closest relationship with religious education in Britain.

Christianity clearly makes normative (epistemic) claims about the existence of God, the incarnation of God in Christ, the death and resurrection of Christ, Christ's atonement for sin, justification by grace through faith, the nature of the after-life; these also include normative moral claims about how one should live and relate to others. Granted, there may be differences of emphasis and interpretation between different traditions of Christianity, yet few would deny that there are certain beliefs that shape Christian identity and are shared by most committed Christians. A denial of one of these beliefs in the context of a presentation of Christian teaching would properly raise the question whether Christianity was being faithfully represented. The normative claims of religious studies are different, while acknowledging that under the influence of the phenomenology of religion the distinction between it and theology became questionable. In recent decades, however, religious studies has been without an overarching theoretical commitment or a single methodology that determines and regulates the study of religion; this is because it has become more secular, and liberal theological commitments no longer provide a shared theoretical foundation. Currently there is no common set of normative commitments in religious studies. Perhaps one may want to refer to certain procedural norms, like attention to evidence and argument and faithful representation of religions and religious phenomena, but it is doubtful if such commitments distinguish religious studies from theology in any significant or meaningful way. There are different currents of thought and different varieties of normative thought that influence, and are expressed through, religious studies. On almost every issue there is argument and debate, where different normative commitments interact and sometimes clash, for example, on the nature of religion (see Pals 2014), on the methodology best suited to interpreting religion (Wiebe 1999), and on the social and political stance of the scholar of religion (McCutcheon 2001; Arnal & McCutcheon 2012). There is, nevertheless, much to be gained from a dialogue by religious educators with religious studies. Religious studies is eclectic in a broader sense than theology and there is greater freedom to choose which substantive normative commitments to follow and use in one's research and writings. The Christian theologian by contrast is constrained, to the extent that he or she professes to interpret and articulate Christian beliefs. The distinction between the two may not be absolute, but they do have implications for education.

What role then for theology in religious education? My first comment does not answer this directly, but it is an important implication that follows for religious education from recognition of the normative claims of Christianity and Christian theology. There needs to be a critical element in religious education in which pupils have the opportunity to consider the truth claims of different religions and the kinds of appeal that are made to justify particular religious commitments. Religious truth claims should be presented and considered in an open and fair way, with opportunities for debate, reflection and criticism. Religious education should not set out to determine the choice of pupils, rather it should provide them with the knowledge, abilities and skills to enable them to make responsible, self-critical choices about their participation in and attitude toward religious beliefs and practices. This recommendation receives further support from recognition of the plural nature of late modern Western societies—where the same society can legitimately be characterised as both religious and post-religious and as both secular and post-secular, albeit in different ways. Young people live in a world where they are increasingly faced with choices and decisions in matters that are central to their sense of self and personhood. Religious identity for most of us is now a matter of choice among competing options. The constraining factors of family and of community have become less under the influence of modernity, that of urbanisation, secularisation, individualisation, and so on. The educational challenge is to enable pupils to make responsible, self-critical decisions about their ultimate commitments and values. This stance is not only consistent with Christian commitment but required by it. For religious faith to be genuine, it must be freely chosen. Our modern concept of liberty owes much to the Protestant Reformation and the importance attached by Luther to the need to commit oneself individually and existentially to the cause of Christ, and by others who extended the concept to include social and political freedom. Christian faith demands that pupils choose freely whether to embrace or to reject Christianity or any other religion or non-religious worldview; and consequently, even confessional religious education ought to include a critical element.

The truth claiming nature of a religion assumes that there are things to be believed. Beliefs are constitutive of religion and of religious experience (see Barnes 2014: 113–125), or if this is too forceful a statement for some, the weaker and less controversial position that beliefs are an important dimension of religion is sufficient to justify giving serious attention to religious concepts and beliefs in religious education. Pupils (and students of religion) 'must seek to understand the conceptual as a crucial dimension to understanding the reality' of religions (Helmer 2011: 253). Christianity, for example, revolves around the concept of the Triune God who revealed himself in the history of Israel and sacrificed himself in the person of his Son to gain human salvation. Individuals become Christians when they come to accept the Christian interpretation of their existential needs and the Christian account of how their needs are met in Christ. By contrast, to be a Muslim is to believe in the revelation vouchsafed to Muhammad and subsequently recorded in the Qur'an.

At one point in *Philosophical Investigations* (1958: 116, §373) Wittgenstein spoke of 'theology as grammar' (*Theologie als Grammatik*). His wider use of the term grammar in the *Investigations* draws attention to the fact that speaking a language is, among other things, a rule guided activity: his reference to theology means that there are rules that regulate how theological language is used and the senses that can be expressed through it. Theology articulates the rules that govern how doctrines are related to one another and, by extension, how the rules relate to practice. To understand a religion or a religious phenomenon one must appreciate the beliefs that are expressed and their relationship to other beliefs within the overall web of belief. This is an important aspect of the acquisition of religious literacy (there are other aspects, I grant). One can not claim to understand the concept of forgiveness, for example, if one does not appreciate not just its role in Christian life but how its meaning relates to and is determined by other beliefs, about God, repentance and sacrifice (Barnes 2018) Religious educators must draw on the discipline of theology and the work of theologians to be educationally equipped to do this.

Wittgenstein also reminds us, however, that beliefs and doctrines are embodied and expressed in religious forms of life. Religion is not just about believing, it is about acting in the world; it is about rituals and practices; it involves values and attitudes and belonging to a community. While beliefs and doctrines are important in religion, their importance should not be over-emphasised in educational presentations. Consequently, while teachers should look to theology in order to gain an understanding of religious texts and the beliefs and doctrines that shape religions, and Christianity in particular, so they should also look to religious studies to gain an understanding of the wider aspects of religions and the religious life—its practices, rituals, historical and cultural significance and its influence on art, music, drama, and in the lives of religious believers.

Theology also has a role to play in assisting religious education to realise the moral and social aims of education. At a theoretical level there are theological resources that enable teachers to overcome British religious education's divorce from morality. Pupils should know that in Christianity there is no dichotomy between facts and values. Ethical imperatives and prohibitions are grounded in Christian indicatives: 'If we live by the Spirit [indicative], let us walk by the Spirit [imperative]' (Gal. 5.25; also 1 Cor. 5:7; Phil. 2:12–13; the same pattern is shown on a larger canvas in Romans, where Chapters 1–11, devoted to Christian indicatives, are followed by Chapters 12–15, devoted to imperatives, and in Ephesians, where Chapters 1–3 are followed by Chapters 4–6). The imperatives of behaviour are based on the fact of the Christian's new nature in Christ. The 'believer's every action is oriented on God's antecedent act in Christ' (Bornkamm 1971: 201). Morality and Christian beliefs/doctrines are intrinsically connected; as Eberhard Jüngel (1992: 36) has said, 'the indicative carries the imperative'. For the Christian the philosophical problem, identified by Hume (2000 [1738]) of 'how to derive an ought from an is?', is a pseudo problem because all facts exist in an ontologically prior universe that was created, sustained, and will be brought to its proper end (telos) by an essentially good God. Facts are value laden!

More practically, the moral content of religion has the potential to reconnect religious education with the interests and concerns of pupils. It is widely appreciated in Britain that by neglecting moral issues, under the influence of the phenomenology of religion, the subject lost much of its relevance to young people; though subsequently, to some extent, some religious educators have made efforts to reinstate the moral content of religion in religious education. Christianity, like other religions, has a vision of 'the good' both for the individual and for society; it has a historically evolving body of moral teachings and it makes important responses to contemporary moral issues. This teaching is necessarily theological: Christian moral teaching cannot be expounded without engaging with (moral) theology.

Theology also has a role to play in developing resources and materials to challenge bigotry and intolerance. For example, respect for others is for Christians grounded in the doctrine that men and women bear the image of God (*imago dei*). Each individual possesses a dignity, that is not natural but supernatural in origin. Nicholas Wolterstorff (2010) has recently argued that this doctrine provides the best foundation for assertions of human rights. He believes that rights are 'normative social relationships' and that 'sociality is built into the essence of rights' (2010: 4). Certain 'goods', including positive ways of treating and respecting others, are appropriate for all human beings because they bear God's image. There is also biblical material in the form of story, poetry, parable and explicit moral teaching that illustrates and commends the practice of Christian love. In other words, use needs to be made in schools of tradition specific materials, such as those provided by Christianity, for furthering the moral and social aims of education.

Finally, there is much within the domain of public theology that is relevant to educators and to religious education. Presumably all theology is public as it is expressed in a public language (again an insight borrowed from Wittgenstein), yet in contemporary usage public theology has a more determinate meaning: it is theology that self-consciously aims to engage with and contribute constructively both to the civil, social and political interests of society and to the 'common good' (see Pirner 2018). Christianity has important things to say about education, just as it has on other subjects of public concern and policy. It has a contribution to make both to the public debate about the aims and nature of education and to how schools, confessional or otherwise, can help to develop personal and civic virtue. Public theology also provides material content for religious education through its reflections and statements, for public theology articulates the social conscience of the church as it relates to such important public matters as justice and peace. Unfortunately, public theology of this kind is more characteristic of German religious educators than British religious educators.

This chapter has covered much controversial ground, from identifying and criticising uncritical appropriations of religious studies in religious education, to flawed readings of the history of post-confessional religious education; it has also identified constructive differences between the aims of religious education and religious studies and concluded with a call for a new dialogue between religious education and theology—illustrated through the example of Christian theology.

Notes

1 By contrast, religious education is compulsory in schools, unless parents exercise their legal right of withdrawal on behalf of their children.
2 Jackson's (1990: 109) review of developments in religious education presents the traditional narrative which equates the transition of confessional to non-confessional religious education with the emergence of professionalism and regards most of the criticism of phenomenological religious education as 'misinformed'; the influence or relevance of theology to religious education is not considered.
3 See http://www.mun.ca/relstudies/about/ (originally accessed on 21 January 2014; more recently revised).
4 See http://fass.open.ac.uk/religious-studies (accessed on 23 March 2019).
5 See https://www.ed.ac.uk/divinity/studying/graduate-school/postgraduate-taught/religious-studies/programme-description (accessed on 23 March 2019).

4

HUMAN RIGHTS, VALUES AND RELIGIOUS FREEDOM

The Twentieth Session of the International Seminar on Religious Education and Values (ISREV), which is the leading international forum for researchers working in the field of religious educators, was held at the University of Saint Mary of the Lake, Chicago in August 2016. The main theme of the conference was 'Values, Human Rights and Religious Education'. The title is indicative of the importance religious educators attach to the development of positive values in pupils and to ensuring that their work is human rights compliant. Interest in values and in rights are not new to religious educators; one may legitimately claim that religious education, like education and schooling generally, have always been concerned with values (at this stage rights can be regarded as enshrining particularly important values). Education is a 'value laden' enterprise, as educationalists keep reiterating (e. g., Hirst 1966: 52; McLaughlin 2000: 444). Nevertheless, it is true to claim that the role of values and of rights, *and* explicit use of the language of values and rights, in British education generally and in religious education particularly, have come to assume much greater importance in the last two to three decades, and some believe that this orientation will give new relevance and legitimacy to religious education, while overcoming weaknesses.

The aim of this chapter is to consider the role of rights in religious education—to assess their relevance and importance, features that are almost universally endorsed by religious educators. More critically, it is asked whether the appeal to rights in religious education ought to chart the future direction of religious education, and whether the promise they hold for the renewal of religious education is as great as is frequently supposed. The argument is structured as follows. The chapter begins with an impressionistic history of the role of values and rights in religious education and how this has increased in the last few decades. Three different versions of the thesis that rights ought to provide the framework within which religious education is pursued are then set out and considered: that of

Robert Jackson's, of Andrew McGrady's and that of the *Toledo Guiding Principles on Teaching About Religions and Beliefs in Public Schools*. Criticism, where appropriate, is integrated into the analysis of each. It is concluded that the importance appropriate to the role of human rights in religious education is in many cases exaggerated; in addition, what can be achieved on the basis of assigning a central place to rights in education is quite limited. It is granted, however, that emphasis on the role of rights in education, often results from the best of motives; for rights are believed to challenge bigotry, intolerance and (immoral) discrimination and to contribute to the creation of a respectful and responsible citizenry. *To a limited extent* they do. But what they do can equally be pursued without reference to rights, and for the most part has been, historically (see below). Yet even while acknowledging that rights have limited, albeit important, relevance to religious education, they are nevertheless unlikely to contribute much to the realisation of liberal educational aims, such as those expressed above. There are convincing reasons for believing that a rights-focused form of religious education will fail to achieve what most of its advocates assume will be achieved by its adoption.

Limitations of space in this context forbid discussion of criticisms of human rights (see Dembour 2010), some of which are important and require careful consideration and extended responses. My argument here, however, does not constitute a critique of the concept of human rights or a rejection of any right in particular. Rights are vital and some are inviolable, except in the most exceptional of circumstances. Human rights provide a bulwark against encroachments both by the state and by other people. Moreover, rights are required for the satisfaction of certain needs, the achievement of certain goods, the protection of certain interests and the attainment of certain values.

The increasing importance of values education and appeals to human rights

In the immediate post-war years, values in British education were believed to be transmitted through the curriculum as a whole, by a process of osmosis. As pupils adapted to the disciple of school life and conformed themselves to the expectations of teachers, parents and society, so they were regarded as acquiring the civic and social virtues that prepared them for adulthood. Similarly, by teaching a broad non-denominational version of Christianity in a nurturing environment, which aimed to inculcate Christian beliefs and values, religious educators believed themselves to be providing pupils with a firm moral foundation that would equip them to meet the challenges of later life and enable them to make a constructive contribution to society. This picture of positive values transmitted effectively, though indirectly, in schools through example and a traditional liberal curriculum could not survive the influence on education and schools of the social and political upheavals of the late 1960s and the 1970s: the increasing pace of secularisation in society, what Callum Brown (2009) has called 'the death of Christian Britain', alongside growing religious and cultural diversity, with the associated evils of bigotry and discrimination; the emergence of more strident and oppositional forms of party politics that stressed class divisions and the differences between workers and management and between the 'haves' and the 'have nots'; and particularly relevant to schools, the emergence of a commercialised youth culture with its own mores, music and fashion, which was a manifestation of the growing spending power of young people and their increasing autonomy as family structures evolved to meet the changing economic and social needs of a post-industrial society—changing needs that on some interpretations sounded the death knell of the traditional family, that of husband and wife following pre-determined gender roles. Like all historically extended social influences, these influences took time to be identified and recognised, and only when recognised can their influence and significance (which may be contested) be assessed and responses considered and implemented. Consequently, it was in the 1980s that educators began to fully appreciate the challenges these influences posed to society and to education. For example, although anti-discrimination legislation was introduced in 1965, it was the Race Relations Act of 1976, which made both direct and indirect discrimination an offence and gave those affected by discrimination redress through employment tribunals and the courts. This Act provided the impetus in the 1980s to antiracist and multicultural programmes in schools, both of which raised questions about prevailing 'conservative' and 'racist' values that characterised the curriculum. Both naturally raised the question about the values that schools ought to be transmitting in diverse and in some respects socially and religiously fragmented modern Britain.

A focus on values in education and schools came from a different direction and with a different agenda with the election of a Conservative government under Margaret Thatcher on 4 May 1979. The most important piece of legislation on education produced under her direction was the Education (Reform) Act of 1988 (which remains one of the most significant legislative documents on education since the Second World War). Although it is best known for the introduction of a statutory curriculum into English education, it also required teaching that 'promotes the spiritual, moral, cultural, mental and physical development of pupils at the school and of society' (Section 1 (2a) of the Act). Since 1992 it has been a statutory requirement for the Office for Standards in Education (Ofsted) to include in its inspection reports an account and evaluation of the spiritual, moral, social and cultural development of pupils, and this requirement obviously ensured that schools attend to this new curriculum initiative (see Taylor 1998: 6), as well as stimulating the publication of books and articles dedicated to explaining the relevant curricular requirements and to clarifying and considering the role of values in schools (see Best 1996; Halstead and Taylor 1996; Bigger 1999).

In 1990, the National Curriculum Council (NCC), which was then responsible for curriculum policy, issued various forms of non-statutory guidance to schools, two of which, that concerned with citizenship and that with the 'Spiritual, Moral, Social and Cultural development' of children, referred to 'values'. Early in 1993 the National Curriculum Council drew up and circulated a discussion paper entitled 'Moral and Spiritual Education', which was reissued by NCC's successor body, the School Curriculum and Assessment Authority (SCAA), in 1995, and used as the basis for a major conference on spiritual and moral aspects of the curriculum in January 1996. A range of 'school values' were identified: these included telling the truth, keeping promises and respecting the rights and property of others. One outcome of the conference was a further discussion paper entitled, *Education for Adult Life: The spiritual and moral development of young people* (SCAA 1996a) that summarised its deliberations. Another outcome was the establishment of *The National Forum for Values in Education and the Community* (1996b). This brought together prominent educationalists, politicians, community leaders, and representatives from the different religions. A consultation exercise was undertaken in order to take account of public opinion on the role of schools in the promotion of spiritual and moral values; its results were published in December of that year (1996c).

These developments occurred against a background of 'moral panic' that focused on the anti-social and criminal behaviour of young people—a subject on which prolonged and graphic media reporting of the abduction and brutal murder of James Bulger, along with the subsequent trial of two ten-year-old boys, Robert Thompson and Jon Venables, brought into public focus. Use of the term moral panic is indebted to the writings of the South African sociologist Stanley Cohen (1942–2013). He originally used the term in *Folk Devils and Moral Panics* (1972) in his analysis of what he adjudged to be an overreaction to seaside violence in the early 1960s between two distinctive and rival groups of youth subcultures, the Mods and the Rockers. He analysed the processes involved in the 'construction' of 'moral panic', conceived (under the influence of the media) as an exaggerated perception of danger by society to forms of wrong doing or behaviour, often considered deviant, that are believed to be threats to the moral order. Moral panics can serve a political function as they become the stimulus for government interventions through regulation and even legislation; in almost all cases such official responses enshrine restrictions on institutional or personal freedom. These comments bears a fruitful application to interpretations of the rise of interest in values in education, throughout the years of Conservative rule (up to 1997, for John Major had succeeded Mrs Thatcher as Conservative Prime Minister following her resignation in 1990), though it is also important to acknowledge, as Cohen does (in the 2011 third edition: vii), that '[c]alling something a "moral panic" does not imply that this something does not exist or happened at all and that reaction is based on fantasy, hysteria, delusion and illusion or being duped by the powerful'. No doubt supporters of the Conservative Party and of conservative social policy viewed values initiatives in education positively, and necessary, given changes in society. The irony is that in substance the documents produced to support curriculum initiatives were not particularly socially or religiously conservative in content or orientation: Robert Bowie (2017: 114) has commented that documents [concerned with pupils' spiritual, moral, social and cultural development] did not advance a strong 'statist' vision of national rights. They did not assert a detailed account of national morality with particular virtues, values or moral norms aligned to a particular system or national narrative. The original NCC/SCAA Discussion Paper on 'Spiritual and Moral Development' (1996a: 2), for example, assigned no special significance to Christianity and maintained that '[t]he potential for spiritual development is open to everyone and is not confined to the development of religious beliefs or conversion to a particular faith'. Spiritual development is regarded as something wider than religious development, the former focusing on experience, creative awareness and human values, the latter on formal or institutional patterns of religious belief and practice. In other words, spiritual development can be completely divorced from religious development; hardly a 'conservative' view of things, but perhaps a realistic view that recognised religious diversity and the growing constituency of those who live purportedly without religious beliefs and practices.

Following an overwhelming Labour election success, Tony Blair became Prime Minister in May 1997. According to David Gillborn (2008: 714), '[i]t is difficult to over-state the sense of widespread relief with which progressive commentators welcomed Tony Blair's election as PM'. In the year prior to his election in his Party Conference address in Blackpool, Blair (1996) famously described Labour's priorities for [future] government as 'Education, education and education'; and within a year of the election, the School Standards and Framework Bill and the Teaching and Higher Education Bill were both successfully enacted. Education was indeed a priority for the Blair government. Those who were expecting a reversal of Tory initiatives on education, which were criticised by the Labour opposition on their introduction, however, soon came to realise that Blair's 'modernising agenda' included retaining most of the Conservative 'reforms': the national curriculum, tests and league tables, financial delegation to schools, and a strengthened inspection service were all enthusiastically embraced by New Labour, as was the emphasis on values and the requirement on schools to promote positive social values. Though, alongside references to values, there also began to appear references in curricular documents to human rights and an increasing use of the language of human rights to frame behaviour and values. This emphasis was to increase, in no small part reflecting Labour's commitment to the introduction of 'education for citizenship' in schools.

In 1997, David Blunkett, then Secretary of State for Education, appointed Bernard Crick as chair of an advisory group to provide advice on the teaching of citizenship and democracy in schools. The report, published the following year, set out the rationale for citizenship being introduced as a National Curriculum subject, and statutory force was given to Crick's proposals through the instrument of The Education (National Curriculum) (England) Order 2000. In the Crick Report (Advisory Group on Citizenship 1998), 'values' are subsumed under citizenship education, which is 'not just knowledge of citizenship and civic society; it also implies developing values, skills and understanding' (1998: 13). Dina Kiwan (2008: 42) has made the perceptive observation that 'the Crick Report emphasises "values" more in terms of "procedural" terms, for example, respect for certain public institutions and the rule of law, although acknowledging more personal, social and cultural values'. According to Crick (1998: 40), '[t]he purpose of citizenship education in schools and colleges is to make secure and to increase the knowledge, skills and values relevant to the nature and practices *of participative democracy*' (my use of italics). Values are set within the context of public life, and education is chiefly concerned with developing the values that contribute to and enhance 'public life' (Crick 1998: 7, 11, 13) and the 'common good' (Crick 1998: 9, 41, 44). This emphasis upon public values naturally supports and gives credence to the importance of rights, which the report frequently associated with 'responsibilities', i.e. 'rights and responsibilities' (Crick 1998: 19, 20, 22, for example). When it comes to the specification of learning outcomes it is the concept of rights that predominates over values (Crick 1998: 45–52). The underlying rationale is that rights are those fundamental values (as fundamental, therefore, deserving the status of rights) that are required to support and participate in a democratic society, and therefore the same values (as rights) that characterise good citizenship.

Few would question the relevance of values and rights[1] to religious education, and both have assumed increasing importance, particularly the latter, in different parts of the United Kingdom and not just England, in the wake of Crick's proposals and subsequent legislation, even though the original legislation applied only to England. Mark Chater (2000), for example, claimed that religious education provides an ideal vehicle for furthering the citizenship agenda. There have been few self-critical discussions of rights by religious educators—about where they come from and how they are grounded, or how they relate to other forms of rights, say social and economic rights, for example. Equally there has been little discussion about the justificatory origins of values or how they are to be applied in contexts where different values are (equally) relevant or where their application is disputed. These observations need not be interpreted overly negatively. For the most part religious educators pursue practical aims, of which developing positive values and respectful attitudes to others are examples, and such are regarded by some as produced by the observance of (human) rights: Robert Jackson (2015b) links rights to the encouragement of tolerance; and *The Human Rights Education Toolbox*, 2013, produced by The Danish Institute for Human Rights, connects them to non-discrimination and equality. There is, however, a convincing case for a more critical analysis of the role and relevance of human rights and values to religious education, and to a lesser extent that of the concept of citizenship. The associations are not surprising. Rights and citizenship are closely connected[2]; in modern political discourse, even necessarily connected: to be a citizen is to be a bearer of rights (Kymlicka & Norman 1994: 354), and rights have priority in legislation (and *human* rights can have further priority over other legally constituted rights, given their inclusive denotation as applying to all persons). Talk of values typically includes democratic values; and in education democratic values are often assigned prominence over other values; and democratic values are often given legal expression and translated into rights; hence the educational triad of rights, values and citizenship, with human rights as the foundational concept, as one would expect given their moral and legal force. The focus in what follows will fall chiefly on the subject of rights in relation to religious education.

Human rights as a framework for religious education

In this section three different variations on the theme that an orientation to human rights provides an intellectually credible and 'forward looking' foundation for religious education are considered.

Robert Jackson

The following series of quotations is taken from a summary statement of three pages by Jackson (originally in 2013) on the relationship of human rights to religious education, which was delivered as a contribution to a Westminster Faith Debate on 'What's the place of faith in schools?'

> Above all, I [Robert Jackson] suggest that – along with key European Institutions – we need to ground our thinking about religious education in a human rights framework.... What this amounts to is a recognition that every young person in Europe has a *right* (author's italics) to hold a particular view, whether religious or secular, within the limits of the law.
>
> *(Jackson 2013: 1)*

Jackson (2013: 1) goes on to assert on the basis of his 'team's recent research' that 'many adolescents interviewed give strong support to applying democratic principles in classrooms', which is to be equated with a 'safe place' for 'dialogue', 'peaceful coexistence', 'knowledge about each other's religions and worldviews' and 'sharing common interests'.

> As for justifying publicly-funded faith-based schools in a democratic society, I [Robert Jackson] return to my starting point: We need to refer to international law, based on human rights principles, concerning the rights of parents and the rights of children.
>
> *(Jackson 2013: 2)*

He concludes:

> [A] European perspective reminds us that the right to hold a particular viewpoint within the law, and parents' right to have their children educated in their religion, are fundamental freedoms which we must respect within the context of our different national histories of education.
>
> *(Jackson 2013: 3)*

According to Jackson, human rights provide the framework for the principles and the practice of religious education.

Andrew McGrady

A similar position to Jackson's is espoused by McGrady. He identifies '[a] new framework... [that is] evolving for the consideration of the role and nature of religious education in the "public space" based on the work of various United Nations agencies concerning the definition and promotion of human rights'(2006: 978). He notes that '[r]eligious freedom constitutes a fundamental human right and can certainly be considered one of the cornerstones of the edifice of human rights' (2006: 981). In relation to freedom in the public square, he adds that '[n]ot only does the state have a duty to ensure the religious freedom of citizens but it also has a right to expect that the exercise of such religious freedom contributes not only to the good of the individual but to the common good' (2006: 983). Some development and qualification of this may be needed both to clarify what is meant and to pre-empt criticism. The state has a duty to uphold (the individual's right of) religious freedom, few disagree, but immediately McGrady goes on to speak of a 'right' of the state 'to expect that the exercise of such religious freedom contributes not only to the good of the individual but to the common good'. Much depends on the force of the word *expectation*, which in this case is expressed in the form of a right—a right of expectation! This right, which he ascribes to the state, is not a right that is enunciated in the *Universal Declaration of Human Rights* (if he believes it to be derivable from the Declaration then an argument needs to be made to this effect). In justification of his position, McGrady refers to the *Declaration on the Elimination of All Forms of Intolerance and of Discrimination Based on Religion or Belief*, which was produced by the United Nations in 1981 to complement the *Universal Declaration*. It, however, is more circumspect and does not ascribe a right (of expectation) along the lines suggested by McGrady. The relevant portion of Article 1.3 states (expanding upon an earlier statement on freedom of religion in the same article)[3]:

> Freedom to manifest one's religion or beliefs may be subject only to such limitations as are prescribed by law and are necessary to protect public safety, order, health or morals or the fundamental rights and freedoms of others.

The limitations imposed by this article are not as narrow as McGrady's view that the state has a right to restrict religious freedom or some aspect of religious freedom if it is believed that such freedom does not contribute to the good of the individual and to the common good. There are two critical issues here. First, McGrady does not seem to appreciate that there may be a conflict between what individuals view to be good for themselves in terms of interests, beliefs, practices and commitments and what the state views as good. The purpose of many of the freedoms (including religious freedom) protected by human rights declarations and related legislation is precisely to allow individuals to accept or reject beliefs and commitments and their associated practices as they see fit and to espouse whatever set of values they want (albeit with the provisos listed above in Article 1.3). The individual has the right to live by the principles he or she chooses, without censure or discrimination by the state. Second, and implicit in what has already been said, McGrady's framing of the right suggests that the issue of who finally determines what constitutes what is good for the individual is not the individual but the (nation) state: he speaks of the rightful expectations of the state 'concerning the good of the individual and that of the common good'. The nation state is given the power to determine what is good for the individual and for the commonweal (if both 'goods' are to be satisfied), and consequently the effective power to curtail or censure any exercise of religion (and other freedoms as well) that, in the view of the state, does not contribute to either. In attempting to apply the *Universal Declaration's* right of religious freedom to 'the public space' (2006: 983), McGrady has inadvertently creating an opportunity for the state to limit the free exercise of religion. This is probably not what he intended, but it is what has resulted.

Implicit in McGrady's position is recognition of the fact that the exercise of religious freedom can result in negative as well as positive behaviour, both from a personal and from a social perspective, and his strategy to counteract this is to place conditions on its exercise. This he does by framing an additional right. As we have noted such a right, in the terms in which he conceives it, does not exist, and secondly his restrictions on religious freedom are too extensive. Nevertheless, concern about the deleterious effects of religious freedom is appropriate and some degree of protection for the individual and society is warranted. McGrady correctly recognises this. The state can have a reasonable expectation that religious freedom will be exercised in ways that are compatible with the rule of law, the protection of minors and the security and safety of individuals. This list is not meant to be exhaustive, but whatever restrictions are imposed on the right of the freedom of religion ought to fall short of those countenanced by McGrady. This is because the state should acknowledge that individuals have the right to pursue their own religion and to frame what is good in religion in their own terms. It may be that some personal (and community) religious choices do not contribute to the common good, but this does not justify all such preferences being legally sanctioned (though some preferences might, in view of the restrictions already supported above) or penalised in some way. It is a well-established legal fact that citizens in a liberal democracy have the freedom to engage in practices that others may view as immoral or socially unacceptable or as subversive of community values; citizens also have the freedom to hold beliefs that others may regard as unwarranted or distasteful or irrational.

A more defensible approach to use as a starting point for restrictions on freedom of religion (and that of other freedoms as well) than that countenanced by McGrady, and one more consistent with the principles of liberal democracy, is Mill's (1974: 68–69) 'one very simple principle'[4] in *On Liberty* (for commentary, see Riley 2015):

[T]he sole end for which mankind are warranted, individually or collectively, in interfering with the liberty of action of any of their number is self-protection... the only purpose for which power can be rightfully exercised over any member of a civilized community, against his will, is to prevent harm to others.... The only part of the conduct of anyone for which he is amenable to society is that which concerns others. In the part that merely concerns himself, his independence is, of right, absolute. Over himself, over his own body and mind, the individual is sovereign.

In this passage Mill rejects moralistic and paternalistic restrictions on liberty and proposes that 'the harm principle' is the only proper basis for restricting personal liberty. There is much that can be said positively about this principle and there are objections. One important consideration that requires clarification is how the concept of personal liberty relates to public/private distinctions, and how this in turn relates to the legitimate concerns of the state and state institutions. One important criticism is whether Mill's commitment to utility enables him to provide an account of harm that could render the 'harm principle' morally coherent (personally I think not). Nevertheless, the harm principle provides a much better starting point for discussion about the nature and extent of religious freedom than McGrady's view that restrictions should be based on the extent to which the exercise of such freedom contributes to the good of the individual and to the common good. A more liberal account of religious freedom is needed. The following is proposed as an initial formal principle to stimulate discussion on these admittedly complex matters: restrictions on religious belief and practice (and the focus should be on practice) should, for the most part, mirror the restrictions and be no more severe than those imposed on individuals by the state in other areas of their lives.

Toledo Guiding Principles

The most important and influential document calling for the orientation of religious education to international and European standards of human rights is the *Toledo Guiding Principles on Teaching About Religions and Beliefs in Public Schools*, produced in 2007 by the Office for Democratic Institutions and Human Rights Advisory Council of Experts on Freedom of Religion or Belief, on behalf of the Organization for Security and Co-operation in Europe (OSCE). The fact that the Principles find their institutional origins in one concerned with security deserves comment, but this is not our current interest; see Gearon 2012 and 2015; and the response by Jackson 2015b. The *Toledo Principles* publication includes chapters on the human rights framework which is appropriate to 'developing or implementing curricula for teaching about religions and beliefs' (2007: 12), on the relevance of human rights to teacher education (2007: 52–62) and on the key legal issues that may arise in implementing how religion should be presented and taught on the basis of the *Principles* in public (state) schools (2007: 2 and 17):

[T]eaching about religions and beliefs [should be] through the lens of religious freedom and a human rights perspective that relies on OSCE commitments and international human rights standards.

Quality curricula in the area of teaching about religions and beliefs can only contribute effectively to the educational aims of the *Toledo Guiding Principles* if teachers are professionally trained to use the curricula and receive ongoing training to further develop their knowledge and competences regarding this subject matter. Any basic teacher preparation should be framed and developed according to democratic and human rights principles and include insight into cultural and religious diversity in society.

There is much to praise in the *Toledo Principles*, which are chiefly intended to ensure the rights of freedom of religion or belief and of freedom of speech. The Principles are concerned solely with teaching '*about* religion and beliefs' (2007: 33), while acknowledging that the UN Human Rights Committee in its General Comment no. 22 grants 'that it is also permissible for public schools to be involved in *religious instruction*' (2007: 33; my emphasis throughout); this may be interpreted as an oblique reference to the educational legitimacy of (some forms of) confessional religious education by the Committee. The fifth Key Guiding Principle of Toledo (2007: 16) also affirms the educational legitimacy of what is described as 'not sufficiently objective teaching'; again, in all probability an oblique reference to confessional education. The legitimacy of such religious instruction, however, *seems to be* questioned in other statements, for example:

While international norms do not rule out various forms of co-operation with religions and belief systems, they do require 'neutrality and impartiality' in the sense of ensuring the tolerance that is vital to pluralism, and in the sense of protecting freedom of religion or belief for all individuals and groups on an equal basis.

(2007: 34)

There are a number of ambiguities and confusions here. Does 'co-operation with religions and belief systems' include in its denotations, confessional religious education/religious instruction? Are 'neutrality' and 'impartiality' to be distinguished in meaning, as some have recently argued (Gravel & Lefebvre 2012: 199; also Jackson & Everington 2017: 10, who distinguish the terms differently) or do they carry the same meaning? Equally, of what is 'neutrality and impartiality' required? Is it the teacher or the content or the methodology? And if teaching is to be neutral and impartial, is this intended to rule out or to caution against any element of religious nurture in *public* education? This is the impression given by attention to the use of the term public and the distinction that is made between public and private schools in the document (see 2007: 15, 16, 19, 20, 33, *et passim*; though again there are ambiguities). The suggestion that 'international norms' require neutrality and impartiality appears to be a statement that is rooted in a more naïve and less reflexive philosophical age.

The myth of (secular) public education as objective, neutral and impartial is difficult to maintain in the wake of the post-structuralist philosophies of Foucault, Lyotard and others (see Barnes 2014: 159–179). Foucault, in particular, has drawn attention to the ways in which power is diffused, disguised and embodied in all discourse, knowledge and 'regimes of truth', including, and equally perniciously so, public institutions and the organisational apparatus of the nation state, including schools (Foucault 1991; Rabinow 1991). Every methodology and pedagogy in religious education assumes and employs an interpretation of religion; none is neutral—phenomenological approaches, experiential religious education, the interpretive approach and so on. The distinguished sociologist, David Martin (2016: 69–170), speaking in the context of religious education, has recently identified 'a general truth that neutrality is always in the eye of the beholder and not all it is cracked up to be'. That British religious education is anything but neutral, despite all protestations to the contrary, and in addition has espoused commitments and strategies that, again all protestations to the contrary, effectively frustrate the attainment of liberal educational aims are themes that I have pursued elsewhere in some detail (see Barnes 2014). The challenge for religious educators is not about developing neutral presentations of religion, it cannot be done, it is both about which educational representations are faithful to the nature of the different religions; and about which educational aims and values are appropriate to and best realised through religious education in different types of school in a pluralist, liberal democratic state.

Perhaps these critical comments, though justified on the basis of what is actually said, are not what is meant by the need for neutrality and impartiality in religious education, as the passage quoted goes on to specify the two aims that this requirement is meant to facilitate and realise: that of ensuring tolerance and protecting freedom of religion and belief. Yet this is problematic as well. Both aims are legitimate. There is no empirical evidence, however, that neutral and impartial religious education (which in this context may be equated with non-confessional religious education) is any more successful at developing toleration in pupils of other people's viewpoints, traditions, cultures and religions than confessional education, at least as religious education is practised in democratic societies. Furthermore, international norms, if by this is meant human rights and their associated embodiment in international protocols, neither require states to impose a neutral and impartial form of religious education (even assuming that there is such) on parents and their children in order to protect freedom of religion nor to exclude all forms of confessional religious education from public schools. Matters are a good deal more complicated and qualified than this. It may be granted that some confessional forms of religious education can be indoctrinatory but there are no good reasons, including reference to human rights considerations, for equating all forms of confessional education with indoctrination (see Chapter 8), or for that matter to deny necessarily public funding to confessional schools.

Results of our review

We are now in a position to draw some conclusions on the basis of our review of a number of proposals that look to human rights as providing a framework or foundation for religious education. The obvious point to make is that appeals to human rights in religious education seem to be of *limited relevance*, at least to religious education as practised in contemporary liberal democracies. There are three reasons for reaching this conclusion: the first is essentially positive; the second and third are negative.

The positive reason that recent appeals to the importance of human rights are of limited relevance, is not because rights are irrelevant, for they clearly are, it is because both the broader and the narrower concerns raised by human rights have already been debated and integrated into provisions for religious education. Rights focusing on the freedom of religion and on children (while taking account of their developing autonomy) have long been a concern of politicians and educators in liberal democratic societies, such as the United Kingdom, Germany, the Netherlands, Australia and elsewhere. The description of these countries as liberal democracies already informs us that there has been a long and developing tradition of personal freedoms that enjoy legal protection accorded by the state. Such personal freedoms (as 'goods' entitled to protection) have evolved over centuries and pre-date the prominence that human rights have come to acquire in the post-Second World War world. The freedom of religion, the right of free assembly, for example, are not new ideas that had to await their 'invention' and publication by the United Nations. The modern idea of freedom of religion arguably traces its origins back to the Protestant Reformation and the forces unleashed, both for good and evil, that emerged in its wake. Allied to this are changing and evolving ideas about the nature and limits of liberty and how these relate to the emergence of the modern nation state. This story need not detain us. The point is that modern education systems in democratic countries developed in the context of increasing recognition of the importance of freedom of religion and typically took steps to accommodate religious diversity and to be inclusive of those pupils in national systems of education whose parents in good conscience could not endorse the beliefs and practices of the culturally dominant form of religion—in Western Europe typically some form of Christian state religion. Take England, for example; since 1870 there has been 'a conscience clause' that allows parents to withdraw their children from religious education, coupled with the requirement of non-denominational teaching in all 'county' schools (see Chapter 8, for discussion).

The story of on-going legislation to protect freedom of religion in education and elsewhere is a feature of liberal democratic states, but unfortunately it is not universal. In 1990 45 member states of the Organisation of the Islamic Conference (now Organisation of Islamic Cooperation, some of which did not subscribe to the Universal Declaration on Human Rights) officially endorsed the Cairo Declaration on Human Rights in Islam, which states that rights and freedoms 'are subject to... Islamic Shari'ah (Article 24): neither freedom of belief nor the right to convert from Islam to any other religion is recognised as a right or enjoys protection under the law'. Clearly, there is a strong case for the introduction of a human rights foundation and framework for religious education in countries where religious freedom and other freedoms are not protected by statute (or where such rights are not enforced) and where public institutions and schools by constitution and/or practice require conformity to the official religion of the state. The problem is acute in Muslim countries where there is no analogue to Christianity's gradual separation of temporal from ecclesiastical power (influential in this separation was Aquinas's fundamental distinction between natural and supernatural orders, and Marsilius of Padua's view that the pope is not the source of the government's power and authority; see Canning 2005; Miethke 2000).

The second reason why appeals to human rights have limited relevance to religious education, even in liberal democratic states, is again not because they are unimportant but because a human rights framework provides only a minimum threshold for the practice of religious education. That human rights provides only a minimum threshold is shown by the observation, already discussed, that in democratic states, additional legislation and rights have evolved to protect religious freedom in education. Just as appeals to human rights do not extend sufficiently to protect our developing appreciation of the concept of personal agency, liberty and autonomy, so they do not extend sufficiently to produce the kind of religious education that can realistically hope to contribute significantly to the realisation of liberal educational aims. Legal protection for freedom of religion and the rights of children, by itself, will contribute little to the creation of good religious education. Commitment (whether explicit or implicit) to human rights is a necessary but not a sufficient condition of good religious education. Human rights are concerned with basic protections under the law; and there is a case for watchfulness to ensure that new policies do not compromise them. Human rights legislation, however, has limited relevance to actual ongoing debates in religious education—to its nature and purpose, its pedagogies and commitments, assessment techniques, to the number of religions to be studied, whether the study of non-religious worldviews such as Humanism and Marxism should be required of all pupils, to reporting on academic progress or contributing to the spiritual and moral development of pupils. What is said here needs to be interpreted correctly. It is not claimed that considerations of justice are irrelevant to many of these issues and debates, it is that adherence to specific human rights will cast very little light on the issues, and fail to justify one conclusion or position over others. In any case, considerations of justice are much wider than what may be regarded as the basic and minimum principles of justice enshrined in human rights.[5] The concept of justice does not reduce without remainder to human rights but extends much further beyond them: it should also be noted that there are different conceptions of justice: libertarian (Nozick 2001); contractarian (Rawls 1971); and communitarian (MacIntyre 1988), to name the main ones. Furthermore, justice is not the only consideration that is relevant to the provision of good religious education. Account needs to be taken of the conceptual development of pupils, their interests and concerns and the aims appropriate to religious education in different types of school, among other considerations.

There is a third reason why appeals to human rights in religious education are limited in force and relevance, which follows on from what has just been said. This is because human rights are formal and abstract (it is this that makes them universal) and require application. As Pamela Slotte (2011: 45) has recently remarked, 'in human rights documents, legal rules are formulated in such general terms that room is left for a number of different interpretations'. Rights can be observed and expressed in different ways in different contexts, and even in contrasting ways in the same context. There is no direct line, for example, from the right of freedom of religion to one particular educational policy in schools (see Pépin 2009: 19–22). Attention has already been drawn to the right of withdrawal from religious education by parents in the United Kingdom, which is intended to protect the principle of freedom of religion. In Germany this same principle is protected in most *Länder* by the opportunity for pupils whose parents do not wish them to receive religious education to avail of a course on ethics (*Ethik*) or philosophy (*Philosophie*). In some countries freedom of religion is protected by the exclusion of religious education as a formal subject from state schools, as in the USA and France, though factual aspects of religion (*faits religieux*) can be integrated into relevant subjects (see American Academy of Religion 2010, and Hanf & Mufti 2015). In this case, as in numerous others that are relevant to religious education, the point is not that human rights are irrelevant, they are relevant; it is that a wide range of policies, procedures and practices are human rights compliant, i.e. consistent with what human rights require. An appeal to rights does not move debates forward because most of the contending positions have originated within a liberal political framework, where the kinds of interests and goods that rights are believed to serve are already factored into educational policies and positions.

The last two negative points can be summarised in this way: human rights have only a limited relevance to many of the issues that relate to teaching and learning in religious education, in the first instance, because the issues concerned extend beyond the protection of the fundamental freedoms that rights are intended to provide, and secondly, because the broad, formal nature of statements of human rights, entails that a range of different policies and practices are compatible with a human rights framework.

The inherent limitations of appeals to human rights in religious education do not seem to be recognised in the examples considered above. The impression is given that a human rights framework is a sufficient condition of good religious education. This impression is reinforced by exaggerated claims for the form of religious education that is required by commitment to human rights. For example, Jackson (2013: 1) moves seamlessly from an acknowledgement of the importance of human rights in education to a description of the religious education classroom that provides a 'potential "safe space" for dialogue, and… peaceful coexistence [among pupils] based on: (a) knowledge about each other's religions and worldviews; (b) sharing common interests/doing things together'. These he equates with 'democratic principles'. What needs to be appreciated is that this broad form of religious education, with which few would disagree, neither requires an appeal to human rights or democratic principles for its justification, nor is entailed by commitment to human rights. What Jackson describes is good practice in religious education. He might contend that his proposals are consistent with human rights, but so are numerous other proposals, some of which may give priority to other values or differ in detail from his own. Most legal jurists dispute the claim that a study of secular worldviews is required alongside the study of religion by human rights: how is this derivable from commitment to the freedom of religion and to children's rights? Whether secular worldviews *ought to be* incorporated into religious education can not be settled by appeals to human rights, but by an appeal to broader moral and educational considerations and arguments (see Chapters 5 and 6).

McGrady's also exaggerates the relevance of rights to religious education, only this time in a negative way. In unpacking the meaning and importance of the universal right of freedom of religion he places unwarranted restrictions on the practice of religion and by extension religious education—he speaks of the 'right' of the state 'to expect that the exercise of such religious freedom contributes not only to the good of the individual but to the common good'. It has been argued that this position is not required by a commitment to human rights and that it is over-restrictive. Any restrictions that the state imposes on religious educators should be a matter of public debate, and while acknowledging a case for some restrictions (as discussed above), the severe restriction countenanced by McGrady goes far beyond what a proper interpretation and application of the Declaration on Universal Human Rights requires. Equally, the Toledo Principles' espousal of 'neutrality and impartiality' and the (at best) equivocal status it grants to 'religious instruction' goes beyond what a human rights framework requires.

Some may react defensively to the conclusion that human rights have only a limited relevance to the theory and practice of religious education, perhaps feeling that the work of those who contend for human rights is impugned, or the impression given that rights themselves are unimportant. This is not the case. That appeals to human rights have little relevance to ongoing debates in religious education is not because rights are unimportant, rather it is because the principles, values and goods protected by rights are often already integrated into its practice. There are countries where appeals to rights will have significant relevance to religious education; and this because the kinds of protections that rights afford are not constitutionally granted or where 'lip-service' is paid to freedom of religion or where rights are 'trumped' by political and social considerations. Yet even where rights are relevant their espousal 'underdetermines' the policy, theory and practice of religious education. Rights by their nature provide only a minimum, albeit essential standard for religious education; for example, human rights in education are consistent with both religious nurture and nurture in liberal humanism, and with other forms of nurture, say that of the values of the liberal democratic state; but all such forms of education must not become indoctrinatory and subversive of the right of freedom of religion and children's rights.

It is concluded in relation to religious education in liberal democratic states: *either* not much of consequence follows for religious education on the basis of appeals to rights; and this because there is a long and evolving political tradition that has sought by legal and judicial means to safeguard the freedoms, interests and goods that are commonly now enshrined in human rights; *or* where rights are of consequence for religious education they require interpretation and application in specific contexts, and typically draw on broader considerations and forms of argumentation to have effective force. This later conclusion is salutary because part of the use and attraction of an appeal to rights by some religious educators (as in some of our examples above) is to bypass argument and debate and proceed directly to some preferred conclusion—the actual justification of which is much more debateable and finely balanced. The impression is sometimes given that the appeal to rights is made to reinforce an already accepted conclusion and by giving it quasi-legal force to frustrate dialogue and debate. Most contentious matters and debates in religious education, however, do not admit of such easily achieved conclusions, and this because legitimate competing aims, influences, goods and freedoms appropriate to education and schooling have to be reconciled with each other, and all are susceptible to different emphasis and forms of integration. Progress in religious education proceeds by public debate and argument: the collection and weighing of evidence; identification of relevant considerations; the development of an argument that moves validly from premise to conclusion, and so on; and so progress ought to proceed. A democratic society should resolve issues through debate and dialogue, compromise and synthesis, rather than through legal fiat, other than on those occasions where fundamental human rights are at stake.

The question with which we are left is if human rights has such limited relevance to religious education in liberal democratic states, why do they currently assume such prominence for some religious educators: why has rights-talk become the moral vocabulary in which curriculum content, pedagogy, teacher training and other matters are discussed? A proper response to this requires a long genealogical, historical survey that attends to the ways in which our contemporary moral situation, political practice and education systems illustrate and express the ongoing travails of post-Enlightenment liberalism; an account of which will have to be pursued on another occasion (see Barnes 2015a, which provides a summary account).

Notes

1 It is important in some cases to distinguish human rights from rights: human rights give expression to entitlements that apply to all persons, whereas rights can be used to refer to the entitlements that persons enjoy in a particular state. Educators often conflate the two, as do I; where the distinction is needed the context usually makes it clear.
2 In the British context, the ratification of the 1950 European Convention on Human Rights into British law in the 1998 Human Rights Act gives added impetus to the connection between citizenship and human rights.

3 It is becoming increasingly customary to refer to 'freedom of religion and belief', presumably to indicate that one is free to hold and manifest non-religious beliefs, worldviews and philosophies; such is I believe already denoted by the principle of 'freedom of religion'; consequently, I shall use this latter expression and assume its wider connotations.
4 We will forgo discussion of whether the *simple principle* is truly a principle or simple.
5 The clearest and most philosophically sophisticated appreciation of the relevance of both human rights and the wider concept of justice to religious education is Pirner 2016.

5

WORLDVIEWS, JUSTICE AND INCLUSION

The purpose of this chapter and the next is to consider if there are convincing educational reasons for the inclusion of worldviews in the religious education curriculum. Much of the focus will fall on Humanism, as it is the secular worldview that is most frequently cited as warranting inclusion in its own right by those who believe that the traditional category of religion unduly limits the relevance and achievements of religious education. Reference will also be made to other secular worldviews as appropriate.

Humanism in the curriculum: An historical perspective

From the 1960s onwards, Humanists in England have been campaigning for the inclusion of Humanism in the religious education curriculum (see Freathy & Parker 2013). As early as 1964, the Executive Director of the British Humanist Association (which was founded the year before, though it has longer historical roots), Harold J. Blackham (1964: 20) called for the inclusion of 'politico-cultural absolutes (e.g. Marxism and Fascism) and Humanism', a view reiterated 3 years later in the British Humanist Society's report, *Religion in Schools: Humanist proposals for state-aided schools in England and Wales* (1967). Surprisingly to some, the influential Church of England Report of 1970, *The Fourth R: Durham Report on Religious Education* (so named after its Chairperson, the Bishop of Durham, Ian T, Ramsey), while defending Christian nurture in schools and exonerating it from the charge of indoctrination (353–358), in an important appendix contributed by Basil Mitchell, also endorsed the study of secular alternatives to religion, such as Humanism. More significantly historically was its support for the teaching of world religions, a view that quickly came to chart the future direction and orientation of religious education through the work of Ninian Smart, on behalf of the Schools Council (1971), and the Shap Working Party on World Religions in Education, (founded in the village of Shap in Cumbria in 1969, following a conference on 'Comparative Religion in Education'; see Hinnells 1970) and others.

Educational controversy was aroused about Humanism in 1973 with the publication of the then first version of the new Birmingham Agreed Syllabus (see Parker & Freathy 2011: 251–254). It pursued an 'educational' rationale for religious education that eschewed all forms of religious nurture while endorsing a multifaith approach, which covered six world religions, from the first year of primary school. It also required a study of '[n]on-religious stances for living, their basic assumptions and their outworking in personal and social life' (quoted by Cole 1976: 127). Humanism was specifically mentioned in the syllabus and in support material Communism was identified as an alternative 'non-religious life stance' to 'religious life stances' (Stopes-Roe 1976) that could be studied. Such was the 'outrage' in some quarters that the matter went as high as Parliament (see Priestley 2006: 1010). To assuage criticism, the Local Education Authority sought legal advice which concluded that the proposed syllabus was probably not legal (and certainly open to a legal challenge), given the terms of the 1944 Education Act. 'As a consequence… the aims and content of the syllabus were extended and clarified to ensure that the non-religious subject matter was only used to advance instruction in religion rather than taught for its own sake' (Freathy & Parker 2013: 249; see also Hull 1984: 82–86). The term 'non-religious stances' was omitted from the final Agreed Syllabus, published in 1975, although reference to Humanism remained, it was now regarded as a critical source that is relevant to considerations of the nature and truth of religion. Until 2004 and the publication of the non-statutory framework, little progress was made in convincing religious educators that Humanism deserved a necessary place in religious education. Its inclusion is now *de rigueur* in all quasi-official reports and is supported by the major organisations that represent religious educators.

Whose religion, which worldview?

Some will feel that enquiring about the reasons in support of including Humanism in the religious education curriculum is redundant, as the matter has already been settled positively. The 2004 National Framework for Religious Education (Qualification and Curriculum Authority 2004: 12) recommended (as noted above) that 'secular philosophies such as humanism', ought to be included in religious education alongside nine other religions and religious traditions. *A Review of Religious Education in England* conducted by the Religious Education Council of England and Wales (2013: 14), recommended the study of 'a range of religions and worldviews' at all stages of pupils' educational careers, while again expanding the overall number of 'traditions' to be covered: Humanism is recommended throughout, as is the study of a further secular worldview, though no guidance is provided as to what it could be. The legal position is summarised in the *Review* as follows:

The law requires that local authority RE agreed syllabuses and RE syllabuses used in academies that are not designated with a religious character 'must reflect the fact that the religious traditions in Great Britain are in the main Christian, while taking account of the teaching and practices of the other principal religions represented in Great Britain'.

(2013: 15)

This accurate quotation from the 1988 Education Reform Act is immediately glossed as meaning 'that from the ages of 5 to 19 pupils in schools learn about diverse religions *and worldviews* including Christianity and the other principal religions' (my emphasis, 2013: 15). This misrepresents the law, as there is no reference to worldviews in the Act and *ipso facto* no mention of worldviews such as Humanism requiring to be taught. In the sentence immediately following the glossed explanation of the Act, it is stated that 'some schools with a religious character will prioritise learning about and from one religion, but all types of school need to recognise the diversity of the UK and the importance of learning about its religions and worldviews'. What is not made explicit, and arguably overlooked, is that all schools (maintained or academy), which, according to the Act, are not designated with a religious character, must prioritise Christianity.

The Commission on Religious Education's *Final Report: Religion and worldviews: The way forward. A national plan for RE* (2018), again a project initiated by the RE Council of England and Wales, also affirms the central importance of learning about non-religious worldviews for all pupils. Here are some representative quotations:

[W]e propose that there should be a statutory National Entitlement to the study of Religion and Worldviews which applies to all publicly funded schools and is subject to inspection.

Programmes of study must reflect the complex, diverse and plural nature of worldviews. They may draw from a range of religious, philosophical, spiritual and other approaches to life including different traditions within Christianity, Buddhism, Hinduism, Islam, Judaism and Sikhism, non-religious worldviews and concepts including Humanism, secularism, atheism and agnosticism, and other relevant worldviews within and beyond the traditions listed above, including worldviews of local significance where appropriate.

In order to understand the full diversity of religious or non-religious worldviews, pupils may also benefit from awareness of a broader range of worldviews.... This is not intended to be a comprehensive list but rather an illustration of the scope of the subject that teachers and curriculum planners may draw from. These may include ancient (and still living) traditions from China (e.g. Daoism, Confucianism), Japan (e.g. Shinto), Africa, Australia and New Zealand, and the Americas as well as Zoroastrianism and Jainism.... Historical and contemporary paganism in the UK may also be included, as this is both growing and influential beyond those who identify as Pagans. The range of worldviews may also include groups formed more recently that pupils may meet or belong to themselves, including Baha'i, Latter Day Saints (Mormons), Jehovah's Witnesses and Rastafari.

(2018: 3, 13 and 77)

After reading this it seems entirely understandable why the Commission proposes that the subject title of religious education ought to become 'Religion and *Worldviews*' (2018: 3), since all (that they regard as) worldviews are endorsed as potential subjects for study. Controversially, this is the first time Paganism has been recommended for inclusion in the curriculum. One can envisage conservative religious parents using their current statutory right of withdrawal to prevent their children being exposed to pagan beliefs and practices.[1] A further worldview that is mentioned as 'appropriate for study' is existentialism, whereas global capitalism, Communism and nationalism, are designated as inappropriate as they do not qualify as worldviews (2018: 75); interestingly, Ninian Smart did recognise nationalism as a worldview (1999: 2). One wonders whether Platonism and Aristotelianism qualify as worldviews, given the inclusion of existentialism. Do such possibilities orientate religious education to the study of philosophy?

The triumvirate of Humanism, Secularism or Atheism are always listed together throughout the document (2018: 4, 26 and 28); sometimes agnosticism is added (2018: 13, 35 and 75): as presented, the option is there to study all four. It may be asked what positive content can be given to an agnostic worldview, since as its name implies it eschews knowledge and is usually taken to express the view that all religious claims lack the status of knowledge—perhaps we do not possess the requisite capacities to assess or to possess knowledge about religion (in a strict sense, Kant is properly interpreted in this way), or simply that the evidence for religion knowledge falls short. What is the positive content of agnosticism? Furthermore, has serious attention been given by the Commission to the distinctions between these worldviews? It is a moot point how atheism and agnosticism *as* worldviews are to be distinguished for educational purposes, and whether a study of the latter would add much to a serious study of the former. Is there not obvious duplication of content? Ought either be properly considered a worldview? The identification of Secularism as a worldview is equally controversial, as it is often characterised as the view that public and political institutions should be independent of religion. It does not constitute a worldview as such, only that there should be strict limits to the public role of religions in society and in political and public institutions.

'In order to understand the full diversity of religious or non-religious worldviews' (as already quoted above, 2018: 4, also and particularly 75), the Commission Report, *Religion and worldviews: The way forward. A national plan for RE* sets no limits to the number of religions and worldviews that can be studied, and it fails to specify minimally how many religions and worldviews should be studied. A careful reading of the document suggests that by the end of Key Stage 4 a pupil could be obliged to study a minimum of fourteen different religions and worldviews—an onerous task, perhaps an impossible task, given that the law as commonly interpreted up to the present expects significant teaching about Christianity at each Key Stage. What will appear unbelievable to some is the further demand that account is taken of 'the… diversity within worldviews' (2018: 5). However charitably one interprets this broad-ranging and open-ended approach to content, it ought to have been obvious to the authors of the Commission Report that the religious education curriculum will inevitably become a summary review or a Cook's tour of religions and worldviews that will necessarily result in superficial teaching, simplistic learning and confused pupils.

Becoming aware of the broad range of religions and worldviews to be studied may explain, in part, why the RE Commission never explicitly states how many traditions in total it believes ought to be covered: if there is not a sense of embarrassment (that some will conclude ought to reflect a perception of educational irresponsibility) there should be. The same 'inconvenient' awareness may also, in part, explain why the Commission Report does not fully engage with the legal position of religious education in schools. The following is almost all that is stated about the legal position:

> The nature of RE has changed over time to reflect new understandings and new social realities. At the time of the 1944 Education Act, it was known as Religious Instruction, was limited to Christianity and was the only compulsory subject. Over time, subject experts came to recognise that young people needed to understand both a wider range of religious and non-religious worldviews and the idea of diversity within worldviews. This was reflected in the Education Reform Act of 1988, which also changed the name of the subject to Religious Education. Thirty years on, the local, national and global religious landscape and academic understandings of the subject have changed significantly.
>
> (Commission on Religious Education 2018: 5)

Whereas the RE Review mispresents the legal position of the 1988 Act, the Commission Report *merely* obfuscates. Yes, the Act extended a requirement to incorporate other 'principal religions' (unspecified in the Act) into religious education, but it made no refence to non-religious worldviews as appropriate for inclusion: some 'experts' may have contended that religious education should attend to non-religious worldviews. The Education Reform Act of 1988 did extend the curriculum to include non-Christian religions, which is 'reflected in the… Act' (Commission on Religious Education 2018: 5). The Act, however, does not provide any provision for extending the scope of the subject to incorporate non-religious worldviews; this hope is not reflected in it.

One might think of obfuscation about content in the RE Commission Report as a lesser evil than the RE Review's misrepresentation, but the former has mis-interpretations of its own elsewhere. Forgive the brief digression to illustrate the point. In a section devoted to discussion of the right of parental withdrawal (2018: 65–68), the Commission recommends that '[t]he DfE should review the right of withdrawal from Religion and Worldviews and provide legal clarification'. Reference is made to David Lundie's empirical research findings (discussed in Chapter 8): the view is expressed that when '[t]he majority of schools in Lundie's survey invited parents to discuss their request [for withdrawal of their child] and find out more about the RE curriculum. *Most parents withdrew their requests following these discussions*' (2018: 67; my emphasis). Lundie's survey provides no evidence for this conclusion, nor does he claim such. This is a careless 'school boy' error of interpretation (excuse the use of the male gender here!). We may surmise how this egregious misinterpretation was made. It is stated by Lundie (2018: 5) that '[o]ther than with Jehovah Witness (*sic*), all concerns have been solved with a discussion about what the school is teaching/offering and sometimes some reasonable adjustments made'. This quotation from a 'school leader' is about the situation in his or her school (an individual school), yet it is presented by the Commission as a general truth. Lundie's findings are misinterpreted and one is left with an example of an uncritical appeal to evidence and the research of others.

Before moving on, it is worthwhile adding some broadly-based critical comments about the three documents to which reference has been made in this section. First, what is troubling about the misinterpretations and obfuscations discussed above is that they all serve the agendas of the positions that the documents propose. Are these honest mistakes or is something more ideological going on? Second, the documents speak of an entitlement by pupils to religious education: the language of entitlement is particularly prominent in the 2004 National Framework (Qualification and Curriculum Authority 2004: 9), and more recently and prominently in the RE Commission Report (2018: 17, 20, 31, 32–36, 38–41, 43–44, 47, 49–51, 55–56, 58–59, 62, 65–66, 69–70). What is overlooked is that there is already a legal entitlement to religious education and inspection mechanisms to ensure conformity to the law, its quality and effectiveness. Use of the language of entitlement may give the impression these currently do not obtain and something new is needed to make them so. Third, attention needs to be given to the issue of content and its rationale. Apart from differences between the content proposed by the three documents, its wide-ranging nature and continual expansion in each historically successive document undermines the educational credibility of the subject and gives the impression that the subject has cut itself off from self-criticism and theoretical understandings. Finally, there is the issue of coherence and progression. One of the four main reasons for the production of the non-statutory national Framework of 2004 (9), it tells us, is 'to contribute to a coherent [religious education] curriculum that promotes continuity. It helps the transition of pupils between schools and phases of education and can provide a foundation for further study and lifelong learning'. The RE Review also justifies the case for a national curriculum framework for religious education on the grounds that it 'creates coherence in what is taught in schools... to ensure that all children are taught essential knowledge in the key subject disciplines' (2013: 11): progression is conjoined with coherence in numerous other places. The RE Commission does not make any appeal to coherence in its case for a statutory, national form of religious education. How could it, given its open-ending approach to content, with (individual) schools able to choose which worldviews to study from the huge range on offer? If coherence, however, is believed to constitute a good reason for a statutory form of religious education, this surely makes it more difficult for the RE Commission to advance its claim that its content, programmes of study and recommendations ought to have statutory force: it lacks 'coherence' in terms of content!

The Humanist case for the inclusion of Humanism in Religious Education

In October 2014, Ricky Thompson, then Campaigns Officer (now Director of Public Affairs and Policy) for the British Humanist Association (BHA), contacted RE teachers by email who were 'recorded' in their 'system' to request endorsement of its campaign to 'allow non-religious worldviews as an option to be studied alongside religions' at GCSE and at A Level.[2] The context need not detain us. More relevant to our concerns is that the email explicitly addresses the issue 'why Humanism should be included in RE' and sets the positive reasons out in summary form. These reasons will be considered systematically in turn, so it may be assumed that these are the reasons believed by campaigning Humanists to best advance their case for the compulsory inclusion of secular, non-religious worldviews and of Humanism in particular, in the religious education curriculum. The actual wording of the reasons is retained in full to ensure that the Humanist case is faithfully and accurately represented:

(i) All the usual contemporary justifications for the subject of RE in the school curriculum—its contribution to social cohesion and mutual understanding, its presentation of a range of answers to questions of meaning and purpose, and its role in the search for personal identity and values—can best be served by including humanist perspectives and non-religious students.

The Humanist statement is probably correct when it records that contemporary justifications of religious education refer to its moral and social contribution to the curriculum. This focus is entirely predictable in the politically charged domain of modern education, where religious educators want to assure politicians and the education establishment, which is mainly secular, that the subject has relevance to current concerns and therefore should retain its compulsory status in the curriculum. Religious education often advertises itself as counteracting religious extremism, challenging bigotry, and producing 'good' citizens who respect the ever-expanding realm of rights, as overseen and interpreted by the secular state. Understood in this way religious education is of instrumental value only. It is this narrow vision of religious education that the Humanist statement (chiefly) expresses. It suits Humanist purposes to present the aims of religious education in terms that connect only contingently to religion. What it overlooks is the main educational rationale for the inclusion of religious education in the curriculum, which is to provide an understanding of the nature and character of religion. One thinks here of Ninian Smart's (1968; 1971) dimensional model of religion which was widely influential in 1970s and 1980s and of Robert Jackson's interpretive approach (1995; 1997), which came to prominence in the late 1990s and raised the issue of how religions are represented in the classroom. Understanding and interpreting religion and the religions is the central aim of religious education, though this can be expressed and expanded in different ways: some may want to speak of religious literacy at this point (see Barnes 2014: 240). To conceive the aims of religious education exclusively in terms of its positive moral and social effects overlooks this, and therefore facilitates the ideological manipulation of the religions for immediate political and social advantage. The content of religion has educational worth and it is this that the subject of religious education seeks to convey through faithful representations of the different religions and religious phenomena: just as science education seeks to convey the educational value of science, so religious education seeks to convey the educational value of a study of religion(s).

To claim (as above) that the social and moral aims of religions education are best served by a study of Humanism is contentious. What evidence is there for this? It is not at all obvious that a systematic study of Humanism will result in higher levels of moral development by pupils, which in time will generate greater social cohesion in society.

(ii) Humanism has long been part of Religious Education and the Religious Education Council has long supported this inclusion. Successive Government documents have recommended the inclusion of non-religious worldviews such as Humanism, and the 2013 Curriculum Framework is as inclusive of teaching about non-religious worldviews as it is of teaching about religions. This is also reflected in locally agreed syllabuses, the vast majority of which include the teaching of Humanism with many having extensive modules dedicated to its study. The REC's vision is that 'Every young person experiences a personally inspiring and academically rigorous education in religious and non-religious worldviews'.

The fact that the Religious Education Council and the 2013 RE Review support the teaching of Humanism in religious education does not constitute an independent reason for its inclusion in the curriculum of religious education. The RE Review was commissioned by the RE Council and we are informed that '[th]e final text of the Review was agreed by the REC Board' (2013: 6). Furthermore, the British Humanist Association had representation on the steering group for the RE Council's Review. One may conclude on the basis of these observations that the RE Council's position on the inclusion of Humanism in religious education may not be impartial and objective.

To state that the RE Council endorses something and therefore you should too as an educator (given that the email by the BHA was sent to religious educators) is essentially an appeal to authority. In the matter of religious education, religious educators are invited to defer to the authority of the RE Council. Serious consideration ought to be given to the views of religious education associations and those that purport to speak on behalf of the subject on the basis of experience and expertise; yet this falls short of accepting uncritically what is claimed on this basis alone. Humanists need to adduce evidence and employ arguments, not attempt to secure agreement by appeals to the authority of the Religious Education Council, local agreed syllabus committees or any other group or organisation with a vested interest in religious education. As Immanuel Kant (1999 [1784]: 17), (italics in original) said, '*Sapere aude!* Have courage to use your own understanding!'

> (iii) It is vital that Religious Education remains relevant to young people and with surveys suggesting that between 31% and 65% are not religious, this means including non-religious worldviews. RE struggles to engage these young people when their beliefs are excluded.

The point that religious education should be relevant to young people is well taken, though the issue of what *seems* relevant to them should not be the only or most important determinant of curriculum content. Education is about widening the intellectual horizons of pupils and sometimes this can be accomplished by introducing them to concepts and ideas whose relevance they do not appreciate immediately. The implicit assumption that 'young people' find relevance in religious education only when their own particular worldview, which is often inchoate or implicit, is identified and considered must be challenged. Pupils are just as likely to find interest and relevance in what is religiously new or novel as learning about their own beliefs.

There is some truth in the comment that 'RE struggles to engage... young people' (though not necessarily because 'their beliefs are excluded', see above). This reminds us that the content must be made meaningful to the aspirations, values and experiences of pupils, who can be hostile to religion, particularly formal and institutional religion. Yet to make connections between religious content and the lifeworld of pupils does not necessitate a systematic study of Humanism. Is there evidence that a systematic study of non-religious philosophies engages pupils' interest in religious education more than a study of religious or moral issues for example?

Furthermore, to record that between '31% and 65% [of young people] are not religious', in itself, does little to further the case for including a study of Humanism in religious education, as does the fact that 25.3 per cent of the British population identified themselves as 'non-religious' in the 2011 Census (for discussion, see Barnes 2014: 29–30 and 43–47). What this may show is that there is an even greater need for education about religions, so that pupils begin to become religiously educated. Furthermore, it would be unwarranted to interpret any of these statistics as evidence of positive commitment to Humanism. Humanists constitute a small sub-group within the group of those who are 'non-religious'. In symbolic terms where p is 'those persons who do not belong to a religion' and q is 'those persons who are adherents of Humanism': 'all q are p', but 'not all p are q': to conclude otherwise is a fallacy. In all probability, on the basis of what we know from surveys of religious belief, identity and commitment, it is the case that many of those who identify themselves as non-religious actually hold religious beliefs, but beliefs that are unorthodox (from the perspective of orthodox interpretations of the different religions), internally inconsistent, ambiguous and shifting; and such beliefs are often held tentatively or implicitly. A non-religious response in the Census can denote indifference to religion or indicate a lack of formal allegiance to any religion and its integrated set of beliefs and practices. It does not mean that the person is without beliefs or convictions that are properly described and classified as religious; and it certainly does not mean that the person subscribes to a deliberately chosen worldview that provides a 'relatively coherent view of life [such as Humanism]' and 'incorporates an opposition and antipathy to theism and traditional forms of religious life' (Felderhof, 2012: 148). The non-religious category comprises all those who are non-religious, of which Humanists will form (in relative terms) a very small number.

> (iv) International agreements all recommend the inclusion of non-religious worldviews alongside religious beliefs and in fact the UN Special Rapporteur on Freedom of Religion or Belief specifically recommended it in her last report on the UK.[3]

Some ambiguity attaches to what is meant by 'international agreements'. If it means that there are agreements between nations or official government representatives of nations to implement and ensure the teaching of non-religious worldviews alongside religions, specifically in religious education (and not, say, in intercultural education), which is the kind of agreement that is relevant, then the Humanist statement is factually incorrect. No British government has entered into a policy agreement with an international partner to ensure Humanism is taught in religious education. Alternatively, if 'international agreements' means that there are religious educators from different countries who have come together and produced joint documents to encourage the inclusion of non-religious worldviews in education, this is in all probability the case. Some prominent religious educators in Europe support the inclusion of Humanism in religious education and some do not. The matter should be decided by appeals to reason and argument, taking account of the educational, national and historical context of schools: there is no need to endorse a 'one size fits all' solution. In any case, as the argument in (iv) is expressed, it amounts to another instance of an appeal to authority—the authority of so-called 'international agreements'—of their nature, constitution, representation and status we are not told.

> (v) The BHA has long played an active part in the RE Council including at the Board level and has been involved in the steering groups of all relevant government and quango reviews for the last decade. Almost six out of seven English SACREs now include a humanist.

Here is the argument broken into its constituent parts:

Premise 1: The British Humanist Association has been involved with and is represented on the Religious Education Council.

Premise 2: The British Humanist Association has contributed to 'government and quango reviews.' Therefore,
Conclusion: Humanism can be taught to all pupils in British schools.

The argument is so obviously fallacious that it merits no further discussion.

(vi) The Independent School Standards require schools to 'actively promote the fundamental British values of democracy, the rule of law, individual liberty and mutual respect, and tolerance of those with different faiths and beliefs.' Departmental advice recommends that schools meet this standard by using 'teaching resources from a wide variety of sources to help pupils understand a range of faiths, and beliefs such as atheism and Humanism'.

It is appropriate for all schools to endorse the 'fundamental British values' listed above and to seek ways to instil these values in pupils. This commitment, however, does not advance the case for teaching the beliefs of Humanism through religious education. The document (DoE 2013: 7), from which the first quotation is taken, does not draw this conclusion. There are many ways to support and commend fundamental British values through education and schools: there is no evidence to suggest that the teaching of Humanism *in religious education* is essential to this role. For centuries the values of democracy, citizenship, the rule of law and religious toleration have been pursued and conveyed through education without the systematic teaching of Humanism.

The second quotation (DoE 2013: 8) in (vi), like the first, does not have any relevance to the case for the inclusion of Humanism in the religious education curriculum. In the first instance the 'advice' quoted 'is non-statutory' (2013: 3). More importantly, the advice does not have anything to do with religious education: it is concerned with 'Improving the Spiritual, Moral, Social and Cultural (SMSC) development of pupils' in independent schools, academies and free schools through the whole school curriculum. The document makes no reference to religious education; it is unfaithful to its meaning to interpret it as supporting systematic teaching about Humanism in religious education.

In this section the reasons proposed by the British Humanist Association to best advance its case for the compulsory inclusion of Humanism in the religious education curriculum have been considered. A certain degree of charity should be shown toward their assessment. The reasons were incorporated into an email and presented in condensed and summary form that would ensure that busy teachers would find them accessible and not unduly demanding on their time: their summary form possibly fails to do justice to some of the points adduced. For example, it is conceded that (iii) has greater force than my response acknowledges, and for this reason I will return to consider it further in what follows. Nevertheless, the reasons, singly and cumulatively, are not compelling: points are tendentious and there are ironically too many appeals to 'authoritative sources', such as the work and pronouncements of the RE Council, for example, and not enough appeals to reason and argument. The Humanist case for inclusion falls short of securing a place for the inclusion of Humanism, as a subject in its own right, within religious education.

Are there better arguments to which Humanists could have appealed?

The obvious issue to raise is whether there are better reasons and arguments to which Humanists and others can appeal. In this section and the next two sections this issue will be explored.

> As religious leaders we are writing to express our support for proposals to allow students to have the option for systematic study of Humanism in GCSE, AS and A level religious studies.... Such a change would not compel anyone to systematically study non-religious worldviews or make it possible to do so for the whole of a qualification, but it would allow young people to study a more representative sample of major worldviews that are common in Britain today. It would reflect how RE is taught in many schools, the position taken by an increasing number of locally agreed syllabuses, and the 2013 curriculum framework.... In short, it would be fair, popular, and add rigour to the subject; we see no reasonable or persuasive argument to oppose it.[4]

In an open letter to the (then) schools minister Nick Gibb, published in *The Times* on 5th February, 2015 (reproduced, in part, above), a number of prominent churchmen, religious leaders, and religious educators, including the former Archbishop of Canterbury, Lord Williams of Oystermouth and Professor Trevor Cooling, Professor of Christian Education and Director of the National Institute for Christian Education Research, Canterbury Christ Church University, called for the inclusion of Humanism as a possible subject for systematic study in all formal state regulated school examinations in religious studies. The case for Humanism, which is here confined to formal external examinations, will be considered within the broader context of our discussion of Humanism as appropriate to religious education at all levels of schooling in all types of schools. Although this is a broader aim than that supported by Lord Williams and the other signatories, it is not unreasonable to conclude that most of the signatories would support this extended position (though it does not follow necessarily); in any case the reasons advanced in support of teaching about Humanism has a much wider application than the use to which they are put by the signatories.

The issue of fairness

According to the signatories 'it would be fair, popular, and add rigour to the subject' of religious education for pupils to study Humanism, and they 'see no reasonable or persuasive argument to oppose it'. It is indeed a terse statement of things. The appeal to fairness (or justice) is not developed, though it has obvious rhetorical appeal. What form might an appeal to fairness in this context take? Before attempting to consider this, it is necessary to voice some initial misgivings about the appropriateness of appeals to justice and fairness in public debates of this kind. To state that something is just and fair is by implication to claim that alternatives are not just and fair; presumably in this case that not teaching pupils about Humanism is unjust and unfair: I have also heard this view expressed by some religious educators. Such language, however, adds an unnecessarily adversarial and strident tone to the debate and to public debates more generally. The discussion is cast in binary terms—just and fair or unjust and unfair. Given the pluralist nature of modern Britain such oppositions, even if implied or implicit, are not always helpful. The claim that justice is being denied naturally attracts public attention but at the cost of exacerbating distrust and heightening tension between those on different sides of an argument, and in some cases where contrasting cultural beliefs and values are brought to bear on issues, it can contribute to the alienation of one community or other from the rest of society.

Appeals to justice (and even human rights) can also lend encouragement to legal and judicial resolutions of issues that further polarise public opinion. In short, it would have been more socially responsible (and I think philosophically more plausible) for the signatories to frame their proposals in terms of what is good for education and society, rather than what is just and fair—in terms of the 'the good', rather than in terms of 'the right'. Framing a debate in terms of 'the good' can allow for a diversity of different opinions to be aired, endorsed and appreciated, for they may all properly encapsulate and express some aspect of what is good for society and for social institutions in different ways. Such a process could illustrate what political philosophers and commentators mean by democratic deliberation: a process that is inclusive, dialogical (even dialectical), potentially open-ended, and encouraging of one to take account of new evidence or to revaluate the significance of contrasting evidence and appeals. To state, as the signatories do, that it is just and fair to teach about Humanism in religious education fails to appreciate the requirements of responsible, public debates on education in a pluralist, liberal democracy such as Britain.

John Rawls's justice as fairness

While misgivings about framing the debate on the inclusion of Humanism in religious education in terms of fairness have been registered, an attempt will now be made to construct as positive an argument as possible within these terms. This is to do what the signatories of the letter have failed to do and to overcome their omission in the most plausible and convincing way. The best and most philosophically sophisticated candidate argument to advance the cause of Humanism in religious education is John Rawls's celebrated interpretation of (social) 'justice as fairness', as set out in *A Theory of Justice* (1971). Justice, for him, is when 'the proper distribution of the benefits and burdens of social cooperation is achieved'. Rawls

(1971: 17–22) postulates 'an original position', where individuals deliberate about the rules appropriate to society behind, what he calls (1971: 136–142), a 'veil of ignorance', in which they are ignorant of their natural endowments, environmental advantages or disadvantages and of their 'comprehensive concept of the good'. The agreement that should result from deliberation on this basis, Rawls contends, will be impartial and hence fair to all.

The principles of fairness

The principles of social justice that result from Rawls's hypothetical dialogue between appropriately ignorant (as defined above), free and equal citizens can be summarised as follows:

> (1) Each person is to have an equal right to the most extensive system of basic liberties compatible with a similar system of liberty for all.
>
> (2) Social and economic inequalities are to be arranged so that they are both (a) attached to offices and positions open to all under conditions of fair equality of opportunity; and (b) to the greatest benefit of the least advantaged members of society.
>
> *(1971: 60–75; 298–303)*

A constructive application of his principles to religious education will be attempted: the discussion and debate that surrounds Rawls's conception of justice will be overlooked.

Principle (1) states the need for an extensive system of basic liberties, compatible with a similar system of liberty for all. While it is difficult to see how this could advance the case for a study of Humanism, the principle does have some relevance to religious education. If a state legislates for compulsory religious education, it seems reasonable that there should be a right of withdrawal as a liberty available to all parents. This position, while not deducible from (1) is consistent with it, and arguably captures its spirit, which is to enhance the range and scope of civil liberties in society (while acknowledging that an exemption from religious education may not constitute a *basic* liberty; see Chapter 8 for discussion). The law in Britain currently upholds the freedom to withdraw one's child from religious education in the form of a 'conscience clause', and the continued existence of such can be supported by an appeal to Rawls's first principle of justice as fairness.

Implicit in the first part of Rawls's second principle, namely (2a), that social and economic inequalities are to be arranged so that they are attached to offices and positions open to all under conditions of fair equality of opportunity, is that justice is a quality of human relationships; 'offices and positions open to all', means open to all persons. Justice has principally to do with persons. Justice regulates human relationships, and even when it is concerned with resources, burdens and benefits, the focus is on how these are distributed among people.[5]

We are now in a better position to connect the case for the study of Humanism with Rawls's principles. To state that fairness requires Humanism as an examination option in religious education (or/and by extension a study of Humanism by all pupils at all stages of schooling) most naturally and sensibly means that justice is owed to certain people, in the first instance Humanists and Humanist parents. Is this appeal to fairness convincing? What it overlooks, however, is Rawls's inclusion of a reference to conditions of fair equality of opportunity in (2a). The line of reasoning assumed by the signatories seems to be that it is only fair that Humanist parents and pupils should have the right to have their fundamental beliefs and convictions studied and examined in schools. This may initially sound plausible, but as Rawls fully appreciates there has to be some account taken of the principle of equality. For him all people are equal behind the veil of ignorance, in the sense that everyone is equal with regard to respect and dignity in a free democratic society. If a claim to fairness requires that the curriculum of religious education ought (used here with a moral sense) to reflect what Humanists want, then the principle of equal dignity and equality of opportunity also means that a similar claim can be advanced by all others: all ought to enjoy a similar right, say those who espouse Wicca or Satanism, or Pentecostalism. This is unrealistic education-ally. Why should Humanism be favoured?

One response to this critical question might be that there is a democratic ('popular') mandate for Humanism to be included in religious education: fairness attaches to numbers. The following comments are also relevant to point (iii) above in our discussion of the reasons advanced by Humanists in support of the com-pulsory inclusion in religious education, and to which a commitment was made to consider it further. On its website the British Humanist Association claims a membership of 40,000[6] and the National Secular Society is usually accredited with about 7,000 members, a calculation made on the basis of its published finances in relation to membership fees.[7] Both groups together can claim 47,000 adherents, which is 0.073 per cent of the total population in Britain. It should be obvious from this that on the basis of membership and committed followers there are numerous religions that have a much stronger democratic claim to be included in religious education before Humanism; the Church of the Latter Day Saints, for example, has over 150,000 members, Jehovah's Witnesses has 136,000 members; furthermore, both of these are examples of religions, unlike Humanism, which is a secular, non-religious worldview.

Interestingly, at the time of the 2011 Census the British Humanist Association advised its members not to record their allegiance as Humanist but to register themselves as possessing 'no religion'[8]; perhaps this represented an awareness that the number of Humanists was small as a percentage of the population and that the political and social influence of the Association would be undermined by public recognition of this fact. As noted in discussing (iii) above, the British Humanist Association on is website claims to represent 25.3 per cent of the British population that identified itself as 'non-religious' in the Census. This is tendentious, for, again, as noted above, on the basis of numerous surveys of religious belief, commitment and practice, we know that many of those who describe themselves as non-religious hold a range of beliefs and practices incompatible with Humanism, say belief in ghosts, in flying-saucers and in horoscopes. Many actually hold religious beliefs, such as belief in God[9] or in angels; such commitments are again incompatible with the tenets of Humanism. A non-religious response in the Census does not equate to commitment to secular Humanism; to claim such is a clear case of creative accounting.

This brings us to the second part of Rawls's second principle, i.e. (2b), which states that social and economic inequalities are to be arranged so that they are to the greatest benefit of the least advantaged members of society. Some creativity is required to relate this to the content of religious education. The social inequalities to which Rawls refers may be regarded as including educational inequalities, but not (what may be termed) 'first order' inequalities, which have to do with such things as differential access or provision or even outcomes, but with 'second order' inequalities, which, among other things, can include curriculum preferences and content: not all knowledge can be imparted to pupils in schools and not every subject or theme can be covered: decisions have to be made about what to include and what to exclude in any curriculum. There are constraints on what pupils can know and how much they can know at different stages of schooling—determined by the available time, mental and psychological maturity, and so on. Patently, not all religions or worldviews can be studied in religious education, but which ones should be? A reframed version of (2b) may help.

(2b.1) The content of religious education should be chosen so that it is to the greatest educational benefit of the least advantaged members of society.

Given that only a limited range of religions or worldviews can realistically be studied in religious education, greatest educational benefit will accrue to pupils who gain knowledge and understanding of those that are most relevant and significant in a British context, where relevance and significance express an overall composite judgement based on the number of adherents, historical and social influence nationally (also taking some account of the international situation), and potential contribution to the realisation of the educational, moral and social aims of schooling. It is difficult to give a definitive list, yet the religions of Christianity, Buddhism, Hinduism, Islam, Judaism and Sikhism would seem to constitute strong claims for inclusion, though, apart from Christianity, not all need be studied at every stage of education or at equal depth; local context ought to be taken into account. There is room for debate and discussion. Greatest educational benefit will also accrue to pupils who have the opportunity to study (at least some) individual religions in sufficient breadth and depth to enable them to appreciate their distinctive beliefs and values, their diversity and relationship to modern culture and society, and their contribution to the personal development of individuals and to the social development of communities. Pupils should also be acquainted (at an appropriate stage) with criticisms of religion and objections to religious belief (for which current legislation makes provision)—this seems reasonable in a liberal society where most of the population have the opportunity to accept or reject religion, to pick and choose in relation to religious beliefs, and thus we can speak of personal religion or a personal worldview. In the early stages of education, in the interest of inclusion, recognition ought to be given to the religions and beliefs of pupils in particular classroom groupings. The religions and beliefs to be so considered cannot be identified in advance and efforts of this kind cannot to be used to support compulsion beyond the individual classroom: the emphasis should be on flexibility and contingency as schools respond to the religious constituency of the local community. One of the further advantages of studying a limited number of religions in detail is that the skills acquired in doing so can be applied to the study of other religions and non-religious worldviews that are not formally included in the curriculum.

Which individuals constitute the least (educationally) advantaged members of society in relation to religious education in terms of their knowledge and understanding of the most influential and significant traditions? It is those that follow minority religions or secular worldviews that are indifferent or hostile to religion (as is the case with some non-religious worldviews). Individuals from such groups will have much to gain educationally and socially from acquaintance with the religious beliefs and practices that are held by the majority of their fellow citizens and that historically have shaped and continue to shape the nature and character of British society and its institutions.

But if the choice of content of religious education is partly determined by social influence does this not reinstate the case for a study of Humanism that takes account of the influence of Humanists? The obvious objection, already stated, is that the number of Humanists is tiny compared to other groups whose beliefs and practices are traditionally ignored in religious education; not every religious tradition or worldview can be studied. The wider the religious education curriculum, the greater the dangers of truncated teaching and superficial learning leading to confused pupils. Second, religion is sufficiently important of itself to warrant study and there is enough relevant content to cover—too much, as we have noted—and a revised version of (2b) has been used to provide a fair way of determining (in broad terms) what should and what should not be included in the curriculum.

An appeal to Rawls's concept of justice would seem to fall far short of justifying a compulsory study of Humanism for all pupils. Equally, if the issue of compulsion is removed, it also falls short of deserving a place in the religious education curriculum over larger and typically excluded religious traditions.

An appeal to the principle of inclusion and toleration

Could a case for the study of Humanism within religious education be advanced on the basis of an appeal to the principle of inclusion? The Humanist Statement considered above argues for the inclusion of Humanism in the religious education curriculum but does not explicitly appeal to *the principle of inclusion*. Perhaps the principle is to some extent implicit in what is said, and for this reason is worth considering.

An appeal to inclusion assumes some ground or foundation for inclusion. In this respect an appeal to inclusion is like an appeal to rights: to say that something is a right assumes that there is some justification for the right and some reason for its bestowal. Historically fundamental rights were believed to have a moral justification. It is difficult to know what to make of a claim that a principle of inclusion requires all pupils in British schools to study Humanism. The basis for this conclusion might be that there are pupils in schools who are or whose parents are Humanists and therefore Humanism should be the object of study. This form of argument has already been considered and found wanting because it justifies too much—every single worldview and religion that is represented in Britain has an equal right to be included in the content of religious education and this unrealistic.

This raises the issue of what determines inclusion and exclusion (and by whom). One modern answer, advanced by Paul Hirst in the 1960s, is that (what he calls) liberal education is initiation into knowledge and that religion constitutes one of a number of logically distinct forms of knowledge (Hirst 1965). Hirst (1972) later expressed doubts about the distinctive nature of religious knowledge, though he continued to support the inclusion of religious education in the school curriculum, chiefly on the basis of the cultural significance of religion. Belief in some kind of divine reality is widely shared, whether the divine exists or not, and in the form of organised religions has exerted profound influence over human affairs. Politics, history, society, literature, jurisprudence, the arts and much else besides cannot be appreciated and interpreted without knowledge and understanding of the different religions, and of their past and continuing role in society; this is even apart from taking account of the distinctively spiritual aspects of religion and the truth claims of the different religions. Furthermore, there has traditionally been a close connection between religion and morality and this connection, which religious believers view as intrinsic to religion, provides resources to educators for the moral development of pupils and the social development of communities. It is educationally defensible to frame the aims of religious education exclusively in terms of religion and there is certainly enough content to cover without extending the subject to include non-religious worldviews and philosophies.

There is a further principled reason for confining religious education to the religions and to religious interpretations of life and reality. The curriculum of British schools, with the exception of religious education, is almost exclusively devoted to secular interpretations of phenomena and to secular approaches to knowledge and belief. The teaching of science is a clear example, where religious perspectives are deliberately and formally excluded. Teaching and learning in other subjects such as History, English and Geography are equally pursued along exclusively secular lines without reference to religious interpretations. Furthermore, a secular system of values is assumed and transmitted through Citizenship Education and through Personal, Social, Health and Economic Education. Secular or non-religious approaches to 'knowledge' are constitutive of school subjects, with the (traditional) exception of religious education. To the extent that a secular approach to education corresponds to a Humanist approach, which is precisely the claim made by many Humanists, it can be said that the modern British school curriculum is mainly a transmitter of Humanist beliefs and values. The secular commitments of Humanism enjoy a privileged position in British education. Perhaps what is needed is greater transparency about this role and recognition of the fact that a secular view of education is for the most part equivalent to a Humanist view. Once this is acknowledged, proper application of the principle of inclusion gives some support to the case for a subject exclusively concerned with religion and with providing pupils with a clear contrast to other subjects that focus on secular knowledge and on non-religious interpretations of reality. This gives some element of balance to the curriculum, while acknowledging that the balance will continue to favour secular forms of learning.

The appeal to inclusion, however, may be construed in a different, less formal way. Some religious educators may view the addition of secular worldviews to the list of religions to be studied in religious education as the next natural step. Since the demise of confessional religious education and the shift to multi-faith religious education, the number of religions taught to pupils has increased steadily. The trajectory of English religious education is the increasing addition of new religions (and worldviews in some Agreed Syllabuses) to the content to be covered: by incremental steps in terms of statute and recommendation it has moved over a period of 50 years from one to six (1988 Education Reform Act), to 11 (the 2004 Framework) to 13 (2013 RE Review), and potentially a greater number still if the advice of the RE Commission Report (2018) is followed. This incremental trajectory gives a form of credibility to the process, which in turn acts to legitimise future increases: each new addition has historical precedent and difficult questions about justification and relevance are ignored. The process is conceived, in Foucauldian terms, as a 'natural' line of development. To add secular worldviews to the religious education curriculum is regarded as the next step. But it is not a 'logical' or a 'natural' step, precisely because the complete process and line of development is not logical or natural. Both terms, logical and natural are metaphors to describe a process that is neither logical in philosophical terms nor natural in biological terms. There is no inner logic or dynamic that requires religious education to include more and more religions and worldviews in its purview. Foucault has warned of the dangers of so called 'natural' developments that institutions and disciplines make in their pretensions to power and influence.

If one looks dispassionately at this line of development it should be obvious that too many religions are already prescribed for study, and to add worldviews makes an already bad educational practice worse. How can it be otherwise? Ironically, both the 2004 Framework and the 2013 RE Council Review are replete with references to the need for pupils to acquire the necessary skills to study religions, yet this insight is not recognised as raising questions about the ever expanding range of belief systems these same documents recommend or require pupils to study. Religious educators sometimes ask why their subject is not regarded as rigorous and challenging by other educators, yet fail to appreciate that depth has been sacrificed for breadth, rigour for superficiality. The skills necessary to interpret, understand and evaluate religion are best acquired by a detailed study of a limited number of religions, not by facile acquaintance with ten or more. Religious literacy requires pupils to have the opportunity to explore the various dimensions and aspects of a reasonably limited number of religions, as chiefly dictated by the findings of cognitive and educational psychology: their beliefs, practices, rituals, historical origins and development, sacred narratives and moral teachings; how the different parts of a religion relate to each other; contemporary interpretations; historical divisions; the relationship of a religion to culture and to the nation state in different contexts; the process and impact of secularisation, and so on. Religions need to be studied in this kind of depth for pupils to understand their nature and relevance, to appreciate their challenge and to become familiar with their inner diversity. This position does not necessarily exclude from study brief 'pen-portraits' of other religions where there are overriding social or educational reasons to do so. One of the weaknesses of studying a wide range of belief systems is that stereotypical representations inevitably result: a false sense of unity and agreement between fellow believers is conveyed because time is only available to cover the essential beliefs and practices. Religious educators and policy makers need to take seriously the idea of transferable skills: analysing and interpreting texts, synthesising information and views from primary and secondary sources, developing a critical argument, assessing beliefs and values, etc. Such skills in religious education can be developed only in the context of detailed knowledge and understanding of a limited number of religions.

If there are educational disadvantages to including more and more religions and worldviews in religious education what then drives this expansion? One plausible answer, for there must be an answer, is that the gradual increase in the number of religions to be studied has resulted from recognition, often implicit or inchoate, that multi-faith religious education has been much less successful, among other things, in challenging and undermining religious prejudice and bigotry than it anticipated it would be. One response to this has taken the form of adding to the number of religions to be studied, in the hope that by acquainting pupils with more and more religions they will become more tolerant of difference and less bigoted; an extension to this strategy is to add secular worldviews, in addition to more religions. The proper response and the educationally necessary response should have been to reassess and re-evaluate the fundamental commitments, beliefs and values that determine the practices, pedagogy and character of English religious education in the classroom (see Barnes 2014). This necessary reassessment has proved too challenging and painful for many religious educators, as it requires revising policies and practices that some regard (incorrectly) as constitutive of multi-faith religious education. Based on this misapprehension, the fundamental weaknesses that undermine the contribution of religious education to the curriculum are allowed to continue, for the most part, unaddressed and even unacknowledged.

Notes

1 There are problems identifying Paganism as a worldview. The editors of the standard academic handbook on Paganism (Pizza & Lewis 2009: 2) point out that most pagans identify themselves as members of a particular tradition, i.e. as Wiccan, Druid, Heathen and so on, rather than seeing the pagan movement as one large self-conscious community: 'pagan' is for many so-called pagans not their primary religious identity. Several contributions to the handbook draw attention to the racist roots of some aspects of modern Paganism in the 'folkish movement' in Germany (*'die völkische Bewegung'*) and of 'pagan fascist' groups in the UK and racist Odinism in the US respectively. These are certainly not subjects for primary school pupils. It ought to be acknowledged that all religions have their 'dark' histories as well.

2 All unattributed references are to Thompson's email, 'Will you sign a letter opposing Humanism being excluded from the new GCSE Religious Studies?' sent on 23 October, 2014, to RE teachers: a copy is in the possession of the author.

3 None of the Annual Reports by the Special Rapporteur on freedom of religion or belief specifically commended the teaching of non-religious worldviews in British RE; the reports are available at http://www.ohchr.org/EN/Issues/FreedomReligion/Pages/Annual.aspx (accessed 25 March 2019). Furthermore, the 2008 Report that deals exclusively with the UK also does not recommend the teaching of non-religious worldviews in RE; see http://da ccess-dds-ny.un.org/doc/UNDOC/GEN/G08/105/17/PDF/G0810517.pdf?OpenElem ent (accessed 17 November 2014).

4 A full version of the original letter is available: http://www.politics.co.uk/opinion-form ers/humanists-uk/article/rowan-williams-heads-religious-leaders-in-call-for-fair-stud (accessed on 10 February 2019).

5 The classification of justice as an abstract noun can cause us to overlook its personal character and orientation.

6 See https://humanism.org.uk/about/ (accessed 6 May 2015).

7 See http://starcourse.blogspot.co.uk/2009/06/national-secular-society-has-fewer-than.html (accessed 6 May 2015).

8 See https://humanism.org.uk/campaigns/religion-and-belief-some-surveys-and-statistics/ census-2011-results/ (accessed 6 May 2015).

9 A 2013 YouGov poll revealed that of those sampled who claim to have 'no religion', 16 per cent believe in God, see http://faithdebates.org.uk/wp-content/uploads/2014/01/ WFD-No-Religion.pdf (accessed 24 March 2019).

6

HUMANISM, WORLDVIEWS AND HERMENEUTICS

The last chapter attempted to identify and assess reasons that can be regarded as contributing to making the strongest possible case for the inclusion of Humanism (and by extension other non-religious worldviews or philosophies) in the religious education curriculum. Some effort was needed to give substance to insights and considerations that in their original form lacked development or substantive form. This is not the case with our next contribution by David Aldridge, which both aims to develop positive reasons for the inclusion of Humanism in religious education and to meet expressed opposition—that my position is one with which Aldridge interacts gives added piquancy! A consideration of his position gives urgency to the issue of hermeneutics[1] in religious education and its relevance to determining the proper role and place for worldviews: attention to hermeneutics can move us in a more positive direction than might have been anticipated up to now. This is followed by a short discussion of the difference between religions and worldviews. The chapter concludes with a summary account of an interesting, recent, cautionary contribution to the place of worldviews in religious education by one of Germany's foremost religious educators, Friedrich Schweitzer.

David Aldridge's positive case for Humanism in religious education

Aldridge (2015: 92) voices his support for Humanism in forthright manner in the first two sentences of his article:

> The case for Humanism in religious education is here advanced in accordance with what I will call a hermeneutic or ontologically dialogic understanding of the endeavour of RE. The term 'ontological' here denotes that learning has the character of a dialogue, distinguishing this from other 'dialogic' approaches that emphasise particular dialogical pedagogical methods.

It is with some relief that we learn a few sentences later that 'a hermeneutic or ontologically dialogic understanding of the endeavour of RE' essentially resolves to

> [t]he simple statement... that learning in RE consists of a transformative dialogical relationship between student, on the one hand, and religion (or religious content, or religious text) on the other, about some subject matter that is of common interest to them.

This is the familiar hermeneutical account of learner and subject matter and the dialogue or relationship between the two in the quest for knowledge and understanding, which in turn raises the possibility of 'transformation of the student' (2015: 93) through the ensuing dialogue. 'An ontologically dialogic account of religious education', Aldridge tells us (2015: 93),

> develops Gadamer's recognition... that there are no 'eternal' or timeless questions, and that subject matter 'emerges' in dialogue. Having a monolithic or 'fixed' understanding of the subject matter at hand will therefore constrain the possibilities for mutual understanding, and ultimately restrict dialogue or stop it in its tracks.

Here Aldridge is drawing on Gadamer's insistence that interpretation is a creative event in its own right. Interpreting a 'text', by which is meant not only literary texts but the wider category of art, symbols and artefacts, creates the possibility of an ontological encounter that effects a new disclosure of truth and a new understanding of reality (ambitious aims for younger pupils!). Aldridge (2015: 93) then identifies the 'interesting pedagogical implications [of this] on two different levels'. The first, at the classroom level, is of individual student learning. 'The moment of understanding', he tells us, 'is the dialogic achievement of student, teacher and religious content' (this seems to personify religious content, which is problematic, but it will be passed over).[2] The 'horizons of understanding' of the participants will differ as each brings a different set of pre-understandings to the learning encounter and consequently each 'understands *differently*' (Aldridge's emphasis, 2015: 93). This might have been an appropriate time to refer to the positive role that Gadamer (1975: 240) believes 'the concept of prejudice' (*der Begriff des Vorurteils*) plays in this encounter. While I agree with the general thrust of what Aldridge has said up to this point, I do not agree with what follows. He goes on in the next sentence to claim:

> that the moment of learning for each individual student is *in tension* with any 'programme of study' or 'scheme of work', since in order to demonstrate progression within subject content a teacher will need to 'move on' to the next item in a methodically pre-determined chronology of content which necessarily cannot take into account the indeterminate fusion of horizons that continuously occurs in learning.
>
> *(2015: 93–94, author's emphasis)*

Learning is always thwarted by a set programme of study! There are a number of issues here. First, I am unsure how this sits with the aim of giving support to compulsory or optional teaching about Humanism if incorporated into a programme of study with determined content, given that, as Aldridge claims (2015: 94) it 'necessarily cannot take into account the indeterminate fusion of horizons that continuously occurs in learning'. Is his case for requiring a study of Humanism in the religious education curriculum not self-defeating? Second, good teaching and learning presuppose progression and development and for best educational effect and achievement these need to be planned and directed. Third, his talk of the *indeterminate* fusion of horizons exaggerates the degree of diversity of understandings that emerge from learning encounters, particularly in the case of pupils in school. Finally, his emphasis on indeterminacy also opens him to the charge that understanding is ultimately subjective, 'in the eye of the beholder' as it were (in contrast to objective), whereas many will want to say that there can be true and false understandings of certain texts, closer and more distant approximations to truth, legitimate and illegitimate interpretations—without the assumption of faithful and unfaithful readings of texts, any justification of examinations in religious studies would presumably not be possible. At one point, Gadamer (1975: 297) seems to warn that an interpreter cannot read into a text what he or she wants; 'the work of application' is not 'making free with the text'. Nevertheless, according to some commentators, Gadamer's insistence that interpretation necessarily involves application opens him, like Aldridge, to the charge of subjectivism (see Hirsch 1967: 245–264). Matters are not straightforward. Whatever view one takes of the position of Gadamer, Aldridge would appear to locate subjectivity at the heart of interpretation; it is on this basis that he identifies a 'tension' with any 'programme of study' or 'pre-determined … content' for the 'individual pupil' (Aldridge 2015: 93–94). It is wiser to distinguish between interpretation and application: one may acknowledge that there is meaning, or more likely multiple meanings in a text, at the level of interpretation, and there can even be new meanings discovered, yet all must be grounded and based on the text and be legitimised by reference to it. Application is a different matter as individuals appropriate these meanings in different and potentially creative ways in various contexts, which may reflect contrasting personal, social, political and religious interests. The distinction between interpretation and application, however, ought not to be regarded as a dichotomy, as in every learning encounter they may not be easily differentiated from each other.

The second level of 'interesting pedagogical implications' that follows from Aldridge's 'hermeneutic or ontologically dialogic understanding of the endeavour of RE' moves from the subject of education, namely the pupil, to the curriculum.

> At the second level, however – the level of what might be called, informally, 'the curriculum' – there may be implications that are particularly significant for religious education as a subject area. We should acknowledge here that by 'curriculum' is intended not only policy or guidance documents, but also the

individual understandings of teachers, schools and departments, the various text books or resources that have become influential, and so on – in fact all of the components that go towards making up the 'commonplaces' of the learner's experience of RE.

(Aldridge 2015: 94)

The essential point he makes is that the religious education curriculum is in a constant state of transition and contestation, historically and contingently evolving, with no abiding structure or even rationale. It follows that '[a]ny elements we fix in place concerning any aspect of the aims, content or proper teaching methodology for RE will lock down certain conditions for our answers to other questions, and foreclose other possibilities' (Aldridge 2015: 95). In my view this is not lamentable but is something that is inevitable: religious education is not the whole of life, or of education or of schooling. Religious education must have some determinate form, alongside some educational claim for inclusion; for aims and content that contribute to, what R. S. Peters (1970: 12) called, the 'family of processes which have as their outcome the development of an educated man', which we would now express as an *educated person*.

[T]he transformative potential of… dialogue, for the students that participate in it, relies on not closing down in advance the paths that the dialogue might take, or the ways that its subject matter might develop and change. I therefore hope to demonstrate that attempts to close out Humanism or other non-religious perspectives as significant contributors to this dialogue are ultimately anti-educational.

(Aldridge 2015: 95)

This again sits uncomfortably with his support for the *compulsory* inclusion of Humanism in the curriculum. This is because this would represent a 'fixed' understanding of the subject matter that, as noted above, he believes, constrains the possibilities for mutual understanding and restricts dialogue. Second, if effective dialogue in religious education is open-ended, what assurance can he give that in every religious education classroom there are pupils who want to enter into dialogue with Humanism; this is surely a contingent matter. I certainly would not want 'to close out Humanism', to use his language, in situations where dialogue between pupils and teachers was moving in that direction; as if any responsible teacher would curtail expressed pupil interest and classroom dialogue by simply referring to the syllabus. Discussion and dialogue in religious education can move in various directions, for the topic of religion is wide-ranging and potentially embraces all of life. The issue is not whether discussion of Humanism is taboo in religious education, it is whether there is a proper educational rationale for compulsory and systematic study of it, beyond those aspects that impinge on consideration of the truth, rationality, meaning and relevance of religions. Finally, Aldridge has much too sanguine a view of curriculum development and 'progress'. He does not seem to appreciate the ideological and political forces and agendas that are constantly working to exert influence and control over the religious education curriculum. Here is one recent pertinent example. The RE Commission Report (2018: 14), initiated by the RE Council concluded that a 'national body should be appointed by the Department for Education on the basis of recommendations from the Religious Education Council of England and Wales, following an open application process'. In other words, the RE Council recommends that it should have control of membership of any new national body set up to determine the nature and content of religious education. It gets worse, for in the next paragraph (2018:14), it is stated that 'Members of the national body should be appointed on the basis of commitment to the approach taken to Religion and Worldviews in the National Entitlement', which is the 'entitlement' that instantiates the curriculum proposed by the RE Commission! Furthermore, only those (ought the term 'comrades' be added here!) who are committed to the RE Commission's/RE Council's vision for the future 'should be appointed'.

To note, as Aldridge does, that the non-statutory Framework of 2004, the RE Review and numerous Agreed Syllabuses require teaching about Humanism hardly clinches the argument. To his credit he recognises this (2015: 98), for he admits that 'it would contradict the spirit of what has been argued so far [in his article that we are here considering] if we were to concede to any of these bodies or documents the authority to offer a final resolution to matters of debate about the RE curriculum'. He continues: 'This observation does nevertheless throw into question the assertion of some critics of the role of Humanism in RE (Barnes in this issue [i.e referring to Barnes 2015b] Barnes & Felderhof 2014) that the burden of proof lies with those who wish to demonstrate that Humanism rightly has a place in the RE curriculum'. I disagree, there ought to be a 'burden of proof' and a 'hermeneutic of suspicion' expressed towards all aspects of the religious education curriculum, not just innovations but equally those hallowed by tradition and practice. In my view every aspect of the curriculum must be justified educationally. My concern over support for the compulsory integration of non-religious philosophies into religious education is not based on animus against their adherents, it is because I believe this broadening requires to be justified, rationally and educationally, and the arguments advanced up to now are unpersuasive. It is not enough to have various national RE bodies recommending a broadening of the curriculum and to expect this to be done on the basis of their status and authority: convincing educational arguments are needed to justify inclusion of all aspects of the religious education curriculum.

Aldridge (2015: 98) identifies current extensions to the curriculum to include non-religious worldviews as 'analogous' to the demise of Christian nurture and the shift to non-confessional, multi-faith approaches in the 1970s and 1980s, as formalised in the 1988 Education Reform Act of Margaret Thatcher's Conservative government. He (2015: 98–99) notes that prior to the 1988 Act this was 'potentially in contravention of the spirit of the 1944 Act', yet what he fails to note is that it was consistent with the letter of the law, an important point to note, and because of this the transition to multi-faith education could proceed. He continues:

> I am aware of no scholar on RE in England and Wales now who suggests a complete reversal of this move: it is widely acknowledged that a responsible approach to religious education must take seriously the range of reasonable faith perspectives that exists and not attempt to nurture students into one of these perspectives.

Greater nuance and knowledge of increasing efforts to centralise control over religious education are needed to appreciate the weak force of this analogy. Aldridge constructs a false dichotomy between religious nurture and multi-faith religious education. While the point is well taken that religious nurture is educationally inappropriate in schools that are by nature, intention and governance intended to cater for a religiously diverse population, this is not the case in 'schools with a religious character', i.e., faith schools, where religious nurture, then and now, continues *alongside* a commitment to include teachings about other religions, i.e., a form of multi-faith religious education.

Another point worth noting is that the transition from Christian nurture to multi-faith religious education came about historically through the innovative work of Local Authority Syllabus Committees in the 1970s that were able to initiate such reforms 'from the bottom up', as it were. The possibility and the reality of reforming religious education were the result of the exercise of local democracy. Multi-faith religious education gradually emerged to become appropriate and successful in an environment where contrasting approaches were pioneered by different local authorities: some syllabuses remained conservatively confessional for a time, some more multi-faith than others. What Aldridge overlooks is that all recent reports and commissions recommend the centralisation of the religious education curriculum and its removal from local influence and local constituencies of communities. All future content will be imposed from above, by what the RE Commission calls 'national experts'. Certainly, if this happens, no future analogy of precisely the same form can be drawn between the transition from confessional to non-confessional religions and a broadening of the content of religious education to include secular philosophies: new developments of this form cannot occur because the democratic element of local accountability and innovation will no longer exist. Aldridge (2015: 99) states that '[it] may be that by a similar "grass roots" transformation we will come to acknowledge that a sophisticated approach to RE must take seriously the existence of perspectives that do not see themselves in religious terms'. A 'similar *"grass roots"* transformation' in the future will not be possible if the curriculum is centralised: 'transformation' can only occur at the behest of national experts! This brings us to the end of Aldridge's positive case for the inclusion of Humanist and other non-religious worldviews in religious education.

David Aldridge's polemic

Aldridge's polemic against an earlier expression (Barnes 2015b)[3] of my opposition to the inclusion of non-religious worldviews in religious education on the same terms as the religions is now considered. For convenience I have itemised his main points of criticism to aid comprehension and assessment (all are direct quotations).

> (i) There is little enough time to take more than one religion seriously, Barnes argues, without also having to deal with secular views, which are adequately represented elsewhere on the curriculum. So the subject matter of religious education is taken, explicitly and inflexibly, to be religions, and the *sui generis* nature of their claims (Barnes and Felderhof 2014, 115 [this reference applies only to the claim of the last sentence; the first sentence is unreferenced, despite appearances]).
>
> *(Aldridge 2015: 99)*

There are two criticisms here, to which I will respond.[4] According to Aldridge I argue that '[t]here is little enough time to take more than one religion seriously'. This criticism is unreferenced, despite appearances, (see below); it must be such because he has attributed to me a position that I do not express in the article that is the subject of his polemic (namely Barnes 2015b), or in any other writing. Here is what I did say about the number of religions to be studied in Barnes 2015b (86 and 88).

> If this form of argument is valid [i.e. if a religion is practised in Britain, how-ever small its number of adherents, it entails that] it has an equal claim to inclusion in the religious education curriculum, then every single worldview and religion that is represented in Britain has an equal right to be included in the content of RE. This is unrealistic for the reason that given constraints of time it is impossible to include every religion and worldview in curriculum content. Choices about what to include in the curriculum and what to exclude have to be made.
>
> Too many religions are currently prescribed for study by both the 2004 Framework and the more recent REC Framework (2013), yet there is no evidence that adding worldviews to the list will enhance the (limited) con-tribution of RE to the moral and social aims of education.

Let us now consider the reference to the *sui generis* character of religion. Aldridge writes that 'the subject matter of religious education is taken, by Barnes and Felderhof, explicitly and inflexibly, to be religions, and the *sui generis* nature of their claims'[5] (Barnes and Felderhof 2014: 115). The first point to note is that in the article in which I argue that the educational case for the inclusion of non-religious worldviews in religious education is unconvincing omits any appeal to the *sui generis* character of religion; no such appeal was part of my argument. Aldridge's chosen quotation, which includes a reference to the *sui generis* nature of religious interests, is taken from an earlier jointly authored article by Marius Felderhof and me (Barnes and Felderhof 2014: 115). This is precisely what is said: 'Religious educators should resist any attempt to diminish the *sui generis character of religious interests* and the way this informs religious education' (my emphasis). What I meant is that *religious interests* have a unique character because they typically refer to a unique object—God, Allah, and Brahman, for example. Such spiritual 'objects' as the philosopher Thomas Nagel says (2012: 26) are 'not part of the natural order'; hence supernatural. This definition (which he overlooks) is used to make the same point in the article in which I reject the inclusion of Humanism in the curriculum, which is the subject of Aldridge's polemic.

An important matter to consider is what use was intended by us in referring to the *sui generis character of religious interests*. The answer to this is simple and straightforward: it is that a principled distinction can be made between religions and non-religious worldviews and that this distinction has relevance (though not determinative) to the issue of whether the latter ought to be included in religious education. This contrasts with the use Aldridge accredits to Felderhof and me by our reference to the *sui generis character of religious interests*. He complains that by it we aim to exclude critical discussions of the truth of religion from religious education. There is no justification for this complaint: it is a restriction on the purpose of religious education that neither of us countenance (see Barnes 2015b: 86 and 89).

> (ii) Another way of looking at this foreclosure of dialogue might be to consider the challenge levelled by critics that Humanism should demonstrate in advance its claim to be a coherent worldview in its own right, rather than a set of negative challenges to theistic belief (Barnes 2015b).
>
> *(Aldridge 2015: 100)*

No page reference is given by Aldridge quite simply because I have never claimed that Humanism is incoherent or that it must establish its claim to be coherent to warrant study within religious education. Such attribution to me of such a viewpoint is simply mistaken.

> (iii) Barnes asks, 'What might pupils "learn from", say a study of National Socialism or Nietzschean "will to power" atheism?' (Barnes 2015b: 80). The implication is that if we admit Humanism, we by the same token admit the study of other secular approaches that we might consider unsavoury.
>
> *(Aldridge 2015: 100–101)*

Aldridge fails to take account of the context in which I discuss National Socialism and Nietzschean 'will to power' atheism. I (Barnes 2015b: 80) was drawing attention to the fact that the document under discussion, namely the 2013 RE Review, 'requires a number of different worldviews to be included in the curriculum (as indicated by use of worldviews in the plural throughout and at each Key Stage), only that of Humanism is cited as an example in the document'. In the absence both of any further examples or of any discussion of criteria for the identification of educationally appropriate non-religious worldviews it is surely legitimate to ask what other worldviews are appropriate for study, and the examples of National Socialism and Nietzschean 'will to power' atheism are cited as possibilities. The view attributed to me by Aldridge is that because Humanism is accommodated, other 'unsavoury' (his term) worldviews must necessarily be included. This is a position I neither express nor hold. My reference to National Socialism was to raise the issue of what constitutes a worldview and what criteria ought to govern its inclusion; and this because the RE Review recommends the study of worldviews but provides only one example, namely Humanism. There is no suggestion that the possible inclusion of Humanism either necessarily or by implication requires the further inclusion of National Socialism in the religious education curriculum.

His misrepresentation of my position continues:

> But Barnes' question ['What might pupils "learn from", say a study of National Socialism or Nietzschean "will to power" atheism?'], presented rhetorically, is precisely the one that would inform our decision about curriculum content. It seems likely that educators would more often decide (as indeed they appear to have done) that a study of Humanism has more to contribute to their students' development than a study of National Socialism, but nevertheless one can imagine situations where students have a great deal to 'learn from' a study of National Socialism. This only becomes an unpalatable consequence if we confuse the aim of engaging students in educational dialogue around religious questions with the aim of commending to them some particular stance on religion. We might engage our students in many kinds of fruitful study of National Socialism without intending or anticipating that they will become National Socialists. In state-funded maintained schools we likewise engage students in dialogue with Christianity without the aim of their thereby becoming Christians. Although Barnes laments its 'demise' (Barnes 2015b: 87), that particular confessional train has now left the station.

First, he omits to mention that the context of my questioning of the relevance of National Socialism as appropriate for study relates to 5-year-olds in schools: 'Specifically, what other worldview should be taught to 5-year-old pupils in primary schools?' (Barnes 2015b: 80). He (Aldridge 2015: 101) overlooks this qualification and with a degree of confidence assert that one can imagine situations where students have a great deal to 'learn from' a study of National Socialism. I agree, but I do not believe that a study of National Socialism is appropriate for 5–6 year olds *in religious education*, perhaps Aldridge does and on this we differ. The further question whether religious education is the best place in the school curriculum to study National Socialism is a matter that need not be considered. Second, why would he think that I entertain the idea that to study a worldview (or a religion for that matter) is to induct pupils into it (no reference is given for his assertion)? Such a position is not credible in two senses. It is not credible in the sense that no religious educator to my knowledge has ever expressed the view that to require pupils to study a religion other than their own necessarily betrays a desire to convert pupils to that religion; this seems absurd! It is also not credible as a position that I hold or have ever expressed, either in the article which is the subject of his analysis and criticism of my position, or in any other writing. Finally, readers are told that I lament the demise of confessionalism—presumably in community schools. What I said was '[s]ince the demise of confessional RE and the shift to multi-faith RE, the number of religions taught to pupils has increased steadily'. This is a factually correct statement, not a value statement.

Why has Aldridge constructed a false portrait of my position? Opinions and positions are accredited to me that I have never espoused in any writing or publication. In the terms in which he interacts with my position he may believe himself to have made effective criticisms, but this is an 'empty' victory, as the criticisms he raises are against arguments and positions of his own constructing, not mine. My position emerges unscathed because it is misrepresented, misinterpreted and overlooked. What Aldridge needs to do is to attend to hermeneutical issues and acquire the skills required to engage with contrary views in academically credible ways. Genuine dialogue assumes that contrary viewpoints and positions are faithfully and respectfully expressed, on such a basis only can progress be made and debates moved on.

The hermeneutical spiral

As a young religious educator in the early 1980s one of the exercises in which I engaged pupils (at the end of Key Stage 3) was to invite them to respond to a list of written statements, the answers to which were kept in their possession: three responses were available: 'Agree', 'Disagree' or 'Don't know'. The answers were recorded and presented numerically by me on the blackboard (yes blackboard, teaching was not 'high-tec' in those days) on the basis of a show of hands, for example, 16 out of 26 (the class total), responded positively to Statement 7; 8 responded negatively and 2 stated they were unsure and didn't know. This was followed by a lively discussion, in which responses were discussed; which extended to identifying correlations, as in who responded positively to Statement 3, 'I believe in God', and to Statement 6, 'I attend church regularly'. Interesting responses and correlations received further attention, such as those who attend church regularly but do not regard themselves as religious; further questions would elicit responses to why this might be the case, and so on. The lesson would end with a summary by me of the findings and some comments about how our prior beliefs 'colour' our attitudes to beliefs and practices that we do not share. This presumably sounds quite amateurish, yet it was an attempt to bring to the attention of pupils an appreciation of the beliefs that they hold and to show how these beliefs relate to other beliefs and how one's beliefs condition/determine why one accepts or rejects certain other beliefs and practices; contradictions were frequently noted as well.

Rudimentary as this exercise was, it does introduce the issue of the perspective of the interpreting subject and the influence our prior beliefs have on our interpretation of religious 'texts', where texts, as earlier in Chapter 4, denote a range of things—artefacts, people, movements and practices. In response the text may modify our prior beliefs and commitments. Some writers express the initial beliefs that we bring to the hermeneutical task as one's 'presuppositions', 'assumptions' (*Voraussetzung*[6]; see Bultmann 1964) or 'horizon' (Gadamer 1975) and more recently, following Heidegger, as one's 'preliminary understanding'(*Vorverständnis*).[7] The idea of preliminary understanding is probably the most helpful term, as understanding is often not static and unchanging: understanding provides a starting point or way into a text that can be subject to correction, revision, adjustment and even rejection in the interpretive encounter, hence *preliminary* understanding. Recognition of the nature of the dialogical encounter between subject and text goes back to Schleiermacher and Dilthey in the nineteenth century and is often referred to as 'the hermeneutical circle', whereby one brings a prior understanding to the task of interpretation, which may then be modified by an encounter with the text. More recently, some (Osborne 2006) speak of the hermeneutical task as, to change the metaphor, more that of a spiral, where understanding of both part and whole develops progressively in tandem with each other, than that of a circle with its potential for understanding to be arrested by a static and fixed interpretation of both the part and the whole.

The RE Commission (2018: 72) has recently and helpfully distinguished two senses or uses of the term worldviews, that of institutional systems of making meaning and structuring how one sees the world, e.g. Christianity, Islam or Buddhism as well as non-religious worldviews such as Humanism are identified here; and that of the process of making sense of life and attributing meaning to experience by individuals. Quite rightly the RE Commission points out that everyone has a worldview and we can conceive of them as high-level preliminary understandings, for understandings operate at different levels: certain beliefs are more important and constitutive of our identities than others. Worldviews can be consciously or unconsciously held; explicitly or implicitly held. Some individuals are more reflexive and self-critical than others of the beliefs they hold, whereas others are less aware of their beliefs and values and how they shape their view of things. Personal worldviews 'may make reference to institutional worldviews,' though 'increasingly young people make less explicit reference to institutional worldviews' (2018: 72). Ideas can be drawn from a variety of sources and in some cases may faithfully reflect the framework of some particular religion or worldview; others may combine sources and beliefs in unusual, hybrid ways, and so on.

At some stage pupils in religious education need to be directed to reflect upon the nature and character of their preliminary understandings and the framework that they bring to the study of religions and religious phenomena. A much more sophisticated 'tool' or 'tools' than that described by me at the beginning of this section could be developed and employed by teachers to identify the preliminary understandings that pupils bring to their study and interpretation of religions. A certain combination of responses could reflect what the RE Commission calls an institutional worldview, whereas other combinations reveal personal worldviews. There need not be a perfect match between responses and an institutional worldview or religion to identify an individual with it. In this way, it can be envisaged that non-religious worldviews such as atheism or agnosticism and perhaps even Humanism will become topics for discussion and analysis and how these worldviews can be brought into dialogue with religions. It is possible that this will capture the essence of the kind of 'open-ended' dialogue that Aldridge believes characterises as 'a hermeneutic or ontologically dialogic understanding of the endeavour of RE'.

What's in a name?

One of the most controversial issues that has arisen in relation to the RE Commission Report (2018: 3) is its recommendation that the subject be named 'Religion and Worldviews'. There are three basic responses to this new title: the first is straightforwardly positive; the second is chiefly negative and the third is ambiguous in an important sense. The first response is that the inclusion of secular worldviews alongside religion are to be studied systematically in their own right in the same way as religions. The second response is that religious education ought to be confined to education about religions, while including secular worldviews at points where they are regarded as relevant for comparative purposes or where they raise criticisms of religions and religious truth claim (some would see this as expressing the current legal framework). The position I have developed in this chapter espouses this second response, though it also argues that some account needs to be taken of the preliminary understandings that pupils bring to their interpretation and (cognitive) attitudes to religions, because of their influence over how religions, religious phenomena and religious texts are viewed. The third response draws attention to the fact that by re-conceptualising religious education as the study of religious and non-religious worldviews, the nature of the subject will be fundamentally changed and this, once it is appreciated, may well be welcomed or rejected. That the nature of the subject will be fundamentally changed by incorporating worldviews is not acknowledged by the RE Commission, either because it has not 'crossed the minds' of the writers or it has 'crossed their minds' but for political or ideological reasons, it is best unacknowledged. Some educators may feel that reconceptualising the subject is what is needed; at least it is something different to try in the hope that it can restore religious education's ability to contribute to the (entirely appropriate) social aims of liberal education, which I have argued elsewhere has been severely limited as a consequence of the two current educationally dominant theoretical paradigms (see Barnes 2014). This third response will be the object of analysis and criticism.

Like religion, worldview has a range of meanings; hence there has historically been some ambiguity and debate that surrounds its usage (see Naugle 2002).[8] The RE Commission Report's usage, however, discussed above, captures and expresses a conventional and relatively uncontroversial account of its meaning. Where it falls short is that it does not identify and develop the different aspects of a worldview that are constitutive of 'systems of making meaning and structuring how one sees the world'. Educators need to attend to this issue for it is not enough to say that worldviews, institutional or personal, enable us to give meaning to life and provide us with a framework for interpreting reality or some aspect of reality. More needs to be said to design and integrate worldviews into a structured programme of teaching and learning that aims to achieve certain outcomes, while being sustainable educationally over 11–12 years of compulsory religious education in terms of depth and of maintaining pupil interest and motivation. James Sire (2009; 2017), for example, has analysed worldviews as providing answers to the following questions:

- What is ultimately real?
- What is the nature of external reality, that is, the world around us?
- What is a human being?
- What happens to a person at death?
- Why is it possible to know anything at all?
- How do we know what is right and wrong?
- What is the meaning of human history?
- What personal, life-orienting core commitments are consistent with this worldview?[9]

Sire was writing for a broadly philosophical audience, and not as an educator. Attention, however, has been given to the nature of worldviews by educators who are aware that imprecision in usage and meaning will frustrate policymaking and educational practice.

Religious educators Jacomijn C. van der Kooij, Doret J. de Ruyter and Siebren Miedema (2013: 214) have helpfully provided 'an outline of the conceptually necessary characteristics for both organized and personal worldviews'.

- An organized worldview prescribes answers to existential questions.
- An organized worldview aims to influence thinking and acting.
- An organized worldview contains moral values.
- Organized worldviews aim to provide meaning in life.
- A personal worldview answers existential questions.
- A personal worldview contains moral values.
- Having a personal worldview means experiencing meaning in life.
- Having a personal worldview means that this worldview influences acting and thinking.

Both these analyses are helpful. They draw attention to an inherent feature of worldviews, which I regard as a weakness in their use and application to religious education: a study of worldviews is a highly ramified intellectual, cerebral and abstract form of study. It represents the imposition of a philosophical, academic approach to religious education, and if this approach is intended to frame how both religions and worldviews are conceptualised, interpreted and presented in religious education, as it seems to be, it will inhibit pupil interest and not be sufficiently broad-ranging to sustain a curriculum over 12 years. In their perceptive review of curriculum change in religious education over the period 1963–1975, Rob Freathy and Stephen G. Parker (2013: 227) point out that Harold Loukes, Richard Acland and Ronald Goldman, on the basis of 'social and psychological research, and in response to increasingly negative assessments of the effectiveness of RI,... sought to make the subject... more child-centred and relevant to pupils' everyday lives, and "less centred on abstract religious ideas or the essentially academic study of the Bible or church history"' (incorporating here a quotation from Parsons (1994: 170–171). The RE Commission Report needs to be attentive to the history of religious education in the 1960s when academic approaches to the Bible and church history were prevalent: the result was widespread disinterest among pupils. There is a case for drawing an analogy between this historical orientation to academic approaches in religious education with the current proposed academic approach of studying worldviews by the Commission; it will also result in disinterest because it is not sufficiently relevant to the concerns and lives of young people. In addition, what conceptual means do Key Stage 1 and 2 pupils have for reflecting on meaning in life, or identifying and considering their own and others' worldviews or how their own acting and basic (religious or non-religious) commitments are connected and how they relate to the acting and thinking of others? One of the strongest criticisms of phenomenological approaches to religion to emerge in the late 1970s and 1980s was that a psychological perspective on children's cognitive development shows that most pupils in primary schools are incapable (conceptually) of considering a viewpoint contrary to their own or of possessing the kind of reflexivity that is required for a truly critical engagement with religions and religious beliefs and practices or with their own inherited beliefs.

Conceptualising religions as worldviews unduly narrows the content of religious education, if we remain faithful to what is typically meant by a worldview. It narrows understandings of the nature of religion and of how religions can be represented. One might contend that there is no intention to truncate the study of religions in the ways that a worldview approach presumes; but what of secular worldviews that lack the features of religions that can be appropriated by younger pupils? What rituals do agnostics and atheists practise? Apart from opposition to religion what beliefs do atheists share? The same question may be asked about secularism, which the RE Commission regards as a worldview. What institutional form does atheism, agnosticism and secularism take? The narrowness of 'vision' of both atheism and secularism has prompted Michael Hand to conclude that '[n]either has anything like the scope and ambition of a worldview'.[10] Curiously and inexplicably the RE Commission Report claims (2018: 39) that 'the shift in language from "religion" to "worldview" signifies the greater attention that needs to be paid to individual lived experience'. Have members of the Commission ever read any of the literature on worldviews? This is precisely what is typically not included.

According to the RE Commission Report (2018: 7) its new 'vision... is... signified by a new name for the subject: Religion and Worldviews'. As well as indicating the future orientation of the subject, it also 'removes the ambiguity in the phrase "Religious Education," which is often wrongly assumed to be about making people more religious'. I have never met any parent or teacher who wrongly believes that religious education in community schools aims to make pupils more religious. Is there any evidence to substantiate the claim that religious education is 'often' taken to denote a form of religious nurture?

It has been argued in this section that enlarging religious education to incorporate worldviews, the study of which is commonly associated with a distinctive form of study and/or conceptualising religions along similar lines, fundamentally narrows the nature of religious education and accordingly limits its educational and social potential.

A continental contribution to the British debate

One of the effects of the internationalising of interest and research on religious education, indicated by such associations as the International Seminar on Religious Education and Values (ISREV) and research projects that engage religious educators from different countries, is that insights can be gained from other national contexts and valuable contributions can be made by religious educators from elsewhere. One such contribution has recently been made by Professor Friedrich Schweitzer (2018) of the University of Tübingen, Germany. He has entered into the growing controversy (see also Hannam & Biesta 2019) that has arisen around the position and recommendations of the RE Commission Report.

Anyone who thought that the 2018 RE Commission Report charts a convincing future direction for the subject and provides an intellectually and educationally credible, research based response to the troubles that beset religious education in England will find Professor Schweitzer's comments salutary reading. He (2018: 516) admits he does not possess 'any first-hand familiarity with the situation of Religious Education in the UK' or 'familiar[ity] with the complex functioning of politics and school administration there'. Consequently, these are not matters he considers, so his lack of familiarity with them is of little consequence. He does, however, question the broadening of the subject to include worldviews:

> Is there really a necessary relationship between the changes needed at system level concerning the curriculum and supervision of Religious Education on the one hand and changing from Religious Education to Religion and Worldviews on the other?
>
> *(2018: 518)*

Framed in terms that I have been pursuing in this book: is there any reason to think that broadening the religious education curriculum to include worldviews will do anything to overcome the weaknesses many identify in its current practice and the theoretical commitments that currently guide its practice? More widely, the question relates to many of the proposals considered in different chapters: is there any reason to believe that they will overcome the weaknesses and transform the subject into one that can truly realise, entirely appropriate, liberal educational aims that combine faithful representations of religions while contributing to the development of a respectful, responsive citizenry? Schweitzer (2018: 520) raises the critical question already asked by me, and like me finds that they are typically unanswered.

> The obvious problem remains which worldviews deserve a place in the curriculum and what qualifies the encounter with them as educational. What should be the criteria for treating worldviews at school? What does education mean in relationship to different worldviews? The report remains rather vague in this respect, referring to 'refinement' as the aim of Religion and Worldviews (cf. 5: 'young people come to a more refined understanding of their own worldview'). What does this mean concerning, for example, fundamentalism and ethnocentrism, racism or, to mention some examples from different fields, neo-liberalism and evolutionism? Is 'refinement' an adequate aim in the case of 'prejudice and discrimination' (28)? It is obvious that the Report does not have in mind that education should function according to such worldviews. Yet nevertheless, any decision concerning the content of teaching and the criteria applied in teaching is neither obvious nor innocent. All choices and selections of topics should be transparent, democratic and based on participatory procedures. Moreover, they should be informed by scientific analysis concerning both, the respective worldviews themselves (including their implications for society) as well as education referring to worldviews.

How will extending religious education to incorporate worldviews further the aims of religious education, or will the aims be reconfigured in ways that will actually fail to overcome current weaknesses and re-orientate the subject to new aims and procedures that undermine the subject's justification and its educational credibility? Like Schweitzer, I am concerned that the study of worldviews is advanced in the cause of making pupils more aware of diversity and 'for young people [to] come to a more refined understanding of their own worldview', that is, to a better understanding of what they already believe. These are not good enough reasons for expanding the curriculum. Where is the research base for expanding the religious education curriculum? Is there research that shows that the systematic study of secular worldviews contributes any better than study of a range of religions to challenging discrimination and bigotry (in particular against Jews and Muslims, against whom these are most often directed) in society? Let us not as educators fall into familiar clichés about how effective religious education is in helping pupils to understand others and prepare them for life in a diverse society if current approaches have never been tested and new understandings are advanced on the basis of a few experts, who may have ideological axes to grind. The story is often repeated that the atheist philosopher Bertrand Russell was once asked what he would say if he found himself standing before God on judgement day and God asked him, "'Why didn't you believe in Me?" to which he is said he would reply, "Not enough evidence, God! Not enough evidence!'". The response sounds less convincing now than when it was first expressed, since the emergence of sophisticated philosophical challenges to the whole concept of evidentialism in the philosophy of religion (see Plantinga & Wolterstorff 1984). In relation to religious education, however, the request for evidence (empirical evidence would be good) and argument are entirely appropriate.

Schweitzer is not unacknowledging of good ideas contained in the RE Commission Report or unwelcoming of all its recommendations, yet the fact that one of the most internationally prominent and influential religious educators raises criticisms ought to cause serious reflection about the future direction of the subject suggested in this regard by the RE Commission. Let us British religious educators not continue with our self-congratulatory rhetoric, rehearsed for the benefit of government and for religious educators elsewhere, and not retreat further into isolationism that sees no virtue in learning from the experience and knowledge gained from other countries and national contexts.

Schweitzer (2018: 521) can have the last word.

> May one then not... foresee a different future for Religious Education in Britain (and in other countries) as well? Should it not be possible to foresee a future existence for Religious Education, with a clear focus on religion(s) instead of a diffuse mixture of religions and undefined worldviews?

Notes

1 A plural noun usually treated as singular, as here.
2 Presumably the word 'achievement' is to be interpreted literally when applied to student and to teacher and metaphorically when applied to religious content.
3 Aldridge was given access to my article, Barnes 2015b, before publication; I did not see his polemic until after publication; if I had I could have pointed out some of his mistaken interpretations and attribution to me of positions I do not hold.
4 I considered responding in this section to Aldridge's criticism of my claim that 'secular views' are well represented in the broader curriculum, but given that my claim is confined to a few sentences and effectively constitutes an aside to my main argument, I have decided otherwise. To address it fully would give to it a significance it does not warrant.
5 I have never stated that the subject matter of religious education should be 'explicitly and *inflexibly*' confined to religions. If Aldridge had been attentive to what I said in the article to which he refers and to what I have written elsewhere he would know that I have always contended that one aspect of my support for a critical element in religious education is to take account of criticisms of religion that emanate from non-religious sources; his attribution to me of 'inflexibility' suggests otherwise.

6 *Voraussetzung* can properly be translated as 'presupposition' or 'assumption'; this is the term used in Rudolf Bultmann's (1964) influential article, translated into English as 'Is Exegesis with Presuppositions Possible?'

7 The term *Vorverständnis* has a variety of meanings in German and in some contexts 'prior understanding' is not the best English translation.

8 It is commonly accepted that Immanuel Kant coined the term *Weltanschauung*, that is, worldview, in his work *Critique of Judgment*, published in 1790. It originates in a passage that characteristically expresses his view of the contribution of the mind to perception: 'If the human mind is nonetheless to be able even to think the given infinite without contradiction, it must have within itself a power that is supersensible, whose idea of the noumenon cannot be intuited but can yet be regarded as the substrate underlying what is mere appearance, namely, our intuition of the world [*Weltanschauung*]' (Kant 1987 [1790]: 111–112). For Kant *Weltanschauung* means something like a perception of the world gained empirically. According to David Naugle (2002: 59), '[f]rom its coinage in Kant, who used the term only once and for whom it was of minor significance, it evolved rather quickly to refer to an intellectual conception of the universe from the perspective of a human knower'.

9 Taken from Sire's summary of his position; see https://www.christianity.com/theology/other-religions-beliefs/8-questions-every-worldview-must-answer.html (accessed 20 December 2018).

10 Michael Hand, 'Why "Religion and Worldviews" is a non-starter'; see https://blog.bham.ac.uk/socialsciencesbirmingham/2018/10/10/religion-and-world-views/ (accessed 20 February 2019).

7

RELIGIOUS EDUCATION AND A STATUTORY NATIONAL RELIGIOUS EDUCATION CURRICULUM

> So it's published. The long awaited… publication of *A New Settlement: Religion and belief in schools* by Charles Clarke and Linda Woodhead. This is a ground-breaking review which has the potential to shape the future of our subject. If the document is to have the impact it deserves it needs to be understood, debated and supported by the RE community. Supported not in every detail but in terms of its big picture and the opportunity it offers to do something! Things of this stature don't come along often in RE.[1]

With these words, Alan Brine greeted the publication of a reforming pamphlet entitled *A New Settlement: Religion and belief in schools* (2015), produced by the former Labour Education Secretary Charles Clarke and Professor Linda Woodhead of Lancaster University.[2] He then proceeds to give eight reasons why 'he likes it': one of which is that the authors 'aren't in any of the usual RE camps that so often undermine our debates'. This is a perceptive point and one that strikes home. It has been argued elsewhere that English religious education is plagued by ideological disputes about which groups and individuals speak for the profession; about how to gain control over the religious education curriculum; about how best to achieve government funding; about defensive attitudes to legitimate criticism in order to maintain the reputation of the subject, and so on (see Barnes 2014: 10–13, and 177–179). The critical question is whether Clarke and Woodhead, who are not professional religious educators and who up to this point have not published anything on religious education, are best equipped to offer convincing responses to current weaknesses. Brine thinks that their proposals are significant. He concludes his recommendation with these words:

> I genuinely think that this pamphlet… offers the best opportunity in years to take our subject forward. The price of failure could be serious. My genuine

fear is that the current problems facing our subject in many, many schools are not part of a cycle where all recovers in time; I fear the problems are systemic and need radical solutions![3]

What gave added weight to Clarke and Woodhead's proposals, when originally published, is that some regarded them as providing a blueprint for new legislation by the Labour Party on the role of religion in schools, in anticipation of its election to government in 2015. This did not happen, as David Cameron and the Conservative party were returned to power with a sufficient majority to end its coalition with the Liberal Democrats, which had been established when no party gained a clear majority in the 2010 General Election.

Towards the end of 2018, Clarke and Woodhead published a revised version of their proposals, which differs little in substance from the original; difference is mainly confined to recommendations on the practice of school assembly (2018: 32–35).[4] The problem with this later version is that it is ten pages shorter and consequently omits some of the arguments and considerations that are found in the earlier version. This is disappointing from a critical perspective and leaves their recommendations less well supported. Their revised version is more clearly focused on gaining political consensus[5] and less on justifying their recommendations to 'rank and file' religious educators by developing arguments and citing evidence. It appeals for support to recent sources published after their initial Settlement version, such as Baroness Butler-Sloss's (2015) report, *Living with Difference: Community, diversity and the common good*, which in many respects reaches similar conclusions about religious education. Equally their revised version gives less attention to the evolving history and current legislative framework of religious education. In other words, Clarke and Woodhead's 'Revised Settlement' is more user-friendly and direct but less persuasive educationally and philosophically. In some cases one has to turn to the original 'Settlement' document to discover the reasoning behind the position adopted in the later revised document in somewhat stark, unsupported terms. For this reason, discussion of their case for a national statutory curriculum for religious education will be considered by reference to their original, longer version; to indicate that the recommendations and the substance of the original are retained in the revised version, refences to it will occasionally be included.

The Oxford English Dictionary defines a pamphlet as 'a small booklet or leaflet containing information or arguments about a single subject', and Clarke and Woodhead's publication describes itself as a pamphlet. This self-description is not entirely appropriate: it runs to 68 pages, hardly short, in its original form (see above). Moreover, it does not confine itself to one theme: it includes discussion of religious education in schools, collective worship and faith schools. According to them there ought to be a new legislative settlement that subsumes all three elements, as in their view '*there are common principles... and linkages between various elements*' (2015: 9; authors' emphasis). Nevertheless, they subdivide their final recommendation under the three headings of 'Act of Collective Worship', 'Curriculum' and 'Faith Schools' and they (2015: 15) also admit that by 1988, the year of the Education Reform Act, 'few would have seen collective worship as a part of religious education', and acknowledge that '[r]eform in relation to each area needs to be tackled in different ways, and at different paces' (2015: 9). Such comments suggest the plausibility of uncoupling worship in schools, religious education and faith schools from each other and it is this I intend to do. My intention is to deal only with religious education. My experience, competence and interest do not extend to collective worship and it is hoped to consider faith schools on another occasion. No doubt there are connections between all three, but if there are, they will be for others to make and explore.

Setting the scene

Clarke and Woodhead provide some background information as preparatory to their discussion and proposals and some of this may be usefully summarised.

Religion

They state that:

> The last twenty-five years have witnessed some of the most significant shifts in religious belief and practice since the Reformation, as traditional forms of religious authority, and uniformities of doctrine and practice, have given way to a much wider and more diverse range of religious and non-religious commitments.
>
> In this period the churches' religious monopoly has been lost, other faiths have grown in strength and visibility, some elements in all the main religions including not only Islam but the churches are taking more radical 'counter-cultural' stances against a perceived secular mainstream, and there is a growing proportion of people who do not affiliate with any religious organisation, even though a majority of them are not atheist.
>
> *(2015: 6)*

These short accounts are helpful. Although their statement about 'uniformities of doctrine and practice' within religions, including Christianity, existing up to their suggested date of the 1990s is not historically accurate. From the 1960s forward, the effects of the secularisation of church and of society were becoming clear and although there was 'lip service' paid to the importance of religion in national life, this disguised an increasingly disinterested public, illustrated by a significant fall in baptisms and church attendance. In 1969, J. W. D Smith reflected this new cultural situation by advocating a new secular form of religious education, as did the Schools Council's *Working Paper 36: Religious Education in the secondary school* (1971).

Clarke and Woodhead (2015: 6) are certainly right to speak of uniformities giving 'way to a much wider and more diverse range of religious and non-religious commitment', though again this may be dated from the 1960s onwards, rather than as accredited by them to the last 25 years. One wonders whether the late (and frankly inaccurate) dating of these social influences is to give credence to their suggestion that earlier important legislation on religious education preceded secular and multicultural trends in society and therefore failed to consider and take account of them; this conceivably would strengthen their argument for legislative change to be introduced now to accommodate such influences. This is not the case, however, whether legislative reforms are needed or not: the 1988 Education Reform Act clearly responded to the changing social nature of English society by initiating the requirement that all Agreed Syllabuses should take 'account of the teaching and practices of the other principal religions represented in Great Britain' (Section 8.3). Legislative changes were also initiated with regard to collective worship in schools that were intended to respond to the changing and growing nature of the moral and religious diversity represented in schools and in society.[6]

Clarke and Woodhead (2015: 6) identify the existence of counter-cultural stances by some adherents from all the main religions, including Christians as well as Muslims, against 'a perceived secular mainstream'. They leave the matter there, which is unfortunate. They do not ask the question why religious adherents, whatever their numbers and religious affiliation, have this perception, and it is a perception that is growing. Is it that religious adherents feel increasingly alienated from recent social and educational policies, say about sexuality or gender roles, that in their view stigmatise their communities and require them to 'accommodate', however best they can, beliefs and commitments that they adjudge to be contrary to their religious traditions, yet endorsed by public institutions that brook no exceptions?[7] If such measures produce deeper divisions in society, then it may be asked, given that Clarke and Woodhead are aware of the problem, whether their proposals will alleviate or exacerbate the situation. Will their proposals appeal to religious adherents or are they happy to pursue policies that represent a secular mainstream view? They (2015: 6) also draw attention to the fact that there is 'a growing proportion of people who do not affiliate with any religious organisation, even though a majority of them are not atheist'. The 2011 Census for England and Wales recorded that 25 per cent of the population describe themselves as having 'no religion'; and this does suggest that curriculum planning and pedagogy in religious education need to include some reference to the different varieties and degrees of religious scepticism that exist within Britain (cf. Barnes 2014: 241).

History

Clarke and Woodhead provide a useful overview of legislation relating to religion in schools, beginning with the 1944 Education Act and concluding with recent provisions for the expansion of academies and free schools. Important changes are noted. For example, whereas the 1944 Education Act (Section 25) characterised 'religious education' as comprising 'religious instruction', i.e., the classroom-based subject in schools, and 'collective worship'; this two-fold identification was revised in the 1988

Education (Reform) Act, and the term religious education reserved exclusively for subject based teaching about religion. It has already been noted how the 1988 Act required that account be taken of 'other principal religions represented in Great Britain'. Interestingly, the Act did not specify what these religions were, though Agreed Syllabus Conferences and writers of school textbooks followed the late John Hull (1988), then of Birmingham University and an influential commentator on religious education for over 40 years, in designating Buddhism, Hinduism, Islam, Judaism and Sikhism as such. What Clarke and Woodhead fail to record at this point, in relation to the 1988 Act, is that Agreed Syllabus Conferences must include members of the principal non-Christian religions represented in the area. This again overlooks the ways in which the 1988 Act did take account of the changing religious constituency of modern English and Welsh society. Perhaps, and this is conjecture, what Clarke and Woodhead are attempting to do by shortening the time frame of significant religious change in Britain to the last 25 years and by overlooking the accommodations to religious diversity enshrined in the 1988 Education Reform Act, and significantly, by frequent references to the 'historic 1944 agreement' and the fact that it is over 'seventy years' ago, is to strength their case for new legislation, on the premise that legislation dating from toward the end of the Second World War cannot still be relevant. This is not the whole story, for it overlooks important post-1944 legislative developments that have taken account of social and religious change and were framed precisely on account of these developments.

There is one point where arguably Clarke and Woodhead (2015: 14) mis-represent the law when they state that 'the essential legal framework for the religious education curriculum remained in place after 1988… [but] was significantly qualified in 2004 by the publication of a non-statutory national framework for religious education'. Recognition of the *non-statutory* nature of the 2004 Framework indicates that the law pertaining to the provision of religion education was not 'significantly qualified' by its publication. Their (2015: 14) further assertion that 'the locally agreed syllabuses… obviously varied from locality to locality (though there were also many similarities)' does not do justice to the influence of the Framework and the near uniformity it produced. What they could have accurately reported is that the Framework provided a template for Agreed Syllabus Committees that was almost unanimously followed in terms of its structure, proposed content and scheme of assessment. Variation between syllabuses produced after the publication of the non-statutory Framework are for the most part insignificant, with few exceptions. The *Does Religious Education Work?* project (Conroy et al. 2013: 69), after conducting a thorough review of all the Agreed Syllabuses in England, concluded that '*most* hold their content in common, despite legal provision for "local determination"'. The influence of the Framework over syllabuses was not unexpected given that (draft) guidance, which was sent out to schools, from the then Department for Children, Schools and Families, explicitly stated that 'the Framework and its implementation are the basis of Government policy' (Department for Children, Schools and Families 2009: 18) and its use was encouraged by groups representative of the interests of religious educators and more politically motivated organisations, such as the Religious Education Council of England and Wales. Indeed, as Clarke and Woodhead (2015: 14) record, 'some hoped that over time this [Framework] could develop into a statutory national agreed syllabus'; this remains an aim for those who press for centralised control of the religious education curriculum, as Clarke and Woodhead do, as we shall come on to discuss.

Schools today

A further short section provides a brief statistical description of schools in England today, including the place of faith schools in the English education system. This is prefaced by further summaries of the nature of religious change indicated by a comparison of statistics from the two latest censuses (2015: 16):

> Between 2001 and 2011 there has been a decrease in people who identify as Christian (from 71.7% to 59.3%) and an increase in those reporting no religion (from 14.8% to 25.1%).

'Additional research' (which may be granted reliability, given its provenance and quality) is cited by them (2015: 16) 'to indicate belonging to a religious group will become less common than being religious, spiritual or non-religious outside of traditional institutional frameworks' (and following on):

> The influence of traditional religious authorities is likely to continue to diminish, and the authority of personal choice and new, more disorganised, forms of authority is likely to grow. The influence of more conservative and 'fundamentalist' elements of religion relative to less activist liberal or 'moderate' majorities is also likely to increase.

They then document and discuss the numbers, distribution and types of faith schools, i.e., 'schools with a religious character'. It has already been indicated that our focus will be on curriculum religious education and not the propriety and legitimacy of faith schools, though this focus is not as narrow as it sounds, because what Clarke and Woodheadk propose for religious education has profound implications for the nature and legitimacy of faith schools, as we shall see. At one place in their discussion they appear to make a factual error in relation to voluntary controlled schools. After stating (2015: 18) that '[n]early all voluntary controlled schools are Church of England', they add 'but Religious Education *normally* follows the local agreed syllabus, like other local schools' (my emphasis). Now conceivably they might be recording research findings that show that some Church of England voluntary controlled schools *do not follow* the local agreed syllabus, and this would justify their statement, though there is no reference by them to such research (and I have found no reference to such research in a review of the relevant literature). It is more likely that they have misread the legal situation. In a House of Commons Briefing Paper, entitled *Religious Education in schools (England)* (2016: 6), produced by Robert Long to provide accurate official information on religious education, including 'the rules around RE in state-funded schools', it is stated that 'RE in a... voluntary controlled school with a religious character *must be* provided in accordance with the locally agreed syllabus for the area' (my emphasis): Clarke and Woodhead's use of the term normal does not fully capture the legal requirement.

Curriculum Religious Education

There are two straightforward questions to ask about Clarke and Woodhead's proposals. First, do they make a convincing case for a new legislative settlement? Two, are there reasons for concluding that the form of religious education they wish to see established through a new legislative settlement will overcome the weaknesses identified in current provision and discussed in Chapter 1? To do justice to their position it is necessary to quote at some length both from the original official sources they cite (almost exclusively from Ofsted) and from their commentary and interpretation.

The Quality of Religious Education

Clarke and Woodhead (2015: 28) begin their account of curriculum religious education with the statement: 'In recent years criticism of the teaching of Religious Education in English schools has been substantial and authoritative'. They report the findings of the two most recent reports from Ofsted: *Transforming Religious Education*, published in June 2010, and *Realising the Potential* published in October 2013, and while noting (2015: 28) that the 2010 report 'contains some good news, particularly in relation to student recognition of the importance of the subject', the overall picture makes disheartening reading. They (2015: 29–30) list the weaknesses identified by Ofsted (a sample only is quoted and in some cases in abbreviated form; this is because the same weaknesses are quoted in full in Chapter 1 and are included here again for convenience):

- Too many pupils were leaving school with low levels of subject knowledge and understanding.
- In three-fifths of the lessons seen, both in primary schools and throughout Key Stage 3, a key weakness was the superficial nature of pupils' subject knowledge and understanding. Achievement and teaching in RE in the secondary schools visited were only good or better in just under half of the schools. The quality of the curriculum was good or better in just under two-fifths of the secondary schools.
- Inspectors judged pupils' knowledge and understanding of Christianity to be good or outstanding in about 6 per cent of the schools and inadequate in about 10 per cent of them, making teaching about Christianity one of the weakest aspects of RE provision.

- There were... some uncertainties about the relationship between fostering respect for pupils' beliefs and encouraging open, critical, investigative learning in RE.
- Assessment in RE remained a major weakness.
- The effectiveness of the current statutory arrangements for RE varies. Recent changes in education policy are having a negative impact on the provision for RE in some schools and on the capacity of local authorities and SACREs to carry out their statutory responsibilities to monitor and support it.[8]

'From this depressing description of overall failure (despite substantial patches of good practice and excellent teaching), which offers little comfort to defenders of the current statutory framework' (2015: 30), Clarke and Woodhead identify four recurring themes in Ofsted's findings as significant, the first two of which are relevant to our discussion (the third theme refers to the failure to provide adequate curriculum time and the fourth to the lack of focus to put things right).[9] The first (2015: 30; authors' emphasis), 'and most important', is confusion about the purpose and aims of religious education, which has 'a negative impact on the quality of teaching, curriculum planning and the effectiveness of assessment'; and confusion about how religious education relates to ethics, moral guidance and community cohesion, for example. The second recurrent theme (2015: 31, authors' emphasis) is the need for (what is described by them) as 'the need for wholesale reconsideration of the operation of local determination of syllabuses'. This is expanded upon by three further statements (2015: 30–31): (i) 'The effectiveness of the current statutory arrangements for RE varies considerably'; (ii) 'The structures that underpin the local determination of the RE curriculum have failed to keep pace with changes in the wider educational world'; and (iii) 'The gulf between local authorities that support and monitor RE effectively and those that find this role impossible continues to widen'. (Is there evidence for this? Have local authorities spoken of impossibility in this regard?)

They (2015: 32) cite a range of recent changes in education policy that have had a negative impact 'on the provision of and support for RE, both locally and nationally': the exclusion of religious education from English Baccalaureate subjects and from short courses that contribute to published school performance figures; the expansion of academies and free schools that are not required to follow a local agreed syllabus[10]; reduction in local government spending (a common complaint, not exclusive to religious educators) and in publicly funded national support for curriculum development. They also refer to the withdrawal of bursaries (from 2013–2015, but reinstated in 2015–2016; see Long 2016: 17), and to the reduction in teacher training places for religious education. It is important to ask about the nature of the educational changes to which local structures have failed to keep pace, for this is the point at issue, if they wish to challenge (and to end, as we shall see) local determination of religious education. Apart from the expansion of academies and free schools that are not required to follow a local agreed syllabus (though some choose to) and less funding from local government (there is no suggestion that funding to SACREs have been reduced), the remainder of the changes to which they refer do not bear on local determination and it is difficult to know how these points advance the case for its end.

Interest in defending the current legislation governing the local determination of religious education in schools and its appropriateness or relevance to different types of schools is not my main concern, yet clearly it impacts on curriculum religious education. Clarke and Woodhead (2015: 31) make much of Ofsted's calls 'to review the system' of the local determination of syllabuses, given its perceived weaknesses. They (2015: 48; cf. 2018: 29–31) express the negative conclusion that 'the Religious Education syllabus in county and voluntary controlled schools should no longer be set by a system of agreed local syllabuses'. It may, however, be too premature to reach this conclusion, at least on the evidence presented. A case needs to be made to show that ineffective religious education is attributable to local Standing Advisory Councils for RE (SACREs) and not to national policies, ineffective pedagogies and the like. There are two other matters that are worth considering that bring together politics and policy which have a bearing on the case for the end of local determination and the introduction of a nationally agreed syllabus and programmes of work, as recommended by Clarke and Woodhead. Before consideration of this it may helpful to be reminded that Charles Clarke's opposition to local determination goes back beyond the 'current crisis'.

From October 2002 to December 2004, Charles Clarke was Labour Secretary of State for Education and Skills; after which he became Home Secretary, until May 2006. It was under his direction that the 2004 non-statutory national Framework for religious education was produced and promoted: on page 1 of the document it is expressly stated that it 'has been prepared by the Qualifications and Curriculum Authority on behalf of the Secretary of State for Education and Skills'. Clarke and Ken Boston (QCA 2004: 3), Chief Executive of QCA, contribute a forward which makes clear their belief that the Framework 'lies at the heart of... policies to raise standards in the learning and teaching of religious education'; 'It also', they believe, 'provides a framework within which all partners in education can support young people on the road to further learning'; and in addition:

> This framework makes clear the principles that schools should follow in the teaching of religious education, to ensure that all pupils have the chance to succeed, whatever their individual needs or the potential barriers to their learning may be.

The 2004 Framework is also described as providing and defending 'the knowledge, skills and understanding that is the entitlement of every pupil'. The use of the term 'entitlement' occurs four times in Clarke and Boston's single page forward, and arguably is misleading: it is the statutory provisions relating to religious education that strictly provide entitlement, not non-statutory documents, which lack legal force, as we have already noted. The references to entitlement should probably be interpreted as reinforcing the government's hope to exert more centralised control over the religious education curriculum. In any case, this is about as strong a recommendation as could be given to encourage 'those with responsibility for the provision and quality of religious education in maintained schools' (2004: 3) to adopt the Framework and use it to provide the 'structure for ASCs [Agreed Syllabus Committees] and faith communities… [and to use it] to determine what pupils should be taught in religious education' (2004: 10). Agreed Syllabus Committees readily appreciated the message and as encouraged, most revised their syllabuses in the years following to incorporate the detailed prescriptions (including its content) of the Framework into their agreed syllabuses.

What is clear is that Clarke's enthusiasm for a nationally determined curriculum for religious education goes back to his time as Secretary of State for Education and Skills and the production of the 2004 Framework (as the Forward to it states) 'on [his] behalf'. This enthusiasm clearly antedates the reasons that he and Woodhead currently cite as supporting such an initiative. No crisis of confidence or achievement preceded the recommendation of the (then) Department of Education and Skills to produce a Framework to guide and determine religious education in schools. This gives support to the conclusion that the decision to determine religious education through the 2004 Framework was as much for political as for educational reasons; perhaps even chiefly for the political aim to centralise government control over the religious education curriculum. It may be somewhat disingenuous at this point to suggest that a new Framework, modelled on the 2004 Framework, is needed to overcome the weaknesses of current provision, when the original Framework was not advanced on this basis.

We return now to exploring something more about the relationship of politics and policy in religious education under New Labour. In December 2004, Clarke was appointed Home Secretary, a post from which he resigned in May 2006, following a scandal over prisoners who ought to have been considered for deportation, and revelations that he had waited 3 weeks before informing the prime minister and the police of the problem and of possible dangers to the public. Nevertheless, the non-statutory Framework remained central to New Labour's policy to 'modernise' religious education. In February 2006 a joint statement from the Department for Education and Skills and faith communities on the importance of religious education stated that both 'are fully committed to using the Framework in developing the religious education curriculum for our schools and colleges' (quoted in Clarke and Woodhead 2015: 36). Non-statutory guidance in 2009 (DCSF: 18) reaffirmed that the 'Government's commitment to RE is enshrined in the Framework' and that 'the Framework and its implementation are the basis of Government policy'. It vouches the opinion that the Framework 'has enabled RE to keep in step with wider curriculum developments and support schools in planning an integrated and coherent curriculum'.

The guidance also includes the following statement (DCSF 2009: 18):

> The publication of the first non-statutory National Framework for Religious Education (the Framework) in 2004, whose principles have been endorsed by representatives of all major faith and belief communities and religious

education (RE) associations, has provided the basis for a more coherent and consistent RE curriculum across the country.

There are two claims here that warrant comment. The statement that the principles of the Framework were endorsed by representatives of all major faith and belief communities and religious education (RE) associations is to some degree ambiguous. It is true that the religious education (RE) associations, the RE Council of England and Wales and National Association of Teachers of Religious Education (NATRE) endorsed it, for example, though the endorsement of the former was made by the Council on behalf of its member organisations, which were not invited to respond formally or individually. The Council responded positively on behalf of its members without consultation. At the time there were affiliated groups that expressed reservations, but no account was taken of this either by the Council or in the Framework, which gives the impression that the Framework received universal acceptance among the community of religious educators. It is admitted, however, that the Framework was widely accepted within the religious education community. The claim that the Framework provided 'a more consistent RE curriculum across the country' is hardly debateable. In this context it almost amounts to a tautology, for if the Framework was widely used its use alone, whatever its quality, ensures 'consistency' in the relevant sense. The claim to coherence is also worthy of comment. This is not to suggest that the Framework is incoherent, it is to point out that to advance itself on this basis over existing Agreed Syllabuses that differ from the Framework it would need to show the ways in which they are less coherent in structure and content.[11]

Three senses of religious education

According to Clarke and Woodhead (2015: 32), '[f]ailure to discriminate between legitimate and illegitimate forms of RE in schools fuels much criticism and defensiveness about the place of religion in our school system.' To overcome this failure, they distinguish between three different senses of religious education, and conclude that only the third sense is appropriately educationally, and therefore pursuable in schools (cf. 2018: 21-224).

Religious instruction

> Religious instruction is that which takes place from a faith standpoint, and its purpose is to instruct in that standpoint. It does not involve critical questioning or consideration of alternative religious or non-religious options.
>
> (Clarke and Woodhead 2015: 33)

Religious instruction 'does not involve critical questioning or consideration of religious or non-religious alternatives': yet (2015: 33) '[i]n principle,' they affirm, 'there is nothing wrong with religious instruction, or indeed with indoctrination ('doctrine' = credo, a set of beliefs or convictions)', a significant admission. Clarke and Woodhead (2015: 33) are also open to the legitimacy of secular instruction and (even) secular indoctrination, for they acknowledge the propriety 'of trying to embed young people within a particular religious or *non-religious* tradition' (my emphasis). It seems that for them both religious and non-religious instruction and even indoctrinatory instruction can be legitimately pursued. They (2015: 33) overlook the important issue of why instruction is often properly distinguished from indoctrination; according to them there is nothing necessarily wrong with either, albeit 'in a society which upholds freedom of religion and belief', and presumably for them modern Britain is such a society. By contrast, most philosophers of education define indoctrination almost exclusively in negative terms and as always inappropriate, irrespective of context—as violating 'principles of rationality, freedom, and respect for individuals', namely the principles that trace their origin to post-Enlightenment liberalism and characterise (on most definitions) a 'liberal education', say of the kind advocated by Paul Hirst and Richard Peters (1970). Indoctrination then typically carries strongly pejorative and immoral overtones and religious indoctrination is again typically cited as a clear and obvious example. Philosophers of education also usually extend accusations of indoctrination beyond that of beliefs to a consideration of methods, intentions and consequences. Clarke and Woodhead simplify things by not engaging in these issues or with the relevant literature, and there may be good reasons for this, even if something of the nuance of meaning and the sophistication of argument are lost. One possible confusion in their acknowledgement of the legitimacy of indoctrination, religious and otherwise, in a free society, is that the equation of religious instruction with indoctrination may mislead some who have imbibed popular notions of indoctrination (in part reflective of academic debates) as necessarily illegitimate in all social and political contexts, which is not Clarke and Woodhead's position. Religious instruction or indoctrination (as interpreted by them) is legitimate within religious communities and families. I disagree, but the argument is not relevant to education and schools and therefore does not need to be considered.

The problem with religious instruction for Clarke and Woodhead (2015: 33) is not the impartation of religious beliefs, it is not even their impartation without critical questioning or a consideration of alternative positions within the family or a particular community, it is that religious instruction, so defined, is not appropriate to religious education in schools:

> [T]here are legitimate concerns about religious instruction taking place in schools... such instruction or 'indoctrination' should not take place in schools when it (a) allows little or no room for questioning or criticism by pupils and/ or (b) ignores (or even distorts and caricatures) other forms of religion and belief, and grants them no legitimacy.

If the context of English schools is assumed to be a free and democratic political society, whose public institutions reflect this and seek to develop those virtues that are commonly regarded as constitutive of or required by such a society, then their first exclusionary requirement is clearly warranted. Religious or secular instruction in schools that does not give pupils the opportunity to think for themselves and that expects them to believe what they are taught uncritically and not to express criticism, has the capacity to so limit their expectations, beliefs and values as to thwart their growth to intellectual and social maturity, and therefore make them incapable of appreciating and contributing to the kind of open society that is in the general public interest to maintain. This seems a defensible position, even if it is difficult to draw an exact line of demarcation between instruction, which ought not to be pursued in state institutions and education that can be pursued. I have noted elsewhere that religious commitment must be freely chosen to be religiously valuable, while conceding that all too often religious leaders, though aware of this, acquiesce in coercive methods and behaviour for the purpose of 'exaggerating' the social and political significance of religion and/or perhaps to further their own commercial, social or political agendas.

The second requirement that forbids religious instruction in religious education for Clarke and Woodhead (2015: 33) is that it 'ignores (or even distorts and caricatures) other forms of religion and belief, and grants them no legitimacy'. Much depends on interpretation here. At an earlier stage of our social history, perhaps even up to the 1940s, it might have been defensible for religious teaching to ignore other religions and to be exclusively Christian, in the sense of including only Christian content. Moreover, this orientation ought not to be necessarily equated with instruction of a form that is now regarded by Clarke and Woodhead as incompatible with education, namely religious instruction. The processes and content of education are historically relative and shifting and what is appropriate in one place at one time may not be appropriate universally, in all places at all times. Britain in the 1940s and 1950s is not regarded as a pluralist society, morally or religiously, thus contrasting with the 1960s and 1970s, which are typically regarded as the decades when Britain became a pluralist society. It may be, however, that the word 'became' here elides the fact that the 1950s were more pluralist than is often acknowledged. Nevertheless, the religiously plural nature of modern Britain is now beyond dispute and, given this nature, Clarke and Woodhead are right, on their definition of instruction, to deem it inappropriate in public schools. The case for religious education to consider a number of religions is manifestly obvious; even faith schools should pursue multi-faith religious education. Equally, Clarke and Woodhead's point that 'other forms of religion' than that of the religious affiliation of a faith school ought not to be distorted hardly needs defence. The beliefs and values of a religion should be faithfully presented and not misrepresented or falsified in a way that is unfair and sectarian. This commitment may not produce unanimous agreement on the representation(s) of religions appropriate to education among religious educators, even if it can be affirmed as a working principle. There are aspects of religion and of non-religious worldviews that are subject to scholarly debate, e.g., the extent to which religion gives support to violence against 'unbelievers' or the matter of gender equality in Christianity and

Islam, or religious attitudes to homosexuality. Perhaps the best that religious education can do is to represent the range of views that adherents of a religion espouse and profess.

Formation

> It is normal for parents to wish to form their children in certain ways and imbue them with certain beliefs and values, and natural for those whose children attend a faith school to expect that school to form them within a particular religious tradition.
>
> *(Clarke and Woodhead 2015: 33)*

Clarke and Woodhead acknowledge the educational legitimacy of the formation of beliefs and values according to a faith tradition in schools and in religious education. While formation in faith schools is self-consciously religious and typically tradition specific, they also appreciate that non-faith schools also perform a formative role; both are legitimate. Although they do not address the matter, it may be that in many cases the values and social virtues that both faith and non-faith schools seek to develop and inculcate in pupils overlap significantly. Their support for religious formation, both through the formal curriculum and the informal curriculum, is subject to two provisos (but see below): (a) that there is room for agency, questioning and criticism by pupils, and (b) that such formation does not ignore, distort or caricature other forms of religion or belief. Both provisos are entirely reasonable.

Religious education

> Most people accept the need for all children to be brought up to understand the importance of religions; to appreciate their history and social significance; to be familiar with their beliefs, customs and practices; to be aware of the ways in which they have shaped the world and human lives; to be able to understand the meaning of religious language and symbols; to be able to form and articulate their own values and beliefs in relation to such understanding.
>
> *(Clarke and Woodhouse 2015: 34)*[12]

These are admirable aims for religious education; and also (I would contend) for religious formation in faith schools. We live in a pluralist, multi-cultural society and education in faith schools if it is to be relevant to pupils and to enable them to make self-critical and responsible responses to the claims of their own religious tradition, never mind others, requires structured and educationally appropriate exposure to the beliefs and values of others. Choice is a fact of modern British life—in business transactions, lifestyle, recreation, sexual partnerships and in religion. Faith schools cannot closet pupils from moral and religious diversity: religious formation in a religious tradition ought to encourage reflexive commitment and this is best achieved in the context of knowledge and awareness of other possibilities.

Religious education is envisaged by Clarke and Woodhead (2015: 34) as 'critical, outward looking, and dialogical'.

> It recognises diversity, and encourages students to learn 'about' and 'from' religious and nonreligious worldviews. It involves both 'understanding religions' and 'religious understanding.' It develops knowledge about a range of beliefs and values, an ability to articulate and develop one's own values and commitments, and the capacity to debate and engage with others. These are essential skills in a multi-faith society and a diverse but connected world.

Many religious educators would commend this form of religious education. Again, there is nothing here that could not be endorsed by religious educators in faith schools, or in my view ought to be endorsed by religious educators in faith schools that include religious formation as one of its aims, even as an overriding aim. This point is reiterated against those religious believers that advocate a narrow and insular view of faith education, which as such betrays its irrelevance to pupils and to society, and against religious educators who fail to appreciate and acknowledge that faith formation can be genuinely open, dialogical, critical and educational.

Clarke and Woodhead (2015: 35) advocate that 'Religious education should be based upon a commonly understood overall curriculum', by which is meant the introduction of a nationally agreed syllabus and programmes of work with statutory force (cf. 2018: 12–18). This is the subject of the next section of their pamphlet and will be discussed. They add that the:

> state is entitled to insist that it will only fund schools that teach religions in accordance with such a commonly understood overall curriculum and that it will not provide funding for the teaching of faiths which do not genuinely respect the legitimacy of other belief systems.
>
> *(2015: 35)*

This additional comment is significant and possibly controversial. They have already acknowledged the educational legitimacy of the formation of beliefs and values according to a faith tradition in schools. They have now introduce two criteria *for all publicly funded schools* that in one case arguably undermines the nature of religious formation in (publicly funded) schools, and in the other possibly limits such formation: faith formation in faith schools must follow a 'commonly understood overall curriculum', i.e., for them a nationally determined statutory religious education curriculum (Framework); and public funds ought not to be provided for religious education or forms of religious formation in schools that 'do not genuinely respect the legitimacy of other belief systems' (cf. 2018: 21–24). The obvious negative point in relation to the first criterion is that a curriculum that is designed for all schools is hardly appropriate for religious formative educational processes (to which they grant educational legitimacy) in the increasing range of faith schools—at their highest level of differentiation: Christian, Jewish, Muslim schools, and so on. How could a common imposed Framework satisfy the contrasting formative needs of religiously different forms of religion? The second criterion may or may not be appropriate to religious formation in school, it all depends on interpretation. Clarke and Woodhead's claim that the representation of a religion in education must exclude granting 'no legitimacy' to other 'forms of religion and belief'. If by 'no legitimacy' they mean to exclude from a (self-)representation of a religion in schools the belief that it is unique or that it possesses truth to a degree denied to other religions, this should be questioned. In many cases adherents of a religion or a tradition within a religion regard it as uniquely true. There is no reason why such views ought not to be represented in schools and why faith schools that represent their religious commitment in this way ought to be excluded from public funds. It can be admitted that claims to religious truth can be socially divisive and one unfortunate educational response to this has been to overlook religious differences and focus on commonalities; more alarming have been policies and pedagogies that posit complementarity between the different religions, for in this way the nature of religious commitments are mispresented to pupils and they are also deprived of the occasion and context to develop the virtue of toleration and to learn to accommodate diversity and difference in socially positive ways. Inadmissible educational interpretations of 'no legitimacy' should properly include religious claims that deny full civil rights to non-adherents or that accredit irrationality and turpitude to them. Such views should not be represented in schools. What I am suggesting is that Clarke and Woodhead's claim that 'granting no legitimacy' to other belief systems by religious adherents of a religion is subject to different interpretations, some entirely compatible with the principles of freedom of religion and belief in a liberal society and some not. Their failure to expand upon what they mean raises the possibility that what they envisage may be inappropriate educationally.

Significantly, Clarke and Woodhead's 2018 Revised Settlement, while still insisting on the need for an imposed national religious education curriculum on all schools concedes the option 'for schools with a religious character to complement the requirement [to follow the common curriculum] with further provision as required by their religious designation' (2018: 24). This is a welcome concession, though much depends on how prescriptive and how detailed any new national framework is; if it is such it would severely limit and restrict the aims realisable by confessional religious education.

A national curriculum and syllabus for religious education

Clarke and Woodhead introduce their case for a (statutory) national curriculum and syllabus for religious education with a clear account of the relevant legislation set out in Sections 2 and 8 of the 1988 Education Reform Act, namely that religious education should reflect the fact that the religious traditions in Great Britain are in the main Christian, whilst taking account of the teaching and practices of the other principal religions; and that local authority 'Agreed Syllabus Conferences' are required to determine the locally agreed Religious Education syllabus. This summary of the legislation and of their discussion of the role of agreed syllabuses is sufficient for our purpose. They (2015: 36) add that in principle there could be '152 different RE syllabuses in England'; it has already been noted that in reality most Agreed Syllabuses follow the 2004 Framework (up to 2012); those that *differ significantly* from the Framework can be confined to single figures.

Their focus then shifts to publication of the non-statutory national Framework for Religious Education in 2004, which according to them was 'agreed by all the traditional religions in the UK'. This is not exactly accurate, as already pointed out the RE Council leadership responded positively on behalf of the religions and groups affiliated to it. To further their case for a new Framework, Clarke and Woodhead (2015: 36) also quote from a joint statement from the Department for Education and Skills and faith communities in February 2006[13] which states that both parties 'are fully committed to using the [2004] Framework in developing the religious education curriculum for our schools and colleges'. The support of the Department for Education and Skills is unremarkable, given the reasons already considered above. The degree of support for the Framework by representatives of the faith communities on the basis of this statement is more difficult to judge. The faith communities interpreted their commitment to 'using the Framework in developing the religious education curriculum' as indicating their agreement to ensuring that pupils in faith schools are taught about a number of religions and not just the religion to which the faith schools were affiliated.[14] This need not and probably should not be equated with being *'fully* committed' to using the Framework and following it in its entirety.

It has already been acknowledged that the 2004 non-statutory Framework was well received by religious educators and SACREs. What also cannot be doubted is that the centralising agenda implicit in the 2004 Framework has long been supported by the main organs of establishment religious education, the RE Council and NATRE, for example. Their support may be ideological as both groups would regard themselves through their leadership as coming to exert considerable influence over any new (statutory) Syllabus. It hardly requires reiteration, however, that support of this kind does not guarantee the suitability or quality of educational policies. The critical question is, did the 2004 non-statutory Framework provide a positive direction for religious education, and what evidence can be adduced that it alone in a new statutory form best charts the future for religious education? Clarke and Woodhead clearly believe that any new syllabus ought to be an updated version of Clarke's original 2004 Framework. Has there been any impartial assessment of its strengths and weaknesses? This is an important issue. Ought we to believe that only one statutory curriculum form of religious education can fulfil the aims of religious education in different types of schools.

There are undoubted strengths in the 2004 Framework. Recently, Jeff Astley and I (2018) conducted a review of the understanding and significance of the uses of language in three curricular religious education documents from across the United Kingdom, including the Framework. We concluded that the use of religious language and the contribution of religious education to language acquisition and use are prominent themes within the Framework, unlike Scottish and North-ern Irish documents (DoENI 2007), and unlike the later RE Review (2013); all of which are clearly deficient in their understanding of the role of language in reli-gions. The Framework by contrast takes account of the importance of language (religiously specific and otherwise) and how it contributes to religious knowledge, skills and an understanding of religions, and how this comes to a clear focus in the key aspects of learning in religious education. The Framework provides an excellent account of the role of language in expressing religious beliefs and values. There are other strengths in the Framework that could be discussed, but there are also weaknesses. For example, the Framework is over ambitious and prescribes too many aims for religious education and as the *Does Religious Education Work?* project concluded, this leads to confusion for teachers who are unsure where the real focus of the subject lies (Conroy et al. 2013: 41–45). Finally, criticism of assessment procedures in religious education has been a consistent theme in Ofsted reports from 2010 onwards, yet a review of Agreed Syllabuses shows that many syllabuses simply appropriate the eight levels of attainment (Attainment levels) from the non-statutory Framework, often verbatim, sometimes with minor variations. Now to say what will be 'unthinkable' to some religious educators. Could it be that it is the template for assessment in the Framework that in no insignificant part contributes to the weaknesses in this area identified by Ofsted? No doubt other factors may be relevant: teachers may have had inadequate training in using and applying the levels or in designing assessment tasks that show achievement and monitor learning in relation to the levels. Yet the original criticism may be pertinent. Clarke and Woodhouse do not attempt to support their case for an updated 2004 Framework on the basis of its material strengths, but instead refer to formal considerations, such as coherence and consistency (as we have noted). Their case for a new statutory Framework focuses on the deficiencies of locally produced Agreed Syllabuses rather than on the inherent qualities that may accrue to an updated Framework.

There are three distinguishable reasons for Clarke and Woodhead's rejection of the current system of locally produced syllabuses. The first refers to the reasons adduced by Ofsted in its call to reform the system; the second is that local deter-mination is 'anomalous'; and the third is that SACREs and Agreed Syllabus Con-ferences do not find it easy to engage with local and national expertise. In the Revised Settlement document of 2018 the reasons for their rejection of the current system of locally produced syllabuses is omitted. The final recommendations remain the same, only without supporting argument (2018: 29–31).

Let us be reminded of Ofsted's identification of the main weaknesses that moved it to call for a review of current procedures that mandate local authority determi-nation of the religious curriculum: low levels of subject knowledge and under-standing, particularly as this relates to Christianity; poor teaching and achievement in primary schools; weak assessment techniques; and weak leadership and manage-ment. It is difficult to judge how many and to what degree weaknesses are directly attributable to the locally agreed syllabus: poor teaching, and weak leadership and management seem to have little to do with the local syllabus; are they indications of inadequacies in teacher training institutions? Are too many 'non-specialists' involved in delivering the religious education curriculum? Low levels of subject knowledge and understanding by pupils may reflect the quality of teaching and may not reflect poorly on the local syllabus. The issue of particularly low levels of subject knowledge and understanding of Christianity, however, may, in part, be attributable to local syllabuses. A random sample and review of those on the web revealed that although the legislation is quoted that syllabuses acknowledge 'the fact that the religious traditions in Great Britain are in the main Christian', there is rarely any indication of what proportion of the time allocated to religious education ought to be assigned to Christianity; perhaps too little time is devoted to the teaching of Christianity, and this as a result of an already overcrowded religious education curriculum with too much content from other religions to be covered.

Clarke and Woodhead claim that it is 'anomalous' to have different RE curricula in different localities within England. Why is it anomalous? Their answer is that it just 'seems anomalous' in our increasingly national, indeed global, society and culture. To speak of global society and culture is a highly ramified, abstract term. What is meant by it? In broad, sociological terms global society and culture may be regarded as the interchange and sharing of ideas, beliefs and practices across societies, national boundaries and cultures; and this sharing of ideas is in no small measure because states, communities, and individuals have become increasingly interdependent economically. In the last decades of the twentieth century (after the collapse of communism), many governments encouraged free market economic policies and promoted economic liberalisation, whereby local and national markets were opened to competition (and possible exploitation by multinational organisations, it may be added). The free transfer of ideas and beliefs can be regarded as the consequence of the free transfer of capital, goods, and services across national frontiers. It is difficult to assign causal relationships in these complex matters. A longer discussion would need to develop the concept of globalisation, which describes much of what is said here, and consider the role of new technologies, particularly those concerned with communication.

The irony is that Clarke and Woodhead appeal to the reality of a global society and culture as supportive of uniformity of provision in religious education, whereas most social commentators interpret it as a catalyst for diversity and recognition of legitimate differences between the groups, sub-groups and communities that make up society. As well as multiplying economic choices for the individual, the individual as consumer is also exposed to a rich variety of lifestyle choices, which he or she is free to espouse or revise according to individual taste and interest. Alternative lifestyles are fostered by the realisation that there are other people, however remote geographically, who share similar interests. Diversity fosters diversity. Increasing awareness of diversity has a legitimising effect and therefore encourages further diversity. The rich diversity of interests and proclivities that is represented on the internet, for example, has the effect of cultivating and stimulated further diversity. Alternative lifestyles are fostered by the realisation that there are other people, however remote geographically, who share similar interests. Sociologists now refer to 'hybrid identities' and 'blended identities' to describe the process of bringing together elements from different cultures in ways that are novel and individual (see Hervieu-Léger 1999).

The idea that 'one syllabus fits all' with regard to religious education is not advanced by Clarke and Woodhead's appeal to global culture and society, quite the contrary. One could legitimately argue that the differences in cultural and religious constituency in different English regions and the history of how this constituency has changed and evolved provide a *prima facia* case for differences between regions to be reflected in religious education syllabuses: culturally and religiously Cornwall is not the same as Birmingham! Even their brief reference to British culture needs to be interpreted with care. Is there a single British culture that justifies a single religious education syllabus? The line of justification from one to the other looks precarious, even before the debate is joined over the reality of a single British culture, which I for one reject. In conclusion, the reality of a global culture and society or an appeal to a single national British culture and society (which never has existed) does little to justify the claim that one religious education syllabus ought to be available and imposed on all school pupils in England.

This brings us to the last and final reason they cite for divesting local authorities and SACREs of syllabus production powers (2015: 37): 'through no fault of their own, do not always find it easy to engage with the whole of the local educational community, let alone national expertise in religion and education'. One wonders whose fault it is, but like Clarke and Woodhead it is probably wiser in this context not to apportion blame: it is enough to inform SACREs that their powers will be significantly reduced without at the same time blaming them for their reduction! It might be though that different groups in different parts of England would have more opportunities to relate in much greater numbers with 'experts' in education, religious studies and religious education than any centrally based and necessarily small panel of 'national' experts; certainly university expertise in religious studies is widely distributed across England.

There is a more serious issue to be resolved that lies behind Clarke and Woodhead's (2015: 37) comment that some SACREs 'do not always find it easy to engage with the whole of the local educational community, let alone national expertise in religion and education'. One can legitimately ask where did this 'expression of concern' originate? Are there examples of SACREs expressing this opinion? This is not my interest. The issue is that if SACREs have admitted that they have limited engagement with communities and with expertise, and have been unable to acquire such expertise, then this will probably be reflected in the quality of resultant syllabuses. Has Ofsted identified such syllabuses? It is the educational quality of the final syllabus that matters, and Clarke and Woodhead's comment alerts us to the existence of poor quality syllabuses. The claim to limited access to expertise is redundant if the final syllabus is educationally convincing and religiously appropriate. As is often remarked, 'the proof is in the eating' not the preparation. Clarke and Woodhead's argument is *ad hominen*, literally. Whether the persons that produce the syllabus express limitations or not is strictly irrelevant: it is the final result that matters. What Clarke and Woodhead need to do in this case is to give examples of Agreed Syllabuses that contain inaccurate and inappropriate representations of religions, and then develop a causal chain that shows that the writers of the syllabus lacked the knowledge, skills and abilities to produce an educationally appropriate syllabus because they were unable to draw on local expertise to overcome their deficiencies. My own view is that local syllabus committees entrusted with the production of local syllabuses can act as a catalyst for curriculum innovation and change, and by involving faith communities in how their beliefs are represented is an example of local democracy in action, it will give them a sense of empowerment and in this way serve the aims of social cohesion and integration.

In terms of the arguments they advance Clarke and Woodhead fail to provide convincing support for the introduction of a *statutory national* curriculum in religious education and for many of their curriculum proposals. An acknowledgement of weaknesses in their position may even be appreciated by them, given their decision to omit any serious attention to argument and amassing positive evidence for their recommendations in the 2018 revised statement of their original Settlement document (2015). It would be educationally unwise to implement proposals that fail in so many respects to convince.

Notes

1 See http://www.reonline.org.uk/news/alans-blog-settlements-whats-all-this-about-settlem ents-alan-brine/; (accessed 26 February 2019).
2 See http://faithdebates.org.uk/wp-content/uploads/2015/06/A-New-Settlement-for-Reli gion-and-Belief-in-schools.pdf (accessed 26 February 2019).
3 See http://www.reonline.org.uk/news/alans-blog-settlements-whats-all-this-about-settlem ents-alan-brine/ (accessed 26 February 2019).
4 See http://faithdebates.org.uk/wp-content/uploads/2018/07/Clarke-Woodhead-A-New-Settlement-Revised.pdf (accessed 10 May 2019).
5 The term 'consensus' is used five times in the 2018 version and only once in the 2015 version; while too much emphasis should not be places on use of this one word, it is nevertheless relevant to the point at issue.
6 Lack of acknowledgement of the importance and relevance of the 1988 Education Reform Act for religious education is even more pronounced in Clarke and Woodhead's 2018 'Revised Settlement.'
7 At the time of writing a pertinent example of this is in the news. Parkfield Community [Primary] School, Birmingham, where 98 per cent of pupils are Muslim, is pursuing a positive programme to promote same-sex relationships and marriages that parents believe is contrary to the received teachings of Islam, as contained in the Qur'an and Hadith; see https://www.birminghammail.co.uk/news/midlands-news/muslim-mums-protest-outsi de-school-15729135 (accessed 26 February 2019).
8 They also note that both these reports and their predecessor, *Making Sense of Religion* in 2007, called upon the Department for Education to review the current statutory framework of religious education.
9 Discussion of Ofsted's negative findings in relation to the practice of religious education is omitted in Clarke and Woodhead's 2018 'Revised Settlement.'
10 See National Association of Teachers of Religious Education (NATRE), 'Religious Education (RE) and Collective Worship in Academies and Free Schools Q&A'; see

http://www.natre.org.uk/uploads/Free%20Resources/RE%20%26%20Collective%
20Worship%20in%20Academies%20and%20Free%20Schools.pdf (accessed 25 March
2019).

11 Discussion of the 2004 Framework and the commendation of it as a template for any
new framework is omitted in Clarke and Woodhead's new 'Revised Settlement' document (2018).

12 There is very limited reference to or discussion of the overall aims of religious education
in the 2018 'Settlement' document compared with the 2015 document.

13 Referenced in the document (2015: 36) as https://www.churchofengland.org/media
-centre/news/2006/02/pr2106b.aspx, but no longer active.

14 This source summarises the Faith Communities' position and includes quotations from
the original document; one of which is quoted here; see https://www.christianheadlines.
com/scroll-article-list/?pub=33608&art=1381111&format=Text&page=5#british
(accessed 26 February 2019).

8

COMPULSION, CONSCIENCE AND THE RIGHT OF WITHDRAWAL

A recent editorial in the *Journal of Beliefs & Values*, by its editor Professor Stephen Parker (2018: 255–257), raised the issue of the historic right of parents to withdraw their children from collective worship and religious education in schools in England (also known as the 'conscience clause'). He (2018: 255) expresses the view that '[t]he arguments for the clause's abolition seem apposite in relation to curriculum RE'; though, following a short discussion of the issues, this conclusion became arguably more tentative as he (2018: 256) 'wonder[ed] if ... [the] history of the "conscience clause" in England has any traction or parallels elsewhere. I would like to know.'[1] This last comment may suggest a continuing openness of mind on the issue. No tentativeness characterises the position of Charles Clarke and Linda Woodhead's *A New Settlement: Religion and belief in schools* (2015: 26), which calls for the removal of the right of parents to withdraw their children from religious education: 'we would say that there is no case for a right to withdraw a child from "religious education"': 'the right ... should be abolished'(cf. Clarke and Woodhead 2018: 27). The Commission on Religious Education's interim report, *Education for All* (2017: 77) records that

> there were strong calls across the written and oral evidence for the right of withdrawal to be abolished—a significant majority of individuals and organisations mentioned this. NATRE the NAHT [National Association of Head Teachers] and the Church of England—representing three major stakeholders in schools—all called for an end to the right of withdrawal in their written evidence.

These are influential voices.

The question to be addressed in this chapter is whether there are good reasons for abandoning the parental right of withdrawal from religious education. Unlike some other chapters where attention is focused on a single author, book or document, this chapter will interact with a range of articles and texts. The natural place to begin is with the relevant legislation. This is followed by an overview and discussion of a recent and relevant empirical research project before moving on to consider the arguments adduced by two influential reports that call for the absolution of parental rights over religious education in schools. The argument of one is perfunctory and superficial, whereas the other deserves extended consideration. Two historical policy initiatives in post-confessional English religious education are then briefly considered, which if they had been faithfully followed through, would, it is contended, have legitimately justified some parents withdrawing their children from religious education. This lends support to the conclusion that the existence of a parental right of withdrawal, even if rarely exercised, serves a useful purpose in protecting the right of parents from paternalistic educators and the state exercising a disproportionate influence over the religious upbringing of children.

The conscience clause

A 'conscience clause,' whereby parents can exercise a right to withdraw their children from 'religious instruction,' was introduced on a voluntary basis in some schools in the early decades of the nineteenth century to protect pupils from receiving denominational instruction with which their parents disagreed (see Louden 2003 and 2004, for historical overviews). Schools established by the National Society, which was the educational organ of the national church, i.e. the Church of England, required all pupils to receive religious instruction consistent with the affiliation of their schools. Parents who disagreed with the tenets of the Church of England clearly found this situation intolerable: the problem was particularly acute in areas where the only school available was a National school. In no small part the British and Foreign School Society was established in 1814 to provide non-sectarian schools for the children of mainly 'non-conformist' Christians. The seriousness of the controversy is captured by historian Marjorie Cruickshank's (1964: 10) comment that

> nothing in the educational controversies of the nineteenth century did more to inflame denominational bitterness than the Anglican refusal to concede rights of conscience, for it bred deep resentment and distrust which were to rankle in dissenting hearts for many years to come. Herein lay the problem of the single-school area, where there was only one school and that a Church school.

The controversy raged across the decades. In the 1860s it became patently obvious that the churches and voluntary societies could no longer adequately fund their schools or keep pace with the growing number of children requiring education and that the state would have to intervene in more direct ways in education. The challenge of how to accommodate pupils with different religious identities within the same schools became urgent. The solution came in the form of legislation on religious instruction contained in the English Education Act of 1870, which stated:

> It shall not be required, as a condition of any child being admitted into or continuing in the [public elementary] school, that he shall attend or abstain from attending any Sunday school, or any place of religious worship, or that he shall attend any religious observance or any instruction in religious subjects in the school or elsewhere, from which observance or instruction he may be withdrawn by his parent, or that he shall, if withdrawn by his parent, attend the school on any day exclusively set apart for religious observance by the religious body to which his parent belongs … .

The same legislation also included, what is referred to as the Cowper-Temple Clause (so named after its proposer; see Chorley 1984), which excluded from all rate-built schools every catechism and formula distinctive of any denominational creed. Revision of the withdrawal clause in later Acts up to the present has confined itself to updating its language to accommodate the emergence of different types of schools and to the shift of terminology from religious instruction to religious education (with its attendant shift of meaning); in basic form, it remains in place.

Religious education and the right of withdrawal: An empirical perspective

In this section we will consider and interact with an important piece of relevant and recent empirical research, *Religious Education and the Right of Withdrawal*, conducted under the aegis of Liverpool Hope University, by David Lundie.[2] The report of the research project was published in 2018, and though there is no information regarding when the empirical data were collected, internal evidence suggests a very recent date as some of the introductory material reads as if the specific subject of research and the data collection were occasioned by a response to debates about withdrawal initiated by publications in 2015. It is a lucid and informative piece of research, rich in data and detail, which should be required reading by all who are interested in or who intend contributing to the debate about parental rights of withdrawal. The temptation is to quote from it extensively in the attempt to do justice to its breadth and relevance, but the integrity of the original author needs to be maintained, consequently only the nature of the research project and the main findings will be summarised.

In setting the scene, Lundie (2018: 1) notes that the original right of withdrawal was intended to protect the rights of parents from non-religious and non-Christian minorities to raise their children according to their own beliefs. (This is not quite historically accurate as the main issue was the education of children of Nonconformist parents; see above.) Non-confessional religious education today takes account of non-Christian religions, as well as helping to prepare young people for life in modern pluralist Britain by enabling them 'to acquire an appreciation of and respect for their own and other cultures' (Lundie 2018: 1). These developments, as cited in a number of recent reports, raise questions, Lundie believes (2018: 2), 'about the continued appropriateness of the parental right to withdraw'.

Lundie surveyed the experience and understanding of school leaders (Head-teachers, senior leaders or religious education co-ordinators) across England. This, he informs us (2018: 1), represents 'the first systematic attempt to understand the prevalence of parental withdrawal from RE and CW [collective worship], the reasons behind it, and the way these requests are handled in practice'. An online survey was emailed to 25,193 schools across the country, which generated 312 responses: from the primary sector, 51.1 per cent; the secondary sector, 44.1 per cent; and the 'all age', 4.8 per cent sector. Schools ranged in size from 1500 pupils to 200 pupils and included local authority, academy, Church of England, Catholic (10.3 per cent) and independent schools, though only one faith school other than Catholic or Church of England participated.

The main findings of the survey are (Lundie, 2018: 1):

a   A majority (65.8 per cent) of participants support the abolition of the parental right of withdrawal from Religious Education.
b   Confusion exists as to the operation of this right of withdrawal, with a significant minority (36.5 per cent) of participants believing parents had to demonstrate either a specific religious exemption or make arrangements for alternative provision. There is further confusion as to whether parents can withdraw their child from RE selectively, and even from National Curriculum subjects.
c   In the vast majority of participants' schools (94.1 per cent) few or no children are currently withdrawn from Religious Education or Collective Worship.
d   A significant minority of participants (38.1 per cent) have experienced parents request to withdraw their child selectively from part of the Religious Education curriculum. Largely, this seems to relate to the teaching of Islam, with many participants reporting concerns about racism or Islamophobia as a motivating factor for parents seeking to exercise the right to withdraw.
e   In some cases (7.2 per cent) children appear to have been withdrawn from Religious Education to provide extra tuition time for other academic subjects, or special educational needs support.

The research makes clear that very few parents exercise the right of withdrawal either from religious education or collective worship. 94.1 per cent of schools record few or no pupils parentally excluded on this basis. In 61.9 per cent of schools no pupil is currently exempt from religious education or collective worship; and in a further 32.2 per cent of schools between 1–3 pupils are exempt. 1 per cent of schools record over 10 exemptions. One conclusion that can be drawn, if this survey is representative of schools in England, is that the number of pupils exempt from religious education and collective worship is almost statistically insignificant as a proportion of the whole school population. The research further revealed that the few exemptions there are, most commonly come from parents who are Jehovah's Witnesses or members of the Exclusive Brethren and possibly the Muslim community (more detail in the report is required to reach a firm conclusion here).

On the basis of these results, Lundie makes two recommendations (2018: 2). First, legal clarification is needed on three important matters: (i) the right of parents to withdraw selectively from part (but not all) of religious education; (ii) whether parents seeking to withdraw their children from religious education are responsible for providing an appropriate alternative curriculum; and (iii) whether children withdrawn from religious education can access other curriculum subjects or Special Educational Needs (SEN) support during religious education time. Second, on the recommendation of two recent reports—Butler-Sloss's *Living with Difference: Community, diversity and the common good* (2015) and the RE Commission on Religious Education's *Interim Report: Religious Education for All* (2017)— and of the requirement for all schools to promote spiritual, moral, social and cultural development, Lundie (2018: 2) concludes that 'legislators should reconsider the appropriateness of the legal right of withdrawal'.

It would have been more circumspect if Lundie had qualified his legal recommendations by stating that on two and probably all three of these important matters further legal clarification *is not* required; what is required is for Headteachers, senior leaders or religious education co-ordinators to be made cognizant of the existing law. The legal matters identified by Lundie are considered in turn.

In 2010 the (then) Department for Children, Schools and Families published *Religious Education in English Schools: Non-statutory guidance* (2010: 28) that makes clear that parents can withdraw their children from part of the religious education curriculum:

> The use of the right to withdraw should be at the instigation of parents (or pupils themselves if they are aged 18 or over), and it should be made clear whether it is from the whole of the subject *or specific parts* of it. No reasons need be given. (my emphasis)

The document does speak of this as a right. The issue whether parents who exercise their right of withdrawal are responsible for providing an appropriate alternative curriculum is not directly addressed in the guidance, though it can be inferred from what is said about the role of the school that *it* has responsibility for the school curriculum and therefore parents are not required to provide an alternative curriculum (the relevant section of the document on which this answer is based is too long to quote in full; a reading is recommended, see DCSF 2010: 27–29). An answer to the third legal issue may also be inferred from what is stated in the guidance:

> If pupils are withdrawn from RE, schools have a duty to supervise them, though not to provide additional teaching or to incur extra cost. Pupils will usually remain on school premises.
>
> *(DCSF 2010: 28)*

The question is whether children withdrawn from religious education can access other curriculum subjects or SEN support during RE time. The answer provided in the Guidance (2010) is it is not the school's *duty* to provide additional teaching, which doubtless would be in some other curriculum subject or to provide SEN support during designated religious education time, or to incur extra cost, though presumably a school could conceivably act in a supererogatory way and provide more than duty requires. These answers do seem to be based on authoritative legal sources that are still in force.

There are two limitations in Lundie's study (note *limitations*, not necessarily weaknesses) and one possible misunderstanding by respondents that may have (again note *may have*, not has) some minor influence over results. The first centres on the wording of Question 1a; school leaders were asked:

> 1.a Have you ever received a request from a parent/guardian for their child to be exempt from Religious Education and/or Collective Worship?

This question relates to both exemptions from religious education and/or collective worship. Consequently, the answer does not generate specific answers as to whether parents/guardians wish their children to be exempt from religious education but not collective worship or vice versa. Requesting an exemption from one but not the other are not merely logical possibilities. There are school contexts where parents might object to religious education, but believe that the religious element in collective worship is so insignificant or perfunctory in religious terms, or that the social cost of their child being viewed as absent from such collective events could potentially create hostility from his or her peers, that a decision to withdraw from religious education is not regarded as requiring a corresponding decision in relation to collective worship. There are conceivably situations where withdrawal from collective worship is not believed by parents to necessitate a corresponding withdrawal from religious education. The question posed does not differentiate between withdrawal from religious education and withdrawal from collective worship (as separate activities) and this deprives us of data that could serve a comparative purpose by showing that one or the other activity is viewed in more negative terms by parents who exercise their right of withdrawal; and possibly exaggerates the number of withdrawals for religious education, since withdrawal is defined in term of religious education and school assembly.

The second limitation is that the survey was confined to school leaders, defined as Headteachers, senior leaders or religious education co-ordinators. All empirical studies are limited and circumscribed in terms of respondents, and there is nothing unreasonable in the restriction imposed by Lundie. Nevertheless, it is important to note that the views of parents whose children are the subjects of education were not canvassed. To use the language of the market, the consumers' voice is omitted, only the vendors are recorded. It is not difficult to conceive of unworthy reasons why school leaders wish to end rights of withdrawal: perhaps providing alternative arrangements for those withdrawn are inconvenient; perhaps religious education teachers and co-ordinators feel somewhat slighted by any implicit suggestion that they are not presenting a balanced and 'neutral' view of some religion or other, and so on. Nothing is said by Lundie that suggests he is averse to including the voice of all relevant parties to the debate, including parents and prospective parents.

Lundie (2018: 6) records that some school leaders refer to the refusal of some parents to allow their children to attend non-Christian places of worship, particularly mosques.

> I have been very shocked by parents refusing to allow their children to visit a mosque. I found it difficult to understand that the parents thought that this would irrevocably harm their child.... In the end I couldn't take the children to the mosque as parents refused to sign the permission slip, but they had to remain in school and learn about mosques from the internet which included a virtual tour of a mosque. The children were sad that they were unable to go with their friends.
>
> [We have recently had] withdrawal based on erroneous 'facts' or media hype... parents refusing to send their children on an education visit to a mosque.

One can appreciate teachers viewing such refusals as focused on and originating from parents' statutory right of withdrawal from religious education, but this is in all probability based on a misunderstanding of which right accords refusal in this case. The question may be asked whether school trips and other off-site activities *in religious education*, such as visits to places of worship, are properly interpreted as relevant to a discussion of parental rights in religious education. On 21 July, 2014, the Department for Education published on the (official) gov.uk website a 'Consent form for school trips and other off-site activities',[3] which informs parents that their child need not be compelled to participate in off-site activities: 'You can, if you wish, tell the school that you do not want your child to take part in any particular school trip or activity'. This consent form is presented as applicable to all subjects and to all off-site visits, presumably to those concerned with religious education as well; hence the Department of Education does not view off-site activities in religious education as governed by rules any different from all other subjects and therefore not one to which an appeal to the parental right of withdrawal from religious education is needed to justify non-participation.

Support for relinquishing the parental right of withdrawal

The case for compulsory religious education for all pupils in the United Kingdom is 'framed' by the existence of an existing parental right of withdrawal in each of the legally constituted education systems of England, Northern Ireland, Scotland and Wales. Calls for compulsory religious education for all pupils in English schools requires the right of withdrawal to end and thus the loss of a long-established freedom that parents enjoy in relation to the provisions and character of the state education system. Some will point to the irony in this situation. In Chapter 4 consideration was given to how religious educators have focused positively in the last few decades on the relevance of human rights and of legally defined national systems of rights to religious education, whereas in this case religious educators (presumably, in some cases the same people) wish to remove traditional rights of exemption to religious education and to collective worship. The second irony is that British legislation has increasingly regarded religion (particularly its manifestation) as a private matter, yet if religious education is made compulsory under a national compulsory syllabus (that forbids exceptions) there will be certain forms and representations of religion that will necessarily enjoy a privileged position, for all teaching about religion in schools requires limited content and limited, determinate representations to be made compulsory in *public* education and schools.

Given the existing legal position there are four possible responses. The first is to continue with the current legal arrangements: religious education for all with the parental right of exemption. The second is to remove the study of religion and hence religious education from the curriculum of all schools. The third is to remove the right of exemption to parents and make religious education an elective subject throughout the school system. The final response is to remove the right of exemption and make religious education compulsory for all pupils. All responses have their challenges. For example, given the historical and contemporary influence of religions in British society, it would be difficult to develop a convincing case for complete exclusion of the kind favoured in public education by some countries, e.g. the USA and France. Few entertain this as a serious policy proposal in Britain. The idea of religion as an elective subject throughout the years of schooling might resolve some of the criticisms of compulsory religious education and of its character in certain contexts, but only again at the expense of neglecting the importance and influence of religions on British history, literature, culture, politics and social policy; never mind their relevance to wider international issues and the potential they bring to the religious, spiritual and moral development of pupils (and this is a minimum expression of this potential which could easily be expanded to include religious education's contribution to social cohesion, the common good, and so on). The final response, i.e. to make religious education compulsory for all without exception, is a particularly popular option at the current time. As David Lundie's survey revealed, it is the one favoured by most Head-teachers, senior leaders and religious education co-ordinators. Moreover, it is an option that is almost always advanced alongside the introduction of a compulsory national Framework for religious education. Conceivably one could make religious education compulsory and allow different local authorities or newly constituted groupings to devise their own (compulsory) syllabuses. The educationally 'live' options, however, seem to be to preserve the status quo or to introduce compulsory religious education for all under a national syllabus. The remainder of this chapter will critically asses the reasons for and the advantages claimed to follow educationally from this latter position. Since the case for a single national syllabus has already been considered in Chapter 7, the discussion will focus on the case for compulsion in religious education.

Although there are calls for the relinquishment of the parental right of withdrawal in religious education and for the subject to be made compulsory for all, there are few serious discussions of the issues involved. For example, in *RE for Real: The future of teaching and learning about religion and belief* (2015), a recent survey of opinion by teachers and parents towards religious education, one of the 'key recommendations' made by the authors, Adam Dinham and Martha Shaw (2015: 1), is that '[r]eligion and belief learning (*sic*) should be a compulsory part of the curriculum to age 16, and consideration should be given to what, if anything, happens in post-16 learning'. This is based on their survey of teachers' opinions (no other arguments are adduced):

> Of those teachers who expressed an opinion, 99% favour compulsory 'religious education' (of whom 11% specified to age 14, 34% to age 16 and another 38% to age 18). Only one teacher thought 'religious education' should not be compulsory. There is also support for retaining an optional Religious Studies GCSE.
>
> (Dinham & Shaw 2015: 12)

There is no discussion of the existing parental right of withdrawal; it is as if it does not exist. On a cursory reading it could be conjectured that perhaps the authors meant 'compulsion' within the existing legal framework: even though they speak of the compulsory religious education of pupils, they actually mean compulsory religious education in schools, a distinction that preserves the proper legal position vis-à-vis religious education—it is compulsory in schools but, given the parental right of withdrawal, is not compulsory for pupils. A careful reading suggests otherwise, for the statistic of 99 per cent was generated by the answer to the question (Dinham & Shaw 2015: 31): 'Do you think RE should be compulsory *for all students*?' (my emphasis, i.e. compulsory for all students, not all schools). They also record that 94 per cent of parents in the study think religious education should be compulsory. By neglecting to ask the 'balancing' question whether the existing statutory right to parental withdrawal should be repealed, which would have helped respondents to be aware of the implications of their answers (responses might also have revealed inconsistencies), it is difficult to know how much significance to attach to their findings. Omission of such is a serious structural weakness in Dinham and Shaw's questionnaire and one that ought to have been appreciated by experienced researchers. My suspicion, however, is that even if the survey could be rerun, only this time incorporating a further question about the continuing relevance of a parental right of withdrawal, a majority would still be returned in favour of compulsory religious education.

For Dinham and Shaw the argument in favour of compulsory religious education (with the corollary that the existing parent right of withdrawal ought to be repealed) is to be settled by popular vote. This ought to make us uneasy. There are numerous educational, social and political issues where popular votes could *conceivably* challenge and overcome existing legislation, say on the death penalty, on abortion, on gay marriage, on immigration policy, on transgender rights, and so on. Rights of freedom trump popular opinion. Rights are there in many cases to protect personal freedoms against the encroachments of the state and to protect minority concerns and interests from (as Mill said) 'the tyranny of the majority'.

Are there more intellectually serious contributions to the debate that provide support for compulsory religious education? The most commonly cited reason is that the educational (as opposed to confessional) purpose of religious education, under any new national Framework/syllabus entails that it would no longer be necessary to retain the existing parental right of withdrawal. This is not an argument in any developed sense, nevertheless, it has appeal and deserves consideration. Here are some statements of it.

We have already referred to Clarke and Woodhead's view that they cannot conceive of a case for a right of withdrawal from the kind of religious education they envisage; here is a slightly fuller statement of their position:

> [T]he argument for parents to have the right to withdraw their children from this part of the curriculum should no longer exist, as the curriculum would have lost its 'instructional' or 'confessional' nature. We therefore recommend that this right be removed if the changes we recommend are introduced.
>
> (*Clarke & Woodhead 2015: 39; cf. idem. 2018: 27*)

There is a problem here. Clarke and Woodhead support the introduction of a new updated statutory Framework based on the original 2004 Framework, yet as Lundie's research shows parents are up to the present continuing to exercise their right of withdrawal, and in all likelihood disquiet with the current Framework, probably in combination with other considerations, is one of the reasons for this situation. The close relationship they envisage between the 2004 Framework and any new Framework based on the former provides little confidence for their view that the right of parental withdrawal 'should no longer exist' because it will be unobjectionable to all. Their argument is predicated on the premise that only 'confessional religious education' causes the withdrawal of parental support from religious education. This is not the case at present. There are pupils who are withdrawn by their parents from religious education where the local agreed syllabus follows, for the most part, the existing 2004 Framework. It strains credibility to think a new Framework (modelled on the original) will obviate the need for the existing right of parental withdrawal.

The case for compulsory religious education

The most extended case for the withdrawal of the parental right of withdrawal is expressed in a report produced under the aegis of the Woolf Institute, based in Cambridge. In September 2013 the Institute, which promotes the multidisciplinary study of relationships between Christians, Jews and Muslims convened an independent commission, chaired by Baroness Butler-Sloss, a former Lord Justice, to undertake a review of the role of religion and belief in the UK and to make policy recommendations. The resultant report was published in December 2015 under the title *Living with Difference: Community, diversity and the common good.*

Prejudice, ignorance, developing individuals and social cohesion

Chapter 4 of the Report is concerned with 'the place of religion and belief' in education; other chapters deal with other aspects of the place and role of religion and belief in contemporary Britain. A range of 'problems and challenges' (2015: 33–35) are considered in relation to religion; for example, the issue of the admission policies of faith schools and the shortage of well-trained teachers of religious education in England and Wales. In response to the challenges, the report, under the heading 'Ways forward', identifies two reasons in support of ending the current right of parental withdrawal. Here is the first:

> Education about religion and belief is essential because it is in schools and colleges that there is the best and earliest chance of breaking down ignorance and developing individuals who will be receptive of the other, and ask difficult questions without fear of offending. This is vital for the fruition of our vision for a fairer, more cohesive society.... Education about religion and belief must reflect not only the heritage of the UK, with its religious and non-religious traditions, but also the realities of present society.
>
> *(Butler-Sloss 2015: 36)*

Religious education, we are told, breaks down ignorance and makes one more receptive to 'the other'. It could be accepted, however, that religious education does advance good community relations while insisting that the right of withdrawal should not be relinquished. The social 'goods' achieved by religious education need not be denied; what is needed is an argument to show that these goods are of such a character or magnitude as to negate completely the good of parental choice in religious education. Moreover, to be fully convincing, it is not enough to argue that religious education achieves certain goods, to make the subject compulsory and the *case for* compulsion convincing, reasons are needed to show that these goods are necessarily or for the most part achieved, and that they cannot be achieved in any other way than through compulsion for all.

If the case for relinquishing the right of parental withdrawal is more challenging than Butler-Sloss acknowledges, her proposals also limit freedom of choice more than one might appreciate. Not only does she want to relinquish the existing right of parental withdrawal, her proposals for compulsory non-confessional, objective religious education effectively denies parents the freedom to avail of faith education (2015: 8, 33 and 38). She does allow such 'on the school premises outside of the timetable' (2015: 38). The freedom of parents to send their child to a school where the religious education curriculum reflects their religion and values is denied by her. This is an 'odd' position to espouse in a liberal, pluralist society that aims to be inclusive of different religious commitments and persuasions and that usually rejects assimilationist polices that require citizens to relinquish their fundamental beliefs and values in order to take advantage of public services and public institutions such as education. British society has traditionally been supportive of faith schools and religious education consistent with the religious affiliation of the school. The recent emergence of state funded Muslim schools was warmly welcomed by the Muslim community and this new proposal to evacuate their religious education of any confessional element is unlikely to strengthen their commitment to state institutions.

Does religious education provide 'the best and earliest chance of breaking down ignorance and developing individuals who will be receptive of the other'? (Butler-Sloss 2015: 36). The answer is less obvious that Butler-Sloss assumes. One of the criticisms of multi-faith, phenomenological religious education that emerged among religious educators and researchers in the 1980s was that acquaintance with the beliefs and practices of the different religions by pupils was perceived to have limited effect in lessening religious bigotry and intolerance. This observation has relevance beyond that of Butler-Sloss's opinion. Commissions and reviews comprised of members who know little about the history of religious education in England will inevitably be limited in their understanding of the forces, commitments and assumptions that have shaped its current form and practice, and of the weaknesses as a result that have emerged over the decades. In this instance, as in others, it means that their recommendations lack credibility.

Discussing the contribution of 'studies of religion' in Australian schools to overcoming prejudice, Patricia Malone (1998: 13), in the context of a report on an empirical research project, pointed out that '[t]here are many factors involved in the process of developing… prejudice and although ignorance is a contributing factor, simply learning about a religion is not sufficient to change attitudes'. Prejudice and intolerance are attitudes and although attitudes reflect beliefs and may be influenced by education and increased knowledge, additional sources of 'knowledge' can be drawn upon to confirm existing prejudices, which as research shows are often transmitted through one's family and community. Malone refers to the work of Jan Pettman (1992: 56) who made the point that racism is 'not simply a matter of bad, mad or misinformed (or even stupid) individuals', rather the phenomenon of racism is complex and is a product of 'ideology and a whole set of social relations which are historically generated and materially based'. More recent research supports this conclusion. There is no reason to believe that religious bigotry, which often involves racism and sexism as well, is any different. There are material and ideological determinants of social behaviour, including religious prejudice, and it is educationally and politically naïve to believe that religious education and a study of religions is the best and most effective way of challenging bigotry and banishing discrimination. There is little evidence to support this.

Acquaintance with research on how to reduce prejudice in educational settings indicates that there are few certainties. The statement that '[m]ost educational interventions are not properly evaluated' is commonplace among reviews of empirical studies (McBride 2015: 42). Often educational interventions are short term and self-assessed by those who were involved in the interventions; in other cases, self-selection is involved and those who volunteer are those who are already pre-disposed to change; in other cases there is no control group and it is difficult to know whether what is presumed to be 'success' is the result of some particular intervention, or is explicable in terms of the enthusiasm and greater interest shown by teachers and researchers toward the subjects of research. There is also the tendency for researchers to claim greater success than is warranted by the nature of the research design and the results. As is well known, the adoption of a business financial model by universities and institutions of higher learning places increasing emphasis on rewarding positive research outcomes, which in turn help to attract state funding, in the United Kingdom, through Research Councils, or through charitable institutions, which we are beginning to appreciate have their own ideological commitments. In the conclusion to a wide-ranging review of 'the observational, laboratory, and field experimental literatures on interventions for reducing prejudice', Elizabeth Levy Paluck and Donald P. Green make the following observation:

> Notwithstanding the enormous literature on prejudice, psychologists are a long way from demonstrating the most effective ways to reduce prejudice. Due to weaknesses in the internal and external validity of existing research, the literature does not reveal whether, when, and why interventions reduce prejudice in the world.
>
> *(2009: 360)*

With these caveats in mind, it can be tentatively concluded that what good research there is seems to show is that intolerance is best challenged in schools that promote a positive view of minority groups across the different curriculum subjects, where teachers provide clear and consistent examples of positive attitudes to others, where teaching is inclusive and draws upon the values and wisdom of different communities, and where controversial issues are openly discussed in the classroom with sensitivity and care. Personal encounters with those who are regarded as members of an 'out-group' and the objects of prejudice can also alleviate prejudice, as can pupils engaging in 'imaginative' exercises that encourage them to attempt to experience the feelings and attitudes that result from prejudice and discrimination. Acquaintance with and exposure to diversity within out-groups can also help to challenge stereotypes and identify common beliefs, interests and values. A 'whole school' or holistic approach to challenging prejudice and intolerance across the curriculum, in conjunction with an explicit focus on issues of group identity and on different types of intolerance in particular lessons, will probably do more to foster positive attitudes and values to members of minority ethnic and religious communities than explicit teaching on their beliefs and practices, though explicit teaching could conceivably be used as a catalyst to introduce directed teaching and learning strategies to challenge bigotry and develop respect for others.

Nothing that I have said detracts from the view that religious education has a contribution to make to challenging intolerance and furthering the goal of social cohesion. Religious education, like other subjects, has an important contribution to make, and in the hands of good teachers and with good pedagogical initiatives, appropriately inclusive debates that include consideration of critical issues, and properly focused teaching on developing respect for others, there is no reason why religious education cannot in some schools equal or even out-perform other subjects in this regard. These are things that go beyond what mandated syllabus content requires and give attention to the nature of positive relationships and positive teaching and learning in the classroom. What is properly criticised is Butler-Sloss's (2015: 36) claim that '[e]ducation about religion and belief... is the best and earliest chance of breaking down ignorance and developing individuals who will be receptive of the other'. There is no evidence to support this, and in the light of the evidence we have, it is woefully simplistic and naive.

Whose objective, fair and balanced curriculum?

Here is Butler-Sloss's (2015: 36) second reason for concluding that the parental right of withdrawal from religious education should be removed:

> If the curriculum is objective, fair and balanced, and does not contain elements of confessional instruction or indoctrination, then this teaching should be required in all schools and there is no reason for a legal right to withdraw from learning about religion and belief.

This argument can be construed formally as a single premise from which the conclusion follows:

> *Premise*: If the curriculum is objective, fair and balanced, and does not contain elements of confessional instruction or indoctrination. Therefore,
> *Conclusion*: There is no reason for a legal right to withdraw from learning about religion and belief.

Alternatively, the argument may be considered as comprising two premises, from which the conclusion follows. Thus,

> *Premise 1*: If the curriculum is objective, fair and balanced.

Premise 2: The curriculum does not contain elements of confessional instruction or indoctrination. Therefore,

Conclusion: There is no reason for a legal right to withdraw from learning about religion and belief.

This second formulation of the argument has certain advantages for the purpose of evaluation, even though the two premises are not wholly independent of each other.

Premise 2 will be considered first: 'The curriculum does not contain elements of confessional instruction or indoctrination'. Does 'or' operate as an exclusive (disjunctive) or non-exclusive connector? Is the claim that the curriculum (as envisaged by Butler-Sloss) does not contain confessional instruction, neither is it indoctrinatory; or is the claim that the curriculum does not contain confessional instruction, which is (also) indoctrinatory? Much has been written about indoctrination by philosophers of education in the analytic tradition, yet ambiguity still remains as to its precise meaning and application. Nevertheless, even though philosophers cannot agree on a definition, it is almost universally acknowledged that indoctrination carries negative connotations, and however defined, is to be contrasted with education and educational processes. As emotivists in ethics might say indoctrination is a 'Boo-word'. At this stage, let us proceed on the assumption that Butler-Sloss's proposed religious education curriculum is not indoctrinatory. This does not absolve us of further thinking about the nature of indoctrination. It will allow us to focus more closely on confessional religious education and this will provide the context for further reflections on the nature of indoctrination.

Butler-Sloss (2015: 37) believes that confessional religious education is inappropriate in all schools. As noted above, she even believes that parents should not be free to avail of confessional education in any school that receives state funding (2015: 37–38). Why is this? No reason is given for this controversial position. What is it about confessional education that disqualifies it as properly educational? Her answer may be that confessional schools are not inclusive of all pupils, though at present there is a rule, introduced in 2010, that requires oversubscribed, newly established religious schools to keep at least half of their places open for applicants who are admitted without reference to their faith. According to the Catholic Education Service: 'Existing Catholic schools [most of which are voluntary aided and can follow their own church syllabus]… are the most socially and ethnically diverse schools in the country. They also educate more than 300,000 non-Catholics including 27,000 Muslims'.[4] As the same article records, Catholic schools are extremely popular with parents of all faiths and none; and are frequently oversubscribed. There is evidence to suggests that schools that can foster a sense of community that is built around shared values and beliefs are much more likely to develop the social virtues and commitments that are constitutive of good citizens. Religious schools are well placed to do this, and probably better placed than non-religious schools that cannot assume a coherent and extended set of shared beliefs and values, either among pupils or staff. There is some debate over the claim that pupils in faith schools and Catholic schools in particular, all things considered, do better academically. It is probably the case, but better focused research is needed to place it on a more secure footing and to ascertain the reasons for this. As Andrew Morris (2005: 93–94) has commented:

> The findings of higher levels of academic attainment by Catholic school pupils, while not yet beyond doubt, seem to be well established. What is not at all clear are the causal reasons for those findings. It may be that the observed differences are a function of distinctive practices within the schools. They may be linked to the personal characteristics of their intake or, as the indications… suggest, are the product of a complex interaction of the above derived, in turn, from specific world view and understanding of the purpose of education. There are indications that the values, attitudes and practices seemingly inherent in the traditional confessional model of Catholic school can provide a particularly supportive environment for high academic attainment, especially by socially disadvantaged pupils. It is not clear whether the perceived benefits of such a model are easily transferable.

Some may believe that an appeal to inclusion may be relevant at this point. Inclusion, however, is a two-edged sword. It may enhance the relationships between different groups, but it equally can aggravate existing divisions. As already noted above, simply bringing pupils of different religious backgrounds together in a single school or educating them together in religious education, may well achieve little in terms of challenging bigotry and religious intolerance. It would be good to think that such strategies work, but the research findings are slender and not particularly impressive. By contrast, some Muslim organisations have complained that racism and religious intolerance are not uncommon in community schools and that inclusive policies and lack of provision of faith schools have the effect of worsening relationships between communities (see The Association of Muslim Social Scientists 2004).[5] In fact the problem of prejudice in schools is not confined to Muslims, but extends to Christian and Jewish pupils who also report 'criticism of their beliefs or religious affiliations from their peers and sometimes from teachers' (Moulin 2015a: 489, and 2016a).

There are two sides to the argument about the advantages and disadvantages of faith schools and the confessional education that accompanies them. What is worrying about Butler-Sloss's condemnation of confessionalism in education is that no evidence is cited or arguments adduced. To make a convincing case there needs to be evidence of the deleterious effects of faith education. For example, it needs to be shown that pupils in voluntary aided church schools are more intolerant and bigoted than (similar) pupils in secular schools, or that pupils in voluntary aided church schools are more likely to engage in anti-social and criminal behaviour or that religiously educated pupils in faith schools are more likely to fail to develop a social conscience, and are unconcerned about contributing to the common good. Without knowing these things, it is unfair to condemn faith education; to do so without evidence gives force to the accusation that Butler-Sloss is in thrall to a secular prejudice against faith schools.

No-one disputes that religious education in community schools that are by stature and intention open to all pupils ought not to be confessional. The problem is that Butler-Sloss wants religious education in all schools to be non-confessional and compulsory. Apart from the issue of inclusion, what other reasons might there be for condemning confessional religious education? The complaint may be that it is indoctrinatory. Let us be quite candid, this is a possibility; yet the possibility of indoctrination does not mean that it actually occurs. To reject confessional forms of religious education on the grounds of indoctrination either requires evidence to substantiate the claim that indoctrination is actually practised in faith schools (such is unlikely as inspectors would surely have alerted us to what is going on), or that there is some kind of necessary and invariant relationship between confessional religious education and indoctrination (see *Premise 2* above). If there is, what is it? If there is no necessary connection, then practices and methods that are deemed indoctrinatory can be revised or replaced by strictly educational procedures. It has already been noted in Chapter 7 that faith community leaders have expressed their support for covering a range of religions in religious education. It is no more likely that faith schools will misrepresent the beliefs, practices and mores of different religions than non-religious schools: acquaintance with classroom material and textbooks would alert educators, inspectors and parents to this situation, were it to occur. Faith education is just as likely to encourage classroom dialogue and critical questioning of religious and non-religious beliefs as religious education in non-faith schools; perhaps much here depends on the teacher and how he or she relates the syllabus to the interests and learning needs of pupils.

My own view is that the danger of indoctrination in faith schools is greatly exaggerated and although such fears are still voiced, they typically relate to what went on in schools 50 to 60 years ago. Indoctrination is only effective in a closed or uniform society in which the organs and institutions of the state, the media, public representatives and the educated classes are all committed to the same set of beliefs and values; and where contrary voices are stifled and silenced by legal or social and political means. Indoctrination works only in a 'totalitarian' system. The Britain of today is far removed from the Britain of the 1950s and 1960s, where a high degree of public conformity was enforced by various means. Pupils in schools today are exposed to diversity of beliefs, opinions and lifestyles on a daily basis. One only has to turn on the radio or television, access the internet or social media, observe the behaviour and lifestyle of others to recognise the ubiquity of diversity in modern Britain. In such a pluralist context it is virtually impossible to indoctrinate, in the sense of getting young people to subscribe to beliefs and behaviour without informed or reasonable assent. Interestingly, it is now in relation to sex education that the charge of indoctrination in schools is most frequently heard. It is alleged by some, particularly Muslim parents, that educational efforts to convince pupils of the moral legitimacy of same sex relations are indoctrinatory. This is because at no point in education are criticisms of same sex unions introduced and considered. This contrasts with religious education, where criticisms of religion and the need to develop a critical attitude to religious beliefs are included for study. It should also be noted that in some communities the problem is not educational indoctrination but that of parents and others imposing their beliefs and practices on young people who, while disagreeing, are required to obey on pain of physical punishment, family expulsion or community ostracism.

Turning to *Premise 1*, which requires the curriculum to be 'objective, fair and balanced'. The desire to have a religious curriculum that is objective, fair and balanced in schools is a reasonable proposal, though much may depend on the meaning attributed to these terms. It follows from what has already been argued that confessional religious education can equally be fair and balanced, i.e., it can include accurate representations of different religions and it can incorporate the degree of balance required by the current legislation. This leaves the term 'objective' to be discussed. If use of this term is meant to distinguish the form of religious education in non-faith schools (i.e., 'community' schools, most Foundation schools and many Academies and Free Schools) where aims are limited to what is acceptable to diverse religious and non-religious opinions, from that pursued in faith schools, where teaching and ethos reflect a particular religious perspective, this is uncontroversial. Such usage does not commit one to any disparagement of either type of religious education. However, if use of the term objective is intended to be contrasted with subjective in the one case and not the other, or if it is being used to express a value judgement on the inappropriateness of confessional religious education then such usage ought to be challenged. Butler-Sloss would appear to be committed to using objective in a polemical sense, otherwise she would not be opposed to all forms of confessional education and seek to have her 'objective' form of education imposed on all schools and on all pupils without exception.

There is a range of meanings that might be attributed to the word 'objective' that fail to distinguish it from confessional religious education. An objective portrayal of religion would present it from the believer's perspective (though this should exclude critical questions being asked); that an account is taken of diversity and disagreement within a religion, that religious adherents of a religion are not caricatured or stereotyped; that pupils are made aware of different internal opinions within a religion on controversial issues; and finally that one's own cultural values are not assumed to provide a template for the assessment of other religions and cultures. Confessional religious education can share all these features with 'objective' non-confessional religious education. We can only surmise what other meaning Butler-Sloss attributes to objective religious education to distinguish it from confessional religious education. My suspicion is that objective religious education is regarded as neutral in a way confessionalism is not. Confessional religious education is always expressed through some particular form of confessionalism—Christian, Jewish, Muslim or more particularly as Anglican, Catholic, Orthodox or Reform Judaism, and so on. Clearly in such examples certain beliefs and values are presupposed, and these provide the foundation (or one of the foundations) upon which the curriculum is constructed. This need not (and should not) entail that they are treated uncritically or exempt from questioning. In this sense confessional forms of education and religious education are not neutral.

Is religious education in community schools neutral? Butler-Sloss might acknowledge that this is not always the case but insist that it ought to be; hence the need for objective religious education. This is an unsatisfactory reply because there isn't any form of religious education that is neutral; all involve value judgements: value judgements about the selection of content, the aims to be pursued, the methods to be employed, the values that the religious curriculum are meant to instantiate and to inculcate in pupils, and so on. Education is one of the most 'value rich' activities in which state institutions and other actors are engaged. If the postmodern movement in philosophy, particularly as represented by Foucault and Lyotard, has anything to teach us it is that claims to neutrality are chimerical and most likely to be advanced in pursuit of power, influence and control over others. Claims to neutrality are often meant to silence critics or to overlook the difficult and exacting challenge of entering into dialogue with others to produce working agreements, which may involve compromises and reassessments of one's original starting point. In the case of non-confessional religious education, the challenge is to construct a form of religious education that has broad appeal to parents with contrasting religious and non-religious commitments: the result is never neutral; just as confessional religious education, which may not aspire to have broad religious appeal, is also never neutral.

To return to the issue of indoctrination. Fifteen years ago, Terence Copley (2005 and 2008b) alerted educators to the reality of secular indoctrination in British culture and schools, including religious education. The term secular can be used in different ways, and there is a sense in which one can describe non-confessional religious education in England as secular and not mean by this that it is anti-religious or undermining of religious belief and practice. There is also a sense in which the term secular is used to refer to anti-religious beliefs and practices, and it is in this sense that Copley used it. His analysis traced the historical march of seculariation in British society and culture, and concluded with the identification of secular influences in education and in religious education: the deconstruction of religious narratives and teachings of their religious meaning and presentations of them as universal illustrations of non-religious human values; presenting religious figures as exemplars of current secular preoccupations with gender equality, inclusion and social justice, while overlooking the religious foundation for their teachings, and so on. What Copley showed is that there are aspects of non-confessional religious education that present themselves as open, inclusive and objective, yet are hostile to religious beliefs and commitments. More alarmingly, there is evidence (Moulin 2011: 320) to show that some Christian pupils, in community schools, feel not only 'that Christianity was often misrepresented and not shown the same respect afforded to other religions' but 'that teachers could "offend Christianity more than other religions" and that they "wouldn't do that if it was another religion"' (see also Moulin 2015b and 2016b). Butler-Sloss unfortunately neglects to interact with the history of religious education in England or with research that questions the 'objectivity' of much that passes for non-confessional religious education.

Religious freedom

None of those who advocate repealing the long-standing legal parental right of withdrawal from religious education consider the issue of religious freedom or its symbolic importance. It is assumed by Butler-Sloss that there is no need to appreciate why religious freedom is important or what it is about the nature of religion that convinces most social commentators that freedom in relation to it is fundamental to democracy and to a society that aspires to be participative and open, and in which all citizens, with their distinctive and different identities, can feel valued and respected. In a liberal society, individuals are free to choose their own beliefs and values and to instantiate them in practices and behaviour, within the context of the prevailing legal system of freedoms and responsibilities. By neglecting to consider the wider issue of the nature of religious freedom, why it is important, and closely related to this, what it is about religion that makes it so controversial and divisive, Butler-Sloss is deprived of any appreciation of why parents currently exercise their right to withdraw their children from religious education. Hence what is not appreciated is dismissed as unimportant and unconsidered.

Why are rights of religious freedom regarded as fundamental and what is it about religion that traditionally accords it this status? What is exceptional about religion? The first thing to note is that religions can be conceived as total ways of life, which potentially can regulate all of reality: from one's interpretation of the meaning and purpose of life to, in some cases, how one washes; from one's monthly round of devotions to one's eating regime; from one's choice of marriage partner to where one lives: all of these can be determined by religion. This typically relates to the fact that the grounds for religious beliefs and practices are based on claims to revelation from God or to (claimed) self-authenticating religious experiences, say mystical experiences. The force of religion in a person's life depends on the degree of commitment. It would be mistaken to think that religious beliefs and values necessarily regulate the lives of all religious adherents. There are different levels of commitment and there are different interpretations of the requirements of religion. Not every religious adherent is guided throughout or even mainly by religious considerations. Nevertheless, the religions remain important and, in some cases, primary sources of self-assigned personal and group identity. Even those whose practise of religion is selective and inconsistent by the canons of idealised ortho-doxies often identify religion as their chief source of identity; this is particularly the case for members of religious minorities when confronted by majorities of a different religious persuasion, or by what is conceived to be a largely secular majority population.

Closely related to both religious commitment and identity and, what may be regarded as a factor conditioning their personal and social influence, are differing internal interpretations of religions and what they require. These interpretations can be conceptualised in various ways, say as fundamentalist, conservative (the first two are often conflated) or liberal, or on the basis of attitudes within a religion towards the surrounding society and culture, perhaps employing and adapting H. Richard Niebuhr's (1951) five-fold typology beyond its original use to categorise how Christianity and Christians have related to culture throughout history to apply to other religions as well, for example, Islam and Muslims against culture, the Islam of culture, etc. The believer's interpretation of a religion typically regulates how he or she interacts with other individuals, cultures and even towards the nation state and its bureaucratic systems of accountability and control. Moreover, different internal interpretations of a religion can also lead to sharp divisions and even religious conflict between adherents of the same religion. The obvious topical example is that between adherents of Sunni and Shi'ite schools of Islam. Research undertaken by the Pew Research Center (2012: 20), on how Muslims perceive themselves and others, found that Muslims in many Middle Eastern and North African countries held strong views about sectarian differences (with some 40 per cent of Sunnis not accepting Shi'as as Muslims).

The final feature of religion that is relevant to our present discussion is the historically constituted identity of a religion in relation to other religions and cultures. Religions have a natural history and almost all religions have interacted with other religio-cultural groups, for better or worse. There are positive examples of interactions between religions, but equally there are negative interactions, and it is often these that become defining events in the self-perceptions of followers of religions. One thinks of the Christian Crusades against Islam from the eleventh to the thirteenth centuries, the 'historical memory' of which for some still blights Christian-Muslim relations. Christianity's subsequent involvement in the emergence and spread of new empires from the seventeenth to the nineteenth centuries, imperialism and colonialism, along with more recent associations in the minds of many Muslims with Western 'invasions' of Iraq, Afghanistan and Libya that have resulted in newly strained relationships, even in places far removed from the original sites of physical conflict. A history of Islam, as with Christianity, would reveal both positive and negative attitudes toward adherents of other religions and cultures, though it is the negative attitudes that are often best remembered and which condition contemporary attitudes: support for slavery and complicity in the slave trade, forced conversions, the doctrine of dhimmitude, and in recent times the persecution of non-Muslims, particularly in the Middle East and in parts of Africa, and suicide bombings directed against 'non-believers'. Much more could be added to this selective and embarrassingly short account of the historically constituted identity of the religions; and clearly examples of other religions could have been used to illustrate the point. All religions have a material, natural history and the nature of their interactions with other religions and cultures influence contemporary relationships between adherents of different religions.

Acquaintance with these features of religions helps us to understand why freedom of religion and the ability to follow one's religious conscience is so important, just as it is equally important for non-religious individuals. We have already noted how Lundie's research revealed that within Christianity it is the parents of both Jehovah's Witnesses and members of the Exclusive Brethren who are most likely to withdraw their children. Both regard themselves as preserving the true message of Christianity and both can be regarded as opposing accommodations with secular culture and maintaining a strict separation between believers and non-believers and between themselves and other 'so-called' Christians. Islamist attacks across Europe and Asia may also account for requests by parents for their children not to study Islam or to visit mosques. Other reasons for the withdrawal of pupils from religious education may be that parents are opposed to all religions, or that they feel that their own religion or version of religion is not faithfully represented in the class-room and in school texts. In some instances newly arrived refugees that have fled religiously inspired persecution may feel disinclined to allow their children to study a religion they associate first-hand with oppression and bigotry; others may wish to confine religious education (of a confessional form) to the home and community. There are any number of reasons why parents might wish to avail of their right of withdrawal from religious education, whether presumed to be objective or confessional.

Parental withdrawal: The lessons of the non-confessional history of religious education

The aim of this section is to consider two policy initiatives in English religious education, which, if they had been faithfully followed through, would have been sufficient to justify some parents to withdraw their children from religious educa-tion. Both policies, though believed by their proponents to be appropriate to non-confessional religious education, can be legitimately regarded as educationally and religiously inappropriate and therefore would have provided justification for par-ents to exercise their right of withdrawal. These examples, if convincing (or even if plausible), show that based on past experience, there is a continuing need for the right of parental withdrawal from religious education to be retained.

The first example is one I have considered in detail elsewhere and it can be presented in summary form here. In a series of articles in the early 1990s, Professor John Hull (1992: 70; cf. Hull 2000: 76) introduced the word 'religionism' into the lexicon of religious education.

> Religionism describes an adherence to a particular religion which involves the identity of the adherent so as to support tribalistic or nationalistic solidarity. The identity which is fostered by religionism depends upon rejection and exclusion. We are better than they. We are orthodox; they are infidel. We are believers; they are unbelievers. *We are right; they are wrong.* [my use of italics]
> Religionism always involves prejudice against other religions.

Few would question Hull's criticism of religious prejudice, intolerance and bigotry or of tribalistic or nationalistic attitudes that demean others. Equally, few would question his identification of the attitude of religious superiority as one of the causes of religious bigotry. His position, however, is more controversial than this, for he blames the belief that one's own religion is true and other religions are false or less true as the ultimate cause of bigotry. Hull is quite insistent that '[i]t is not enough for religious education to encourage a *tolerant* attitude towards other religions' (Hull 1992: 71, my italics), it is the denial of the truth of 'other' religious traditions that causes religious bigotry; as he says, it is the view that '[w]e are right; they are wrong'. In concluding that those who claim exclusive truth for their own religion are in effect justifying intolerance, Hull has committed the same error as those he accuses of giving support to bigotry, for presumably he believes he is right and they are wrong in their interpretation of these issues, but this is precisely the view (in this case, 'he is right, others are wrong') that he regards as the root cause of intolerance and bigotry!

Hull's analysis and interpretation of the nature and origins of religious intolerance and bigotry can be dismissed as inadequate, unconvincing and even self-refuting. At the time of writing he was one of the most influential voices in British religious education and his voice carried considerable weight among those concerned with developing religious education policies and initiatives. Even this observation fails to capture the full significance of Hull's proposals. He did not present his interpretation of the nature and cause of religionism to the community of religious educators to be debated and considered on its merits, he called for the implementation of special educational programmes in both schools and churches to combat religionism and in the case of the former, that 'anti-religionist education' of the form he supports to become a feature of all agreed syllabuses throughout England and Wales. He wanted his views accorded statutory force. Religious educators ought to be legally mandated (in the cause of reducing religious intolerance and bigotry) to teach that it is mistaken to regard your own religion as exclusively true or true to a significant degree denied to other religions. This exceeds the role and authority of schools in a liberal, pluralist democratic state. Citizens ought to be free to believe in the exclusive truth of their own religious tradition and ought not to be required by the education system to affirm the equal truth of other traditions.

Had Hull's call for his views to be given statutory force through agreed syllabuses been accepted, it would have been entirely appropriate for religious parents who hold traditional views about the truth of their religion to exercise their right of withdrawal. To put the issue in its most pointed and controversial political form: why ought Muslims that belief in the exclusive truth of Islam have their views challenged in public schools? Wisely, Hull's 'anti-religionist' policy initiative was not taken up and endorsed by agreed syllabus committees; yet it is alarming that one of Britain's foremost religious educators should have advocated a patently anti-liberal policy that limited religious choice, and in some cases would have involved the state in contradicting the religious views of parents, who are entitled to believe in the truth of their own religion and in a free society to seek to convert others, through legitimate moral means, to share their belief (see Thiessen 2011 and 2018, who discusses the issues in relation to Christianity).

The second example, which illustrates the continuing need for the parental right of withdrawal, again relates to the post-confessional history of English religious education; this time to the controversy that surrounded the religious education clauses of the 1988 Education Reform Act, both at its parliamentary discussion and amendment stages and in its subsequent iterations. Much has been written about the progress of the Education Reform Bill through both Houses of Parliament, particularly the House of Lords (see Alves 1991). It would require more space than is available here to provide a full picture of the personalities, debates and interpretations. In broad terms, according to the standard interpretation, there was a vocal lobby in both Houses, particularly the House of Lords, that wanted to 'to give religious education a deliberately Christianising role' (Robson 1996: 17) and to identify Christianity as the foundation for British culture; what David Rose has described as 'policy-making cultural restorationism' (Rose 2003: 205); others have spoken of efforts by some members of the House of Lord to revive and reinforce 'the notion of "Christian England"' through religious education (Bates 1996: 97). By common consent their efforts were thwarted by the Bishop of London who brokered an amendment, which, while supported by those pressing for a more Christian version of religious education, did not, when confirmed in statute, achieve what 'restorationists' intended (see Robson 1996: 17).

There is no need to discuss whether this presentation of the issues and debates surrounding the passing of the Education Reform Bill into law as the Education Reform Act of 1988 fully captures the aims and motives of different parties. In other words, it is not necessary to ascertain whether there truly was an attempt to Christianise religious education and to determine the form it would take. The standard interpretation can be accepted. If the 'cultural restorationists' in parliament had their way, religious education would have been transformed into a vehicle for the transmission of British culture, that is, one particularly exclusionary version of British culture that marginalises the contribution of 'minority' cultures and presents an idealised version of the contribution of Christianity to culture. If a religious education curriculum has been instituted on this basis, there would have been legitimate grounds for some parents to exercise their right of withdrawal.

These two historical examples of policy initiatives in post-confessional English religious education that sought legal enforcement, thankfully were never implemented. Both illustrate that even under the guise of being presented as appropriate for all schools and pupils, legitimate educational and religious objections ought properly to be raised. In our examples these concerns would have been sufficient to justify some parents exercising their right of withdrawal of their children from religious education. One response might be to affirm that 'common sense' prevailed and that both proposed policies were ultimately rejected. Yet the fact that such policies captured the minds of influential educational and political figures is disturbing and perhaps ominous. None of us is sure of the educational policies that will be proposed and implemented in the future: the unexpected vote in favour of Brexit, i.e., for the United Kingdom to leave the European Union, and the rise of populist politics, indicate that shifts in public opinion or by contrast shifts of opinion among the intellectual elite (among which the late Professor Hull would have been counted), can take an unexpected and often illiberal turn. Policies could be introduced in the future that at the present time appear unlikely, though given the history of religious education and recent political upheavals, who is to predict what is likely or unlikely. The parental right of withdrawal provides a continuing bulwark against the encroachments of the state and from well-intentioned social projects that are as uncritical in their construction as they are over-confident in the results they will achieve.

There is no simple knock-down argument whether the parental right of withdrawal ought to be removed or not. It is a matter of assembling evidence, constructing arguments, assigning greater or lesser significance to some things over others, and so on, and then reaching a defensible or (all things being equal) reasonable conclusion. The case for removal, however, is not particularly convincing, when shorn of its rhetorical appeal and when set within a wider critical framework that aims to distinguish what is academically fashionable or axiomatic from what is warranted. Some will point to the benefits to be gained educationally and socially from removal; others will point out that the benefits are not inevitable and that there is an almost negligible research basis for such assertions. Ironically, the principle of inclusion can be used to support both positions. Some will see benefit to all pupils, without exception, being required by law to follow the same curriculum in religious education; others will see that by bestowing a right of withdrawal to parents, account is taken of their beliefs, values and attitudes, and that in a liberal (as opposed to a non-liberal) society inclusion of this form is preferable, even required. In some senses the parental right of withdrawal is part of a much wider framework of 'hard-won' rights of religious freedom. Such freedoms of belief (religious and otherwise) are historically constitutive of British identity and also symbolic of a deeper tolerance that lies at the heart of British democracy, which in my view ought not to be surrendered lightly.

Notes

1 The answer at least in relation to the United Kingdom is that withdrawal obtains in Northern Ireland, Scotland and Wales.
2 See https://davidlundie.files.wordpress.com/2018/04/report-on-re-opt-out-wcover.pdf (accessed 14 April 2019).
3 See https://www.gov.uk/government/publications/consent-for-school-trips-and-other-off-site-activities (accessed 28 February 2019).
4 See https://www.telegraph.co.uk/news/2018/03/05/dont-let-faith-schools-take-pupils-basis-religion-leaders-warn/ (accessed 28 February 2019).
5 See https://www.theguardian.com/uk/2004/jun/08/politics.race (accessed 28 February 2019); also http://www.islamicparty.com/commonsense/educate3.htm (accessed 28 February 2019).

9

THE HOLY, THE IDEA OF THE HOLY AND RELIGIOUS EDUCATION

It is refreshing to move from the prosaic and pseudo-objective language of commissions and reviews to a serious, substantive interpretation of religious education that engages with the secondary literature and with the history and development of the subject. *On Holy Ground: The theory and practice of religious education* (2014), by Liam Gearon, is an important study that raises critical questions about the educational legitimacy of non-confessional religious education. If many of the contributions already considered give little real attention to the major weaknesses in religious education and their resolution, preferring instead to focus on what are relatively minor weaknesses or to construct their own imagined weaknesses in keeping with their own agendas, Gearon raises the matter of weaknesses to a higher level: in his view non-confessional religious education in its present form does not have a coherent rationale and an educational future.

Such is the breadth and depth of Gearon's argument that it is difficult to know where to begin and how to structure a review and assessment of his position. In some respects his work can be read as an intellectual *tour de force* and in some respects as a not entirely predictable and in places possibly disjointed journey through 2000 years of religious history, with a particular focus on post-Enlightenment ideas. It is impossible in this context to engage fully with all of what he says, though a serious attempt will be made to represent faithfully the main points of his overall argument and to subject it to the scrutiny it deserves. Attention will focus on Chapter 1, 'On holy ground,' effectively an introductory chapter, and on Chapter 9, 'The holy and the idea of the holy,' the final chapter. I will also summarise Chapter 2 as representative of his approach and method, while interacting with its content. Extensive use will be made of quotations throughout, to do justice to Gearon's argument.

On Holy Ground

> *On Holy Ground* examines the re-reading of the holy through the texts of modernity, not simply in its rejection of revelation as a source of knowledge but, more widely, the loss of the sacred and the conscious removal of the sacred-profane, holy-unholy distinctions. The book demonstrates how such readings have ben refracted, have become a coda for a modern religious education, for the re-reading of religious texts has become as integral a part of modern religious education as it was integral to the coda of modernity.
>
> *(Gearon 2014: 3)*

After quoting from Charles Darwin about his loss of faith—'I [Darwin] gradually came to disbelieve in Christianity'—Gearon continues (2014: 3–4; emphasis in original):

> Darwin here demonstrates in a single instance a whole Western intellectual tradition which has needed to dispense with the holy in order to seek the legitimacy of new forms of knowledge, not to reach heaven but to dismantle it. Modernity began not with an assault on heaven to regain it but to remove it. Modernity is not an attempted recovery of holy ground but its eradication. In its originating impulse, modernity can be *negatively* defined as a cessation of the assault on heaven through the denial of the holy. In its original impulse, modernity can be *positively* defined (against this cessation and denial) as a quest for earthly alternatives to heaven and alternative grounds for being in the world.
>
> If, in its originating impulse, modernity can here be *negatively* defined as a cessation of the assault on heaven through the denial of the holy, *so too can religious education be read*. If in its originating impulse, modernity can be *positively* defined (against this cessation and denial) as a quest for alternatives to heaven and alternative grounds for what once both knowing and being in the world, *so too can religious education be read*.

This is a provocative interpretation of modern religious education: modernity aims to eradicate the holy and modern religious education follows in its wake! According to Gearon (2014: 5), the Enlightenment spirit of enquiry, of philosophy and theology, the natural sciences, the social and the psychological sciences, phenomenology, modern politics, and ascetics as forms of knowledge are rooted in an epistemological distance from religion as a form of knowledge. This list helpfully provides the names and order of successive chapters in *On Holy Ground* (from Chapters 2–8). Our analysis will continue by clarifying and developing his position as he expounds it in Chapter 1.

Das Heilige

Gearon finds inspiration and opposition to the Enlightenment's critique of religion and its appropriation by other disciplines and writers for their non-religious purposes in Rudolf Otto's *Das Heilige*, first published in 1917. He (2014: 5) wryly comments that '[i]n the English translation of *Das Heilige, The Holy* becomes The *Idea of the Holy* (author's emphasis). Otto's (1917) famed treatise has thereby the ironic distinction of manifesting in its English translation the very over-rationalization which he had sought to overcome.'

At this stage I want to break off discussion of Gearon to pursue my own summary of Otto's account of experience of the holy. This is because part of my later criticism of Gearon's analysis is that the reader may not appreciate some of the vulnerabilities that attach to Otto's position and the innocent reader of Gearon may remain ignorant of these on the basis of his account. According to Otto, the experience of the holy, which is to be equated with numinous experience, is 'the innermost essence of religion,' and that which gives religion its distinctiveness. The holy has both a rational and a non-rational aspect or nature. The rational nature of the holy allows it to be described and classified, whereas its non-rational aspect, which Otto believes is the more basic and original, is beyond description and communication. At its deepest level the holy is 'ineffable' and 'inexpressible.' Thus, experience of the holy is similarly beyond description and qualitatively unlike any other experience. Nevertheless, it constitutes the essential source of knowledge of the divine: numinous experience is a unique religious feeling providing a religious knowledge that is inaccessible to ordinary rational understanding (Otto 1958: 153). The holy may defy conceptual and rational analysis, yet is known in numinous encounter.

Otto's account of the holy focuses (as the sub-title of his book indicates)[1] on the relationship of the rational to the non-rational in religion, giving priority to the latter, in contrast to much of the prevailing religious apologetics of his day. His account of this relationship is also integrally bound up with an equally nuanced and controversial interpretation of the nature and function of religious language. For Otto, the truth of religion extends beyond the boundaries of language and is incapable of being grasped by the intellect in its cognitive or rational mode. There are religious truths too deep for words, in the sense that there are certain religious experiences that cannot be described, but which nevertheless convey knowledge of the holy. Religious experience is primarily a feeling which defies conceptual understanding and lies beyond the domain of discursive reason. Consequently, what is distinctive of religion cannot be adequately communicated through language: what is most real in religion is beyond description and propositional expression—ineffable (Otto 1958: 4, 7, 10, 13, 30, 59, 63, and 184–185). Religious language is chiefly evocative rather than descriptive; it seeks to evoke experience of the holy, rather than describe it. The rational dimension of religious faith is 'parasitic' upon a non-rational and non-verbal core. As Leon Schlamm (1992: 533) notes, '[at] the heart of this collection of [Otto's] claims about numinous experience is an epistemological assumption about the distance separating religious language and experience.'

According to Otto, there are two species of knowledge: immediate awareness, which is non-conceptual or pre-conceptual in form, and rational knowledge, which is conceptual. He writes accordingly (1958: 135):

Something may be profoundly and intimately known in feeling for the bliss it brings or the agitation it produces, and yet the understanding may find no concept for it. To know and to understand conceptually are two different things, and are often even mutually exclusive and contrasted. The mysterious obscurity of the numen is by no means tantamount to unknowableness.

At some stage the plausibility of this distinction between non-conceptual and conceptual forms of religious knowledge will need to be considered, but not now. Instead, attention is drawn to the apologetic use to which it is put by Otto, for carefully integrated into his account of the nature of religion is a defensive strategy to protect religious truth claims. That this is the motive behind Otto's distinction is made clear in a number of places; no more so than the one to be quoted in full below. But first the passage to be quoted needs to be placed in context. It comes at the end of a chapter on 'Divination in Christianity Today'— divination here is a technical term for that human faculty by which one 'genuinely' (Otto 1958: 144) recognises the holy. Ironically, Otto is referring to the lack of epistemic force numinous experience has for those without such experience, while implicitly the point is being made that numinous experience has epistemic force for those who do have the experience. From this he goes on to conclude that the rational criticism of those who do not have the experience is of no relevance for those who have, and even more controversially still, and again implicitly, that the truth and proper content of religion entirely depends upon numinous experience (it is after all the essence of religion). Given that what is important in religion is non-rational, it follows for Otto that traditional rational apologetics cannot commend religion, and more importantly, rational criticism cannot effectively criticise religion. On this scheme of things, religious faith and commitment to the holy are compatible with extreme scepticism regarding the historical and literary sources of religion. This is the clear implication, as Otto himself notes (1958: 174, author's emphasis):

> There can naturally be no defence of the worth and validity of ... religious intuitions of pure feeling that will convince a person who is not prepared to take the religious consciousness itself for granted. Mere general argument, even moral demonstrations, are in this case useless, are indeed for obvious reasons impossible from the outset. On the one hand the criticisms and confutations attempted by such a person are unsound from the start. His weapons are far too short to touch his adversary, for the assailant is always standing right outside the arena! But if these intuitions, these separate responses to the impress of the Gospel story and the central person to it—if these intuitions are immune from rational criticism, they are equally unaffected by the fluctuating results of biblical exegesis and the laboured justifications of historical apologetics. For they are possible without these, springing, as they do, from first hand *personal divination*.

From this it is quite clear that Otto is attempting to do much more than accurately describe religion. His intention is quite clearly to defend religion against criticism, and he does this by locating what is essential to religion beyond the domain of rational knowledge—by opposing religious intuitions of pure feeling to our normal categories of knowing. It is at this point that his distinction between non-conceptual and conceptual knowledge is most clearly seen for what it is. It is an apologetic device to safeguard the autonomy of religion and protect religious truth claims from rational criticism. To return to Gearon's position. He (2014: 7) concludes his summary of *Das Heilige* with the comment: 'Otto saw religious experience as an irreducible *sui generis* feature of all religions.'

Implications for religious education

The final section of Chapter 1 is entitled, 'The theory and practice of religious education,' and begins with the sentence, 'The problem of modern religious education,' Gearon (2014: 8) tells us, 'remains how to ground the subject when it is no longer grounded in the religious life, in the *life* of the holy' (author's emphasis). 'The solution' [in relation to non-confessional religious education] 'has been the seeking of grounds for such religious education when religion is no longer rooted in the pursuit of the holy life.'

> The argument is that such religious education has sought alternative grounds in modern, Enlightenment and post-Enlightenment forms of knowledge. Since these have their origins in the critique of religion, modern religious education presumes a critical distance from the holy life. These grounds then are epistemological. How do we understand the holy? The holy is understood through rational grounds, a multitude of rationalizations. To understand the holy, religious education has appropriated frameworks which have their origins in the critique of religion.
>
> *(Gearon 2014: 8)*

The task Gearon then sets himself in subsequent chapters is to show how non-religious forms of knowledge have come to ground modern religious education. He considers the different (non-religious) disciplines and how they relate to religious education: the philosophical and the theological, the natural sciences, the social sciences, and so on. He identifies 'two *ideal types*' (2014: 9; author's emphasis throughout) of response to religion: 'the adversary and the advocate. The *adversary* is not content simply to observe religion. They want something done about it, preferably its removal.' 'The *advocate* seeks not removal but better understanding of religion.' Religion, on this interpretation, according to Gearon, can be advocated insofar as religions 'mirror' the non-religious (reductive) framework. For example, religion is seen as an epiphenomenon of social or psychological factors, yet it can be given a positive sense if it can be configured to serve social or psychological well-being. 'The advocate can, however, also be antagonistic to certain forms of religion' (Gearon 2014: 9): he provides no example, but he may be thinking of forms of religion that advocate bigotry and intolerance against non-adherents.

Toward the end of Chapter 1, Gearon (2014: 14; author's emphasis) summarises the dilemma of modern religious education:

> The problem of modern religious education remains in finding a ground when modern religious education is no longer grounded in the religious life, in the *life* of the holy. The solution has lain or has been sought then in seeking of foundations. The grounds are primarily epistemological: how do we understand the holy? The problem is also moral: how do we live, how does religious education contribute to the educating, to the leading out from knowledge to life? Thus, again, an epistemological problem becomes a moral and existential one.

Gearon leaves the matter here with an implicit dilemma: non-confessional religious education, i.e. modern religious education, for the most part falsifies the nature of religion and is always seeking a foundation which by the nature of the case it cannot provide, whereas confessional religious education when grounded in the holy and the life of the Spirit is an entirely plausible practice. Gearon does not explicitly identify this dilemma, even though it seems to be the clear implication of his argument. There seems to be a coyness about his position, yet it would be better appreciated and served if he did speak more plainly.

A chapter in his narrative of modern religious education

It has already been noted that Gearon devotes a series of chapters (seven in all) to a review of the different ways (what he regards as non-religious) disciplines have interacted with religion and in a concluding section in each chapter he considers how these disciplines have influenced and been appropriated by religious educators. The structure seems straight forward enough, thought is not as helpful or as relevant as one might have anticipated. There are reasons for this, which will become clear if the contents of a representative chapter are summarised. Chapter 2 will serve as an example (it is incidentally also the longest and extends to 28 pages, of which 17 are devoted to expounding the thought of Kant, Schleiermacher and Hegel). It is entitled 'Philosophy, theology and religious education.'

Gearon begins by accrediting the separation of philosophy and theology to the sixteenth-century Reformation, and views this separation as ultimately leading to the Enlightenment critique of revealed religion as philosophy increased its autonomy and established itself as a rival to religion. He then deals with a succession of adversarial thinkers who reflected on the nature of religion and its claims to truth: he deals in some detail with the scepticism of David Hume (1711–1776) and with Immanuel Kant's (1724–1804) denial of knowledge of God in order to make room for faith; brief references are made to the work of Ludwig Feuerbach (1804–1872) and Karl Marx (1818–1883), and finally half a page is given over to a discussion of the ideas of Friedrich Nietzsche (1844–1900). As advocacy thinkers he considers in some detail the positions of Friedrich Schleiermacher (1768–1834) and of Georg F. W. Hegel (1770–1831) and the latter's idea of religion as an integral stage in the development of human consciousness's ascent to the Absolute; a paragraph is devoted to consideration of theologians that accommodated their ideas to modernity; a paragraph summarises Catholic counter-responses to modernity; followed by a shorter paragraph devoted to fundamentalism and the thought of Karl Barth (1886–1968), and finally reference to a range of postmodern thinkers that affirm religion but only for them 'if narrow doctrinal alliances' (2014: 36) are modified. The chapter concludes with an account of the influence of philosophical ideas and thinking over religious education—all other chapters concerned with particular disciplines conclude similarly with a section devoted to the influence of each respective disciple over religious education (in some cases the influence seems tenuous and insignificant educationally). Gearon notes (2014: 37) that, according to supporters of philosophical approaches to religious education, '[b]y presenting religions rationally, assessing their claims to knowledge, their truth claims, we can justify the place of religious education as a subject along the lines of any other subject in a liberal education.' This comment is followed by a brief discussion of the position of John Dewey (1859–1952), an equally brief discussion of the initiative to include more philosophy in schools, a sixteen line discussion of Andrew Wright's efforts 'to counter ... postmodern challenges to truth in religious education' (2014: 39), cursory references to the work of Jeff Astley and other writers, half a page devoted to the work of critical philosophers who believe that moral or ethical education now fulfils any valid role that religious education once had in liberal education, followed by a paragraph that notes how recognition is given to the incorporation of 'agnostic, atheistic, humanistic understandings within religious education curricula today...' (2014: 42).

> Through such pathways, religiously sceptical pathways now have more than a foothold in religious education. They have attained a legal as well as epistemological legitimacy, as law legitimizes religion *or* belief.
>
> It seems that Feuerbach (1854) was prescient in declaring that 'what is regarded as atheism today will be religion tomorrow.' It might have bemused him to think that religious education was one of the means by which this transformation was facilitated.
>
> *(Gearon 2014: 43)*

For the most part Gearon's summary of writers and of positions is reliable, yet some of his interpretative judgements can be questioned—or at least there is room for disagreement. For example, his view (2014: 16) that the Protestant Reformation effected 'the separation of philosophy and theology,[2] which would subsequently define the eighteenth-century Enlightenment' is a controversial judgement. The context makes it clear that for Gearon this is on the one hand a polemical statement against Protestantism and on the other an apologetic statement in support of Catholicism (as well as laying the travail of modern religious educa-tion firmly at the door of Protestantism). That philosophy, as an increasingly autonomous discipline, was the driving force behind much Enlightenment thinking cannot be doubted, and it may even be acknowledged that the Enlightenment critique of revealed religion was indebted in part to some aspects of Reformation thinking. Yet this is not because Catholicism held reason and revealed theology together in a more creative synthesis, as Gearon believes. It is because the Protes-tant Reformation also emphasised personal decision and the right of conscience: the religious, cultural and political structures that took account of these, slowly but surely allowed much greater latitude for freedom of thought and toleration of critical interpretations of religion (see Wilken 2019). It can be pointed out that St. Thomas Aquinas (1225–1274) drew a distinction between propositions to which assent is necessary for salvation and can be established by an appeal to natural reason, for example, the propositions that God is, or that he is one, and proposi-tions about God's triune nature, which are known only by revelation. In the *Summa Contra Gentiles* Aquinas called this a 'a two-fold truth' about religious claims, 'one to which the inquiry of reason can reach, the other which surpasses the whole ability of the human reason' (quoting from Swindal 2019). Clearly in Aquinas we have a distinction between philosophy or natural reason and theology: this distinction was much less influential in post-Tridentine Catholicism because the religious, social and political authorities did not espouse freedom of religion and religious expression to the same extent as Protestantism.

If pressed, a much more convincing argument for the roots of the separation of philosophy from theology can be traced to René Descartes (1596–1650), who like Aquinas professed loyalty to the Catholic Church. Descartes grounded his quest for indubitable knowledge, over against doubt, in the self and its powers of thought—*cogito, ergo sum*, 'I think therefore I am': to the autonomous thinking self, rather than anything revealed by the senses, including one's body. The *cogito's* epistemo-logical significance is supposed to derive from its self-evident truth status. Descartes used this starting point as the foundation of all knowledge, as he moved from non-inferential, foundational to non-foundational beliefs in a series of (presumed by him to be) self-critical steps based on 'clear and distinct ideas.' To get beyond the foundational belief in the 'thinking self' he is required to draw on the existence of God, which he establishes by an appeal to his 'necessary being' version of the ontological argument (and to some extent to the cosmological argument); this allows him to trust the evidence of the senses because God would not deceive us. In Descartes, certainty about the self precedes certainty about the reality of God. What is radical about his position and one of the reasons he is regarded as the 'Father of modern philosophy' is precisely because the being of God becomes superfluous after performing the function of safeguarding the reliability of sense experience. Descartes's successors soon dispensed with any need to invoke God for this purpose. The thinking self could extend itself to incorporate sensory experi-ence without the need for divine assistance. Helmut Thielicke (1990: 52) describes Descartes's emphasis on the human subject and subjectivity as 'the initial thesis of secularization.' Our discussion of Aquinas and Descartes illustrates the point that a separation of reason from theology is not exclusively a consequence of Protestant influence but can equally be traced to Catholic thought, though the extent to which Descartes can be categorised as a 'Catholic' thinker is a moot point.

I have taken issue with a minor theme in Gearon's historical analysis of philosophy and theology and its influence over religious education and arguably given it more attention than it deserves. Yet this admission raises a more important issue, which is what is the relevance of his extended accounts of different disciplines, ideas and thinkers if it is not subsequently shown how precisely they relate to and have been influential over religious education. Why discuss the thought of Hume, Kant, Schleiermacher, Feuerbach, Marx, and others if there is no direct connection made to religious education or to argue for their relevance, positively or negatively, to the subject in some *specific* way? If the point is that there are philosophers and thinkers that have either rejected religious knowledge or have reinterpreted religion to fit the epistemic conditions of modernity, this could be done more briefly; the principle of selection ought to be on the extent to which these thinkers and their ideas have influenced religious education. If Kant has had limited influence over religious education then it is not necessary to develop his reinterpretation of religion at length (over 12 pages), similarly with regard to Hegel (over three pages)—Gearon provides no direct evidence of either's influence over religious education. This weakness is also highlighted in the final section devoted to tracing the influence of philosophical ideas and thinking over religious education. He refers to John Dewey, but arguably Dewey has had little influence on British religious education. Gearon discusses the 'philosophy for children' movement, but no evidence is cited that this has had any influence over religious educators. It may have, but is there evidence? He refers to efforts to develop autonomy in young people in this context, but this aim has been prominent since the 1960s (see Astley 1994: 204–208) and has long been associated with some forms of liberal education; it pre-dates the philosophy for children movement in Britain by 20 to 30 years.

Gearon (2014: 41) comments that '[c]ritical philosophical engagement now means the inclusion [in religious education] of religiously sceptical philosophical stances, which, historically and in contemporary context, remain hostile to religion.' The implication of what he says is that such a situation is to be regretted. But is it? Pupils live in a religiously pluralist world and in a society where the truth of the religious is disputed and where criticism of religion is commonplace. They cannot be shielded from debate about such matters. It is important that pupils are aware of challenges to religion and in turn to religious responses. A consideration of such matters need not be interpreted as the unfortunate intrusion of critical philosophical matters into religious education but as an important theme that is relevant to pupils and their cultural situation. There is much more that could be said about this chapter and I have considerable sympathy with some of Gearon's points, particularly when he refers to the way instrumental or external justifications are now so frequently cited as giving credence to the inclusion of religious education in the curriculum. Like him I would want to say that religions are not *principally* focused on producing good citizens or on inculcating liberal morality; they are focused on 'the divine' and the beliefs, values and practices that express commitment to the divine. Not to focus on these is to misrepresent the nature and character of religions and to create the temptation for educators to interpret religion according to the latest educational fashion in order to show its continuing relevance. The subject will be ever seeking a new foundation by which to justify itself.

Religious education and the challenge of holiness

What conclusions does Gearon reach in his final chapter of his review of the influence of the different disciplines he considers? According to him (2014: 149) these disciplines both aim to and have the effect of creating a 'separation of religious education from the religious life' and this has 'entailed, necessitated, a series of alternate epistemological grounds.'

> Thus, philosophical models see the object lesson of religious education to make thinkers and proto-philosophers; sociocultural models see the object lesson of religious education as creating ethnographic, cultural explores; psychological models see the learner as a seeker after personal meaning and fulfilment, 'spiritual with religion'; phenomenological models see the object lesson of religious education as creating a detached observer of religion who is perpetually distanced from it; ever more prevalent political models, emphasizing the public face of religion, see teaching and learning in religious education as concerned with the creation of citizens and even activists; aesthetic models see a role for the arts in religious education, not simply the noting of art in religious contexts but also religious education classrooms as forums, through the expressive arts, for creativity as spirituality, the artist as spiritual seeker. These approaches to religion have been appropriated by religious education and become the epistemological filters through which religion is conceived and the subject justified.
>
> Modern religious education can thus be defined as the search for epistemological grounds within intellectual traditions which rejected the holy, not only as a form of knowledge but as an orientation to life.
>
> *(Gearon 2014: 149)*

> [S]ecular religious education, in mirroring modern secular thought, attempts to maintain the separation of religious education from the religious life, to guard the epistemological border between the holy and the idea of the holy, constantly attempting to ensure that religious education remains critically distanced from the object of study.
>
> *(Gearon 2014: 151)*

Gearon has drawn attention to a feature of British non-confessional religious education that in his opinion seems to compromise the whole enterprise: 'its rejection of the holy.' Does it compromise the whole enterprise? Presumably there are those who regard all religions as false (or as some form of false consciousness) yet acknowledge some justification for religious education and who accept that it could perform useful functions. It might be good to know something about religions as it may help pupils to become more tolerant of those from whom they differ. Perhaps there are positive models of religion or positive forms of religions (while still believing that all religious truth claims are false) that can be employed in the service of creating good citizens. Gearon (2014: 76, his emphasis) regards such aims as reductionist because '(a) they *reduce* [religion] to a category outside of religion, or (b) theorize religion as a function of … reduced terms.' The virtue of Gearon's analysis for those, who in his opinion hold a reductionist view of religion, could be to clarify to them the basis on which they have constructed and justified the practice of religious education. This performs a valuable service and may even cause some to conclude that it provides an inadequate basis and prompt them to think about religion in a different more realistic way that supports internal reasons for its inclusion in the curriculum; there again it may not. Gearon is also saying something stronger than this, though he does not say it directly: religious education justified on external grounds is epistemically insecure and therefore constantly seeking a firm foundation, which it will not be able to find. The subject is only of instrumental value, for it may be that in the future all the functions currently performed by it can be secured in other ways through other curriculum areas. In this sense Gearon seems to endorse the idea that modern religious education is always in crisis—uncertain of its place in the curriculum and of its value. Further interpretive and critical comments will be added after the remainder of the final chapter is summarised.

A long section of the concluding chapter is devoted to illustrating the nature of the religious life through the examples of St. Bernard of Clairvaux (1090–1153),[3] St. Alphonsus Ligouri (1696–1787) and Thérèse of Lisieux (1873–1897). Their focus was on acquiring personal sanctification and salvation: the religious life is about drawing near to God and experiencing his presence and power. This is followed by a section in which Gearon shows how learning and knowledge in Christianity serve the cultivation of holiness, humility and goodness. In his conclusion he (2014: 164) reiterates his thesis that a 'critical distance between the holy and the idea of the holy soon becomes a moral and existential distance from the holy life, between the learned and the holy life.' Gearon leaves the matter here.

His overall interpretation, however, needs further development on two levels. First, much more attention needs to be given to substantiating the determining negative influence (on his interpretation) of the 'adversary' thinkers he considers *over religious education* (and in too many chapters 'advocacy' thinkers are not really considered). Second, it is not enough to say that modern religious education rejects the holy and seeks external, non-religious grounds for its practice. It must be asked what the implications of this are for religious education. What is wrong with this?

In my view there are two serious issues. The first relates to the misrepresentation of religion. Gearon's point is that by cutting itself off from the source of holiness in religions, modern religious education necessarily falsifies the nature of religion and he leaves the matter here. The problem of misrepresentation, however, is more complex than this. Let me clarify and explain. It is not necessary to believe that religions are true (or any one religion to be true), as Gearon believes, to endorse the accusation of misrepresentation. Holiness may be regarded as what religious believers regard as holy. In order to do justice to religions, in the sense of representing them as they are affirmed and practised by religious adherents, education must take seriously their beliefs, values and practices and the different ways these are expressed in communities, in life and in history; this can easily be extended to include in art and architecture, in politics and so on. Attention needs to be given to the founders of religions (where historically relevant), narratives and religious figures that exemplify the values by which religious traditions identify themselves. The temptation (and the temptation may be irresistible) with wholly external justifications of religious education, and this is easily illustrated from English religious education, is that religions are moulded to fit the external justification or justifications that are used to secure their place in the curriculum. If religious education justifies itself (chiefly or exclusively) by an appeal to the production of good citizens, what is regarded as important in religion is what serves this purpose. If religious education justifies itself through an appeal to spirituality then this feature becomes the criterion that determines what is included and excluded from the representation of a religion in the classroom; the temptation is to exclude from religion those aspects that do not fit the inclusive spirituality that is felt to be appropriate to schools. The religions are misrepresented in order to fit the ruling and constantly shifting external justification. The religions are not regarded as important in themselves, they are only important to the extent that they serve the external reasons and justifications on the basis of which they are included in the curriculum. Modern, non-confessional religious education plagiarises religions for secular uses! The strategy may be counter-productive, once religious believers and communities come to realise that what they actually believe and practice is misrepresented on the basis of a criterion or criteria external to the religion. They will become alienated from religious education as taught in schools and seek to establish their own schools or forms of education outside the school where the religion is faithfully represented. In this way, deeper divisions may be created in society.

It is difficult to know if the second issue is a separate issue or an extension of the first. If religions are misrepresented in education on the basis of external justifications, these external justifications are liable to become ideological and overtly political in a negative sense. Exclusively external justifications of religious education create a situation where the state, or the political or academic elite, or the group that has the ability to control and exercise power over the curriculum, uses this to serve its own purposes. In other words, exclusively non-religious justifications of religious education become the means by which different interested groups vie for educational control and power over the curriculum, secure in the awareness that control of knowledge may enable them to perpetuate their interests and commitments in the young. The argument is not that external justifications of religious education ought always to be rejected and resisted, it is that they need to co-exist alongside the (internal) aim of faithfully representing the religions as they are affirmed and understood by adherents.

As noted, Gearon posits a dichotomy between the religious life and attendant efforts to pursue holiness and modern religious education, which in denying the pursuit of holiness effectively denies the nature of religion. This is my statement of the implication of his position. He is not as direct. Gearon concludes with an implied dilemma or dichotomy: either a confessional form of religion that takes the pursuit of holiness seriously or a non-religious form of religious education forever in travail as it seeks a non-existent secular, non-religious foundation. The choice is not so stark. Before attending to this, a further critical question intrudes.

Holiness and the religions

Gearon's book is exclusively concerned with holiness in Christianity; no other religion is discussed. This must be deliberate, but why? We are not told. There are several possible reasons, some more defensible than others. It is possible that he believes that genuine holiness is exemplified exclusively only through Christianity: it alone is true among the religions and resistant to external non-religious interpretations. It is also possible that he believes that more than one religion is true or that all religions are true, or perhaps theistic religions as a distinct category are true. It may be that he follows Otto's interpretation of the religions, after all Otto's position is central to his theorising about religion and about religious education.

In *Das Heilige*, Otto identifies the *a priori category* of the holy, which underlies religious experience and hence is the foundation of all religions, as an irreducible faculty of the human mind. According to him, religion emerges from the inter-relationship between the faculty of the holy and an objective Other, which he calls the *Mysterium Tremendum et Fascinans*. *Mysterium* emphasises that God as the Holy is Wholly Other, unknowable and ineffable. *Tremendum* draws attention to God's majesty and power; and *Fascinans* develops the inter-related themes of fascination and awe. Otto, characteristic of scholars of religion in the early decades of the twentieth century, favoured an evolutionary model of religious development. Accordingly, he uses the three aspects of the holy, combined with religion's rational and non-rational nature, to construct an evolutionary model of the historical development of the religions.

> The degree in which both rational and non-rational elements are jointly present, united in healthy and lovely harmony, affords a criterion to measure the relative and rank of religions—and one, too that is specifically religious. Applying this criterion, we find that Christianity, in this as in other respects, stands out in complete superiority over its sister religions.
>
> *(Otto 1958: 141–142)*

Otto, like Schleiermacher and others in the Liberal Protestant tradition, while according a limited legitimacy to non-Christian religions, typically concluded with Christianity as the highest exemplification of the religious spirit. It may be that Gearon thinks that Catholic Christianity represents the purest form of religion. It is impossible to tell.

These observations do not constitute criticism of Gearon's appeal to the holy, rather it draws attention to a lacuna in his account. It would be helpful if he clarified his understanding of the role of holiness in the religions. Is holiness instantiated elsewhere apart from Christianity? If it is, he will have provided a theoretical theological foundation for confessional religious education according to the different religions and religious traditions. Given that he also regards non-confessional religious education as practised in community schools as educationally compromised (because it is religiously compromised), the implication of his position is that religiously committed parents of all persuasions ought to consider ways of acquiring religiously appropriate confessional education.

Overcoming Gearon's dilemma and securing a place for non-confessional religious education

Gearon's book effectively concludes with a dilemma—Gearon's dilemma: either a confessional form of religion that takes the pursuit of learning and practising holiness seriously or a non-religious form of religious education forever in travail as it seeks a secular, non-religious foundation. In my view the dilemma can be overcome. Non-confessional religious education can be justified as both educationally and religiously appropriate (though cognisance needs to be taken of my earlier argument that it cannot be justified by an appeal to exclusively or mainly external, instrumental reasons). There are three 'planks' or 'movements' in my argument. The first attends to the distinction between reasons and causes; the second to the similarities and differences between insider and outsider accounts of religion and finally, to the way religious language functions in the religious life.

Reasons and causes

Gearon believes that non-religious explanations of religions necessarily compromise their truth and this, he believes, undermines non-confessional religious education. Hence the dilemma (even dichotomy): either confessional religious education that accords truth to religion or non-confessional religious education that effectively falsifies the authentic truth of religion. The critical question is: do non-religious explanations of religions entail their falsehood? If not, then the dilemma may not exist. It is not an either/or situation that corresponds to a choice between truth or falsehood. One of the 'adversaries' of religion that Gearon (2014: 77–82) considers in detail (in Chapter 3 entitled, 'Psychology, spirituality and religious education') is Sigmund Freud and to contextualise the argument, Gearon's discussion of Freud will be used as a foil for my critique, which follows my summary of the latter's position.

There is scholarly debate on *the nature of* Freud's critique of religion even though there is little debate about its character as a critique. It is not necessary in this context to explore things all that deeply and only a broad, chiefly uncontroversial outline of his position need be discussed. In popular writing, Freud, the father of psycho-analysis, is typically equated with the view that belief in God *is nothing more than* an unconscious projection onto the universe of the human need for a father figure who will be more reliable and faithful than the earthly figure that nature provides. This projection occurs and grows in strength in unison with recognition that our earthly fathers lack the 'powers' and competences that as children are typically accredited to them.

> Psycho-analysis has made us familiar with the intimate connection between the father-complex and belief in God; it has shown us that a personal God is, psychologically, nothing more than an exalted father, and it brings us evidence every day of how young people lose their religious beliefs as soon as their father's authority breaks down. Thus we recognize that the roots of the need for religion are in the parental complex; the almighty and just God, and kindly nature, appear to us as grand sublimations of father and mother.
>
> *(Freud 1957, vol. XI: 123)*

In his two major works on religion—*Totem and Taboo* (1913) and *The Future of an Illusion* (1927)—Freud makes it clear that religious ideas are illusions and projections. He (Freud 1957, vol. XXI: 33) avers that nothing more need be said in favour of religion once we have identified its origins in the human, often unconscious operations of the psyche.

> To assess the truth-value of religious doctrines does not lie within the scope of the present [psychological/psycho-analytic] enquiry. It is enough for us that we have recognized them as being, in their psychological nature, illusions... . We shall tell ourselves that it would be very nice if there were a God who created the world and was a benevolent Providence, and if there were a moral order in the universe and an after-life; but it is a very striking fact that all of this is exactly as we are bound to wish it to be.

Religion is a wish-fulfilment. Gearon (2014: 81), who quotes the last sentence from this extract, states that, according to Freud, '[w]e need an "education to reality," one that rids us of religious illusion. Religion and education are contradictory.' Has Freud shown that religious beliefs have no basis in reality? He has not. Freud has presented a causal account of the origins of religious belief in God, which he takes to undermine religion. The problem is that one would be entitled to draw this conclusion only if there are good reasons to believe that the causes Freud adduces (or any other purported natural causes), when taken alone, i.e. in the absence (among other things) of any divine activity, produce belief in God or more accurately, the experiences that lead to belief in God. As the philosopher,

William Wainwright (1981: 72) notes: 'Without a disproof of the existence of God and other supra-empirical causes, it is totally unclear how we would ever know that this was the case', i.e. that the non-religious explanation alone was sufficient of itself to explain belief in God and that on this basis alone it can be asserted that God does not exist. John Gaskin, who is a perceptive critic of religion (see Gaskin 1987) acknowledges the point. Naturalistic explanations of religion of the kind developed by Freud and others fail to appreciate that causal accounts of religion need not necessarily detract from the truth of religions.

> I say again: to show that there are causes of a belief—psychological or environmental factors which predispose the person to hold the belief—is not *in itself* sufficient to show that the belief is irrational. It has also to be shown, either that the believer has no reasons for his belief, or that he is going to stick to his belief quite apart from what he alleges to be his reason for holding it.
>
> *(Gaskin 1984: 29; author's emphasis)*[4]

Causal accounts of religion of the kind pursued by psychologists, sociologists and more recently that of cognitive scientists of religion are of little or no relevance to assessment of the truth of religion unless they are complemented by valid and sound arguments that disprove and undermine the reasons for religious belief. Psychological or sociological causes may be the mechanism that God uses, as part of his design plan to generate human belief in himself (see Plantinga 2000). That belief in God arises through entirely natural means tells us almost nothing about its rationality or truth. There are probably many causes for belief in God or in the beliefs of the different religions, but this fact alone does not explain away religious beliefs for which reasons are also offered. We may come naturally to believe in God or have a propensity to belief in God; to discover their cause does not discredit religious belief as Gearon assumes. Such knowledge may illuminate how and why people acquire religious beliefs—an interesting subject—what it does not do is (necessarily) detract from the truth of religious beliefs.

Insider and outsider accounts of religion

It is not unusual for scholars of religion to distinguish between insider and outsider interpretations of religion. One can appreciate why this comes about: an insider will have a different perspective on religion than an outsider. A strong form of this thesis seems to be implicit in Gearon's thesis that an acknowledgement of the truth of religion (in his case Christianity) is necessary for a proper interpretation and orientation to the nature of religion, whereas an adversarial account fails to capture the nature of religion; if it is not implicit then at least it is consistent with his position. At this point it would seem there is again a dichotomy between insider and outsider accounts of religion. This is the view of Rudolf Otto, which provides the theological and philosophical foundation for Gearon's analysis of modern religious education. Otto (1958: 7) held that religious experience is rooted in a 'numinous' state of mind.

This mental state is perfectly *sui generis* and irreducible to any other ... it cannot be strictly defined. There is only one way to help another to an understanding of it. He must be guided and led on ... through the ways of his own mind until he reaches the point at which 'the numinous' in him perforce begins to stir, to start into life and into consciousness.... . In other words, our X cannot, strictly speaking, be taught, it can only be evoked, awakened in the mind... .

On this view, insiders have privileged knowledge unavailable to outsiders. In considering this position we may begin with a reasonably modest critical observation. Although Otto can postulate a sharp separation between believers with privileged religious knowledge and non-believers without such access this does not effectively capture the actual situation of many religious believers and non-believers. There are gradations of knowledge and belief in relation to religion: from absolute certainty of religious knowledge avowed by some to tentative religious belief to tentative unbelief and to an absolute denial of religious knowledge. To complicate matters further, people vary not just in the degree of assent they express toward religion but also in the content of what is believed. One may profess to being Christian and believe in God but be unsure about the triune nature of God or be unsure about life after death. One might be a Muslim, yet entertain doubts about certain teachings in the Qur'an, say the eternal damnation of unbelievers. The relevance of these observations is that the difference between insiders and outsiders is not absolute: one can be an insider in certain respects and an outsider in certain respects as regarding both the degree of assent that is expressed toward certain beliefs and in the doctrines to which one gives assent. In fact these observations challenge any simple distinction between insiders and outsiders. Basically, because religious belief is not an all-or-nothing affair (the same point extends to religious practices) so a sharp distinction cannot be drawn between religious commitment and non-religious commitment and by extension between (full) religious understanding of the beliefs to which assent is given and no religious understanding. To express things this way actually raises a further complication for supposing there is a dichotomy between insider and outsider accounts of religion.

Can it be assumed that those who assent to religious doctrines understand them in a qualitatively better way than those who do not? Do all religious believers understand religious beliefs better than non-religious observers or enquirers? I think a negative answer has to be given to these questions. This is because if the questions are answered positively, it would seem to close off the possibility that non-believers can come to an understanding of a religion that would move them to convert to it. Surely the opposite is the case, prior knowledge and understanding of a religion is necessary before one commits oneself to it. Is it not more plausible to draw a distinction between 'knowledge of ...' and 'knowledge about ...' and to regard the former as involving some kind of commitment based on understanding and the latter as involving only understanding?

It may also be asked what kind of knowledge it is that religious believers have and non-believers do not possess. The answer of Otto, Gearon and others is that they possess experiential knowledge of religion. What exactly is the extent of this experiential knowledge (even if genuine), say in the case of Christianity, for example? In a strict sense they have not experienced events in the life of Christ (his ministry, miracles, death or his resurrection), since these were confined to the first century CE; equally they have not experienced the after-life and the events associated with it. Much of what the Christian believes goes beyond what one directly experiences and is believed on the basis of a (purported) revelation in the Bible or on the basis of the teachings of the church. Even certain statements that Christians use to describe their experience, say that one is justified by grace through faith in Christ, are not directly experienced within the self but are a consequence of adopting Christian faith and regulating one's language and expression according to Christian doctrines that are taught in the Bible and in the Christian community. The Christian adopts the 'grammatical' rules (in Wittgenstein's sense of 'theology as grammar') that govern what can and cannot be said meaningfully within the context of Christian commitment. These rules are learnt within the Christian community, yet equally they can be learnt by others who familiarise themselves with the public religious sources of Christianity. There is much more that could be added to this analysis. The point is that direct experience of God, say in the form of numinous encounter, provides limited content for Christianity or for any religion. The full content of a religion cannot be extrapolated from direct encounters with God and what is not attributable to direct experience is learnt and derived for other sources, say that of the Bible or some other revealed source: the content of these sources can be studied and considered by non-believers as well as believers, critics as well as 'caretakers' (to use Russell McCutcheon's phrase, 2001) and more relevantly to present concerns, by both religious and non-religious pupils. The distinction between insiders and outsiders is not absolute.

A post-Wittgensteinian perspective on the philosophy of language

The source of Gearon's dichotomy between faithfully representing the necessarily self-involving nature of religion and unfaithful, non-religious representations is Rudolf Otto's distinction between the non-rational and the rational aspects of the holy, which can equally be expressed as the distinction between conceptual and non-conceptual aspects of the holy. Can the fundamental distinction be maintained? Reasons have already been advanced that question its plausibility: it is now appropriate to challenge it directly.

Otto assumes that one can distinguish between feeling or awareness and thought, and that although both are categories of knowledge, only the latter is conceptual in form. Yet feeling for Otto has an object: in religious feeling this object is the holy. Thus one feels the holy, knows the holy, but one does not have conceptual knowledge of the holy. As he says the holy 'can be firmly grasped, thoroughly understood, and profoundly appreciated, purely in, with, and from the feeling itself' (Otto 1958: 34). He postulates the idea of a domain of experience, independent of the formative activity of the mind in applying concepts, in which there is direct contact with a reality which transcends the human self.

Can there be experience of an external object, as the holy is believed to be, an experience in which you learn something about the object (should it only be its existence), which does not involve conceptual understanding? Otto writes in places as if religious feelings can be isolated from religious concepts without loss of meaning. This is not philosophically defensible. If the feeling of the holy is intentional, then it cannot be specified apart from reference to its object, and thus it cannot be independent of thought. One difficulty for Otto is that religious experience cannot be specified without reference to the holy: experience without reference to the holy is not religious experience. In addition, this reference to the holy also requires, or presupposes, that the feeling, the religious feeling, is the result of divine operation; without this judgement the experience again remains without religious import. (There is no problem with having an experience of x in which you know nothing about x and learn nothing about x in the process, even the existence of x.) To invoke the holy as the cause of experience/feeling is to employ concepts, and quite complex concepts at that, such as the concept of divine agency, the notion of an invisible, powerful, personal spirit, etc. The criteria for identifying religious experience include reference not only to concepts but also to a specific belief about how the experience is to be explained. Explanation and thus conceptual understanding determine experience from the outset.

The essential critical point, based on a post-Wittgensteinian perspective on the nature of language, is that there is (necessarily) a public element to all experiences because language and the concepts that are expressed through language are acquired within a community of language users. Language is public. Beliefs enter into experience and condition experience. Beliefs, as expressed through language and concepts, can be discussed and considered; analysed, reflected upon and criticised. 'The recognition, description, and even qualitative feel of an experience are now recognized to be dependent, to a greater or lesser extent, on the language and concepts one has available' (Murphy 2018: 110). One does not need to share a belief in order to understand what it means and how it is applied; this because beliefs are expressed in a public language. Once this is appreciated there is no insuperable reason why non-believers cannot gain knowledge and understanding of the uses of religious language by religious believers. They too can learn the concepts and come to appreciate the rules that govern religious uses of language, chiefly the beliefs and doctrines that are central to religions. This does not remove the distinction between believer and non-believer, only that it cannot be framed in dichotomous terms, as if one has knowledge and understanding and the other not; in the case of Christianity, it is a distinction between someone who trusts in God, who expresses commitment to certain religious beliefs and who follows the practices of a religion; and someone who has knowledge and understanding of the beliefs and practices of Christianity but does not have faith in God.

An appreciation of these three arguments constitutes a compelling case against the thesis that only religious believers understand their own religion, but not non-believers, and the associated conclusion derived from it by Gearon that confessional religious education alone preserves the integrity of religion and the religious form of life. Non-confessional religious education can faithfully represent the nature of religion to pupils and there is much to be gained educationally and socially in pursuit of this. The dilemma of having to choose between either confessional or non-confessional religious education is not required; both are educationally legitimate in their own ways and both can contribute to a truly liberal form of education.

I have been critical of Gearon's *On Holy Ground: The theory and practice of religious education* (2014) at numerous points and this may disguise the fact that there is much to be admired in it. It is a serious, academic work that pursues a perspective on religious education that contrasts with the bland and often intellectually superficial character of much that is written on the subject. At a time when many of those who respond to the ongoing crisis in religious education feel required to undermine confessionalism and religious nurture in education, it is provocative to consider a contribution that avers the opposite and questions the educational legitimacy of non-confessional religious education.

Notes

1   'An enquiry into the non-rational factor of the idea of the divine and its relation to the rational'.
2   I am overlooking the anachronism of retrospectively applying the term philosophy and philosopher in anything like our modern sense much before the eighteenth century— other designations and descriptions would have been used historically to distinguish between what we know on the basis of 'reason alone', following Kant, from that of 'revelation' or between that of 'the natural light of understanding' and that of 'sacred doctrine'.
3   While acknowledging Bernard of Clairvaux's *On Loving God* (2014 [originally composed between 1126 and 1141]) is an important spiritual text, it is difficult to overlook, as Gearon does, his support for the Second Crusade and his call to kill Muslims in the cause of Christ, an aspect of his life and thought that is virtually overlooked by historical theologians and biographers.
4   I have drawn on Professor Gaskin's (1984: 31–36) discussion of Freud, in acknowledgement of his influence over my writing and thinking as my former post-graduate tutor in Philosophy at Trinity College, Dublin.

10

TOWARDS THE FUTURE

The aim of this book has been to identify the weaknesses in contemporary English religious education and to review the most important responses that claim to provide the resources in terms of policy and reforms to overcome them. Recent admission of a crisis within the subject served as a focus for analysis and discussion. This approach may be characterised as a 'second order' activity, for no attempt has been made to add to, or to offer solutions. My task has been to review the arguments of others and to test their strength and relevance. This does not mean that I have been a neutral observer and commentator—neutral certainly in the sense that no grand solutions of my own are offered—yet the exposure of weak arguments and unconvincing appeals to evidence, does not, in Wittgensteinian parlance (1958: 49, §124), 'leave everything as it is'. An argument that fails to convince entails that its conclusion is less well supported or not supported at all; a position that requires evidence where none is provided ought to be rejected. By contrast, a flawed critique of an existing practice leaves that practice more secure, and so on. For example, if the case for compulsory religious education for all pupils, without exception, lacks argumentative and evidential support (as it does), it follows that the existing right of parental withdrawal is accordingly strengthened. One has to be circumspect here: *perhaps* some of the reforms and positions rejected in earlier chapters would improve the quality of religious education, if endorsed. The problem is that at present the arguments and evidence adduced in their favour fall short and fail to convince. An example of this is the issue of the extension of religious education to incorporate secular, non-religious worldviews, which is considered in Chapters 5 and 6.

In Chapter 1 it was noted how there needs to be a correlation between what are identified as weaknesses and what is offered in response to them. In simple terms responses, to be adequate, never mind convincing, must relate to the weaknesses. Judged by this simple criterion some of the responses to the current crisis are almost totally irrelevant. Some are clearly ideological, some opportunistic and some intellectually shallow. Most responses are unconvincing. Moreover, the history of non-confessional religious education shows all too clearly that policies, pedagogies and practices that commanded broad support among influential religious educators and those who profess to speak on behalf of the profession have contributed significantly to the creation of the current crisis. What has emerged from our review is that perceptions of what is wrong not only differ widely, but often seem to be manufactured to suit pre-conceived solutions. The weaknesses become infinitely malleable to suit the ideological agenda of the writer. One could continue with this line of observation but for those who have followed my argument so far, reiteration is unnecessary. The invitation exists for those who disagree with my analysis and critique to engage in dialogue and show the points at which my argument is weak or unconvincing.

If reiterating the conclusions of previous chapters is not here pursued, then what remains to be said? Although the focus has been on responses to identified weaknesses in English religious education, the material covered can be conceptualised in a different way; that is, as providing an overview of recent contributions and writings within the field of religious education by some of its most prominent advocates and by those who view religious education as having the potential to contribute something important to the aims of liberal education in a pluralist, democratic state. The question then arises what does this overview reveal about the research priorities and interests of religious educators, and about the assumptions and the values that guide their research and theorising. There is a degree of philosophical sophistication in some of the contributions considered in earlier chapters and there is an overall commitment to improvement and progress, and in some cases a willingness to re-consider 'conservative' assumptions and beliefs that are regarded as constitutive of non-confessional religious education. The positive features are obvious; what are less obvious and infrequently the subject of identification and analysis are the weaknesses and lacunas in writings and research on English religious education. What does our overview reveal? An identification of weakness at this point is clearly relevant to the broader subject of the weaknesses of religious education as a school subject, i.e., as it is practised in schools, for the school subject is configured and conditioned by its theoretical and practical commitments, and these reflect academic and scholarly opinion. No serious consideration of weaknesses in religious education can afford to overlook the culpability of the research community and those who contribute to public debates about religious education. What do responses to weaknesses reveal about the current 'state' of research in English religious education?

Historical consciousness: A case of amnesia

One of the most striking features of our review of recent writings on the travail of contemporary English religious education is its lack of historical orientation. This is most obvious in the work of the RE Commission Report (2018), in the 2013 RE

Review document (both emanating from the RE Council) and in Butler-Sloss's Commission Report (2018), though it is not confined to them. There is only limited appreciation by some religious educators of the beliefs and commitments that have determined the character of non-confessional religious education, apart from its non-confessional nature. Part of the problem is that because of a lack of acquaintance with the history of English religious education, or perhaps because it is (ideologically) convenient, the crisis in religious education is regarded as recent; consequently, there is no need to look back beyond the last 10 years or so. This view is not credible, as was shown in Chapter 1, through interaction and discussion of a range of reliable sources. There is abundant evidence to show that the weaknesses in English religious education are systemic and historically extended. It is uncritical to divorce the current ills that beset religious education from its history and instead look to recent political decisions as wholly responsible. This is where the views of Chater and Erricker (considered in Chapter 2) and that of Gearon (considered in Chapter 9) have value as serious contributions to the current debate. These writers, whatever weaknesses there are in their positions, cannot be accused of not engaging critically with the history of religious education.

By engagement with history is not meant simply recited the standard historical facts about how one movement succeeded another, or providing an account that confines itself to a review of the relevant legislation, non-statutory documents and 'circulars' (as in Brown 2002) or recounting the work of a few prominent and influential 'great men', say Ninian Smart and John Hull. Religious educators need to become familiar with the beliefs, commitments and interests that have shaped the form and character of non-confessional religious education and the aporias that have on occasions resulted—it is not a story of rational progress or unmitigated success, as the Whig version of religious education would have us believe. This may be the 'received' narrative that is rehearsed in uncritical texts and passed on to unsuspecting students as they are inducted into the subject, but it cannot be sustained intellectually. The impression is given that weaknesses in religious education can always be attributed to non-specialists or to government interference: if only religious educators could gain complete responsibility for the future of the subject all would be well. The reality is that those who are most vociferous in their call for religious educators to have exclusive control of the subject often mean by this some small interest group, of which they are a member, parading itself as representative of all, that aims to gain power and control.

It may be helpful to illustrate the kind of critical history that is needed by religious educators in order to understand the current crisis by drawing an analogy with the shift of perspective that has occurred in moral philosophy over the same period as the emergence of non-confessional religious education in the 1970s and its history up to the present. If one familiarises oneself with many of the texts in moral philosophy written in the late 1950s, 1960s and 1970s, what is now obvious with hindsight is that they lack a historical perspective. An excellent example of this is Nowell-Smith's *Ethics* (1954, and subsequent editions, up to 1969). Under the influence of some aspects of the philosophy of language, mainly that of 'ordinary-language' philosophy, moral philosophy became fixated on linguistic usage and the analysis of concepts: it was believed that substantive moral conclusions could be generated by attention to the way moral terms are used in a 'natural' language. Alongside this was a disparagement of the work of earlier thinkers who grounded morality and practice in metaphysical theories about what was ultimately real. This whole 'ahistorical' tradition of moral philosophy was challenged in 1981 with the publication of Alasdair MacIntyre's *After Virtue: A study in moral theory* (and arguably anticipated by Elizabeth Anscombe in 1958).

There is a range of statements that could be made about MacIntyre's position: negatively, he wanted to show that modern moral philosophy was deeply conflicted because it combined fragments of opposing philosophies from the past; positively, he wanted to revive a (teleological) neo-Aristotelian account of the good that would ground and sustain a set of virtues. What is relevant to our concerns is that he showed that ideas and concepts are historically and theoretically conditioned. In *After Virtue* (1985; 1st edition, 1981) MacIntyre identified two rival 'traditions' of moral thought and reasoning; two opposing traditions of beliefs and customs, practices, attitudes and institutions, one going all the way back to Homer, the other firmly rooted in Enlightenment rationalism. In his view the Enlightenment tradition of morality lacked the intellectual resources to overcome the problems that it generated internally.

The important point in this context is that MacIntyre's writings underlined the historical nature of moral philosophising and the conclusions reached: ideas are embedded in traditions of thoughts and become meaningful within particular traditions of thought. His writings stimulated and encouraged a new historico-critical, narrative approach to moral and philosophical issues (it also rehabilitated the relevance of metaphysical commitments to moral theorising). His historical approach to moral philosophy and ethics was corroborated and continued by Charles Taylor. In *Sources of the Self* (1989: 3), he similarly identified the narrow focus of contemporary moral philosophy and wrote of its failure to appreciate the historically evolving nature of our 'modern identity': 'you cannot get very clear about ["what it is to be a human agent, a person, or a self"] without some further understanding of how our pictures of the good *have evolved*' (1989: 3; my emphasis). Like MacIntyre, Taylor recognised that contemporary moral theorising and the problems that beset it are the result of the influence of historically extended traditions of thought, in which certain ideas come to be influential, and these, in turn, generate weaknesses and problems that are difficult to overcome with the intellectual resources internal to a tradition. From a Continental philosophical perspective, the work of Foucault and others reinforced the same broad historical ('genealogical', following Nietzsche) orientation to beliefs and, in Foucault's case particularly, to the relationship between institutions, claims to knowledge and power.

Applying these insights to religious education indicates that efforts to overcome current weaknesses on a serial, piecemeal basis will inevitably fail, because some of these weaknesses are in part generated by the historical influence of beliefs and commitments that have shaped and continue to shape its form and practice. It is necessary to trace weaknesses back to their origin in particular theories and commitments. It is too simplistic to think that current weaknesses can be overcome by extending the curriculum to include more religions and worldviews, or that a nationally enforced syllabus will improve matters. The weaknesses are too many and too serious to be resolved in this way. What is needed is a critical, reflexive appreciation of the post-confessional history of religious education and the ways in which its shifting beliefs and underlying assumptions have contributed both to its strengths and to its weaknesses.

Ideology

The term 'ideology' is used in different ways (see Eagleton 2007: 1–31), consequently it is necessary to review some of these meanings before progressing to identify the ways in which ideology and its cognates are appropriately used in English religious education. Most modern interpretations begin (as in Freeden 2003: 5–11) with the views of Karl Marx (1818–1883), and although there is development in his position (see McLellan 1973), his later thought identified ideology with 'false consciousness' (ideas), which results from the failure to appreciate that social and political reality are determined by the means of production (see Bhikhu 1982). This represents a development of his earlier interpretation in *The German Ideology* (1965 [1845]) that equated ideology with any account of ideas that overlooked their origin in historical and social reality. Marx contrasted ideology with genuine science (as do 'orthodox' Marxists), for it was his science of history (*Wissenschaft der Geschichte*) that he believed revealed the connection between forms of consciousness and the material means of production; thus science contrasts with ideology—hence Marx's self-description of his position as 'historical materialism' or the 'materialist conception of history'. Later writers both developed and extended Marx's account in different ways (see Bottomore 1981). Some use the term to describe the way in which social reality simply reflects material interests; others have revived the usage that existed before Marx in which ideology denotes comprehensive political doctrines, such as Socialism, or Liberalism or Conservationism. There is another stream of interpretation that thinks of ideology as an expression of ideas in their capacity as vehicles of gaining and maintaining power and control: 'ideology is a site of "power relations"' (Jakobsen 1996: 148). The focus is not on the truth of ideas and beliefs or the evidence that is used to support them, but on their role in creating and consolidated social significance and influence. John B. Thompson (1984: 4) has written that 'to study ideology... is to study the ways in which meaning (or significance) serves to sustain relations of domination'. It is this interpretation, which in recent times has been taken up and developed by a succession of post-structuralist philosophers (albeit on more sophisticated interpretations of the basic concept than is expressed and used here) that will inform our discussion.

The obvious starting for a discussion of ideology in relation to the sources we have reviewed is the RE Commission's *Religion and Worldviews: The way forward* (2018). The RE Commission was the creation of the Religious Education Council of England and Wales and as noted in the Introduction it was also one of the first organisations to speak explicitly of a 'crisis' in religious education. Its considered response to this crisis, in the RE Commission Report (2018: 14), counsels that 'a national body of a maximum of nine professionals' be appointed 'by the DfE on the basis of recommendations from the Religious Education Council of England and Wales'. 'Members of the national body should be appointed on the basis of commitment to the approach taken to Religion and Worldviews in the National Entitlement', i.e., the form of religious education prescribed by the Commission. Let us analyse this response: the RE Council identifies a crisis in religious education; it commissions a report to make recommendations on how to overcome the crisis; the Report recommends that the RE Council is given sole rights of appointment to those who are given responsibility for introducing the new proposed statutory national curriculum for religious education of the form that the report recommends; those appointed must approve of the 'approach taken to Religion and Worldviews' that the Commission Report recommends. When set out in this way it is impossible not to regard the RE Council's position as ideological. The RE Council wants to gain control of religious education in the first instance from local agreed syllabus committees and secondly, from the Department of Education, which will then fulfil the minor role of funding and presumably servicing the new RE Council appointed 'national body of experts'.

One is tempted to leave these observations without further comment, for it is impossible not to view the recommendations of the RE Council as anything but self-serving and an attempt to gain power and control over the future direction and provision of religious education. It may be pointed out that the RE Council's view that pupils in school ought to be exposed to the greatest degree of diversity of beliefs and worldviews possible within the context of schooling is not matched by an openness to any diversity of views on the nature and future direction of religious education; only those who agree with the proposals of the RE Council deserve inclusion in the committee of experts. The Council does not contemplate the possibility of creative differences being overcome by new syntheses, or of different viewpoints coming together to create new possibilities for learning and teaching. 'In preparing for adult life', we are told (2018: 29) children and young people 'need to learn to respond well to a local, national and global landscape of religion and belief diversity'; presumably the need to learn to 'respond well' to the diversity of views among religious educators about its future is not required. What makes the Religious Education Council's position ideological is not the fact that it makes proposals about the future direction religious education should take or that little evidence is adduced for its 'reforms', it is that it aims to ensure that its proposals and ideas alone are instantiated, and to achieve this it wants to appropriate to itself the mechanisms of appointment and control over any body that is charged with introducing reforms; basically it wants to ensure there is no debate or possibility of dialogue with critics over its proposals.

Ideology, construed as ideas and beliefs that are used to pursue or consolidate social control, power and influence over institutions and organisations, and ultimately over other people, is not, as already noted, chiefly concerned with issues of truth and evidence, though these remain subsidiary issues in some interpretations (see Levine 2007: 92–96). Truth and evidence are important in themselves, however, whatever importance they are granted within the subject of ideology, and this section will conclude with some brief comments on their role in some of the writings and publications reviewed in earlier chapters. The first comment is of a negative nature. Very few of the writings considered give any real attention to matters of justification and evidence. This is particularly the case with regard to quasi-official publications such as the Religious Education Council of England and Wales's *Review of Religious Education in England* (2013), the Commission on Religious Education's *Final Report: Religions and Worldviews: The way forward* (2018), and Butler-Sloss's report, *Living with Difference: Community, diversity and the common good* (2015). The assumption seems to be that eminent intellectuals and experts have considered the issues and these are the conclusions that all should endorse, given they have been produced by a team of 'experts'. In some cases a minimalist justification is given, as when the Commission Report affirms that in order to learn how to respond well to diversity it is necessary to study a wide range of religions and secular worldviews (2018: 29). But there needs to be an argument that connects learning how to respond well to diversity, which presumably includes learning how to respect other people and their beliefs and practices and to challenge bigotry, and the conclusion that familiarity with a large number of religions and worldviews will achieve this. Equally, there needs to an argument to show that an 'objective' statutory, national curriculum of the form Butler-Sloss recommends, will obviate the need for a parental right of withdrawal or that the case for 'objectivity' in religious education somehow undermines the credibility and legitimacy of religious nurture, however attenuated, in schools, which is also the view of Butler-Sloss. In all these cases assertions are made and conclusions reached without any real attention given to their justification or to relevant evidence. Talking about evidence and justification in religious education relates to the sources of these in relevant research and academic writings, and to this we now turn.

Research and debate

Elements of Professor Schweitzer's review and critique of the 2018 RE Commission Report have already been quoted. In this further extract he raises a criticism that will obviously embarrass the 'experts' who produced the report:

> It is another international tendency that evaluations of a subject should not only be based on school inspection or subjective anecdotal evidence but

should more and more rely on transparent and intersubjective investigations and scientific data. While the Report claims to be based on research, this research is not really identified (which, of course, may be explained by the genre of such statements). Yet unfortunately, the Report also does not foresee a serious role for research concerning the future development of the subject.

As mentioned above, such research has remained particularly rare in Britain. … [T]his might indeed be part of the reasons for the deplorable situation of Religious Education described and criticised by the Report. If this holds true one may wonder why this should not also be changed in the future, quite independently of the designation and scope of the subject. Good teaching should be informed by research. Good school inspection needs to have a scientific basis it can rely upon.

(Schweitzer 2018: 521)

Schweitzer is diplomatic in his comments about the lack of reference to research in the RE Commission Report both to its failure to specify the research findings on which its conclusions are based and to its failure to recommend 'a serious role for research concerning the future development of the subject'. There is the possibility that his comments can be interpreted more negatively, particularly his comment that 'evaluations of a subject should not only be based on school inspection or subjective anecdotal evidence but should more and more rely on transparent and intersubjective investigations and scientific data'. There is more here than the suggestion that the RE Commission Report is not sufficiently based on empirical research.

Schweitzer has drawn attention to one of the most serious criticisms of current theory and practice in English religious education, a criticism that should be apparent to readers of earlier chapters—it does not engage sufficiently with research findings (where there are such), or enter into dialogue with critical literature that questions current fashions and ideas. The various reports, initiated by the Religious Education Council, Butler-Sloss's Report and Clark and Woodhead's *A New Settlement: Religion and belief in schools* (2015 and 2018), almost entirely omit any reference to scholarly literature or research findings on religious education, and completely ignore criticisms that have already been raised about some of the positions advanced. Assertions and recommendations are made without any acknowledgement of their source and justification or basis in empirical research, evidence or critical argument. One is tempted to reach the conclusion that some of the positions advanced are based on what Schweitzer refers to as 'subjective anecdotal evidence'. In our consideration of case after case in earlier chapters it has been shown that there isn't any serious attempt to address identified weaknesses in English religious education or to justify responses: weaknesses are either reinterpreted to fit in with an already accepted solution or neglected in whole or in part.

It is on this basis that it can be confidently concluded that none of the suggested efforts to overcome the weaknesses are likely to be wholly successful. This is because the kinds of radical solutions that could work challenge too many 'hallowed' assumptions and would require a more critical, reflexive attitude to the beliefs and commitments that have shaped and continue to shape current theory and practice.

For the most part, critical debates that characterise other disciplines and fields of study are largely absent from religious education, yet it is through such debates that genuine progress can be made. There is a range of factors that inhibit debate in British religious education, particularly debate and criticism of current policy and theory. First, there is a perception of the precarious position of religious education in the curriculum (as not part of the national curriculum), and that internal criticism and debate may be used politically to undermine its compulsory status. Second, the pool of researchers and academics that publish on religious education is small. This, coupled with emphasis upon increasing specialisation in academic writing and the wide range of themes and subjects relevant to religious education, means that few are qualified to contribute to thematically specific debates and even fewer are willing and equipped to engage in broad-ranging discussions about the nature and future of religious education. A further implication of the small number of active researchers is that through attendance at national and regional conferences and meetings of professional associations most are known to each other and this may act as a deterrent for some researchers and writers to engage critically with their peers. At the human level it is more demanding professionally and emotionally to criticise the views of individuals with whom you are familiar and encounter on a regular professional (and sometimes social) basis. Some researchers may also be reluctant to criticise openly the position of others who have been influential in framing policy or who enjoy professional esteem and status on the basis of their position and past contributions: these may be the same people who act as advisors to grant-awarding bodies, to promotion boards and to influential committees and associations that represent religious educators. Finally, there is the possible fear that by voicing criticism of aspects of non-confessional religious education, somehow support is given to confessional religious education, which will be exploited by religiously conservative groups and individuals. The logic of this is not convincing, yet it does seem to be a factor in peremptorily dismissing criticism of the status quo by some.

Expertise

Who are the experts in religious education and how are they identified? The question is prompted by the RE Commission Report's conclusion that only experts appointed on its recommendation should be included in the small national body that it believes should determine the religious education curriculum for all schools in the future. Those so appointed, will have (ought to have), we are told, proven expertise in some or all of the following:

  i. specialist knowledge of Religion and Worldviews with both research and classroom experience

  ii. curriculum development, within or beyond Religion and Worldviews

  iii. initial teacher education or continuing professional development of teachers

  iv. current or recent classroom experience in either primary or secondary phases.

(Commission on Religious Education 2018: 14)

Clearly on this understanding, there are different routes to expertise in religious education; this is how it should be. It would be profitable to discuss the criteria used by the RE Council to identify expertise. There are some interesting and controversial aspects of their criteria. For example, 'specialist knowledge', we are told, must be sufficiently extensive to include that of religion and of secular worldviews—an ambitious requirement. In addition, those with specialist knowledge must have both engaged in research and have classroom experience (presumably this means classroom experience *in schools*). This, however, is not my main interest, for while it is important to have some idea what constitutes expertise and how it is formally identified in religious education, the important issue focuses on the results achieved by 'so-called' experts—on outcomes (while not disputing that 'means' and 'ends' are connected). I have added the term 'so-called' precisely to draw attention to the fact that experts frequently get it wrong, as well as frequently disagreeing with each other—in a number of points in earlier chapters criticisms have been raised against the arguments and commitments of the RE Commission's Final Report, *Religions and Worldviews: The way forward: A national plan for religious education* (2018), a report produced, we are informed, by experts. We live in an age when many legitimately claim expertise, while not all deserve this accolade. Experts can be found to support almost any position imaginable. This does not entail that the accolade of expert is redundant, though it is an accolade better applied by others than accredited to oneself.

The appeal to expertise can be construed in a negative sense as simply an appeal to authority and as we have identified in earlier chapters such appeals in religious education are frequently ideological, mistaken or even question-begging. John G. Stackhouse (2014: 197) has pointed out that 'even communities that pride themselves on their supposed ability to regard persons and ideas critically and without prejudice—demonstrate the common human trait of confusing status with worthiness'. A claim to expertise increasingly provides little assurance that well justified arguments and conclusions will result. One of the challenges that has also emerged recently is that committees comprised of experts are often obliged to satisfy the unstated rules of political correctness and to be inclusive in their membership, say in terms of gender, sexuality, race, religion, and so on, and such criteria can compromise to some extent the overall level of expertise that is available. There is also the possibility that experts are sometimes included in certain committees, in part, on the basis that they are already predisposed to agree with anticipated conclusions, or at least on the understanding that they will not openly disagree. Perhaps the level of expertise available to committees has always been compromised, for one reason or another. As Stackhouse (2014: 198) also states 'let us be careful not to restrict the idea of "possessing authoritative information and judgment" to the higher social classes—or to people of a certain age, sex, and so on'.

The problem of expertise in religious education is particularly acute, as there are so few who are qualified and have the necessary experience to be regarded as experts. Whereas many universities have departments of theology and/or religious studies that are well resourced and staffed, there may be one or perhaps two individuals concerned with religious education situated in education departments (or 'Schools of education'). These individuals, as well as teaching and lecturing, will typically be required to supervise students on their pre-service teaching experience, thus reducing time for research and writing. It would be interesting to conduct a survey to find out what percentage of (the small pool of) university lecturers in religious education publish articles in international peer-reviewed journals or write academic books compared to lecturers in theology and religious studies—my initial and unscientific perception (and it would need to be confirmed by an appeal to evidence) is that in research terms professional religious educators who work in higher education are much less research active than university colleagues who specialise in theology or in religious studies. Twenty years ago, Denise Cush (1999: 42) characterised the relationship of religious education to religious studies as that of 'little sister' to 'big brother'; the characterisation still has merit.

It is experts who often stand in the way of genuine progress in a discipline or area of study, for experts are inducted into 'conservative' ways of thinking about their areas of expertise and to think in terms of the ruling intellectual model or paradigm. Radical new ideas challenge established traditions of thought and the status and power achieved by those who regard themselves as experts and who receive academic, social or political acclaim as so identified. Thomas Kuhn in *The Structure of Scientific Revolutions* (1970) spoke of 'normal science', by which he meant the kind of science that conforms to the dominate scientific paradigm. Similarly, we can think of 'normal religious education' as that which follows the evolving trajectory of mainstream English non-confessional religious education. A convincing case can be made that most of the responses to identified weaknesses in contemporary English religious education considered in earlier chapters are deeply conservative in nature. For example, Butler-Sloss believes that religious nurture is educationally inappropriate in all (publicly) funded schools, thus bringing to expression efforts to remove religious nurture from schools that were first initiated in the 1970s and 1980s on the basis of the equation of faith education with indoctrination. By comparison, the position of Liam Gearon, considered in Chapter 9, is much more radical, for he questions the religious and educational appropriateness of non-confessional religious education. Although his critique of non-confessional religious education is not finally convincing, it does show that he is sufficiently confident of his academic identity to challenge accepted ideas that are foundational to current theory and practice in English religious education. What is convincing is his perception that a radical reconfiguration of the field of religious education is needed to restore its intellectual and educational credibility.

The missing perspectives

One further feature that emerges from our review of responses to weaknesses in English religious education is what can be called 'the missing perspectives', i.e., potential sources of relevant insight and knowledge that have been overlooked.

Comparative research

Attention has already been given to Friedrich Schweitzer's comments about the lack of attention to research findings in the RE Commission Report and in English religious education more widely. He also provides a specific illustration of this limitation, when he notes (2018: 516) that 'more and more the future development of Religious Education has become an international issue, especially in Europe (quite independently of the EU)'.

> The internationalisation of the discussion corresponds to the insight that decisions about Religious Education should be based on scientific analysis and empirical research which can no longer be seen as limited to one's own country. Moreover, international-comparative aspects should also play a role, as a broader basis for considered judgment. From my perspective this holds true although the new Report does not make reference to such considerations but presents itself as a document arising from a broad but only national hearing and drafted by a committee bringing together voices exclusively from the UK.
>
> *(Schweitzer 2018: 516–517)*

Schweitzer is drawing attention to the insularity of much theorising and research in religious education in Britain. Not only does the Commission on Religious Education's Report neglect to include an international perspective or national perspective from outside Britain, such neglect is common to every contribution considered in our review of responses to the current crisis (with the exception of Liam Gearon's). Is there anything to be learnt from a comparative perspective on religious education? It seems not, and the problem is not confined to British religious educators. As Schweitzer and Peter Schreiner have observed elsewhere (2019: 2):

> It seems to be the rare exception that international groups of researchers would be working on certain problems and even more, that the solutions for certain problems or at least the analysis of such problems offered by individuals

or groups in the field would become part of the common cumulative knowledge upon which religious education should built in the future.

Even strategies and curriculum initiatives that have been implemented and assessed in other national contexts, on occasions with negative results, are not deemed worthy of interest or regarded as relevant by English religious educators (see Schweitzer 2018: 518–519). What are the reasons for this form of intellectual isolationism? It may be that we have been telling ourselves for too long that Britain is a 'world leader in religious education in public schools' (Miller 2009: 6); as world leaders, presumably we have nothing to learn from elsewhere. It may reflect the small pool of researchers in religious education; it may be that a lack of facility in foreign languages among religious educators shuts us off from learning about the practice of religious education in other national contexts (though this complaint needs to be qualified by the fact that many religious educators from other national contexts publish research in English; see Altmeyer 2010, for example). Whatever the reasons, it is to be regretted. There is much to be learned from attention to other national contexts. Such studies can be conceptualised into two broad categories: comparative studies that aim (as the name implies) to compare the nature of religious education or some aspect of it in different national contexts, e.g., a comparison of school texts, pedagogy or curriculum content and how it is determined (see Meyer 2001; Schreiner 2017); and studies that confine themselves to one ('foreign') national context, from which British religious educators can draw comparisons and contrasts (see Ubani 2013).

Social and political philosophy

The insularity of religious education from other disciplines and fields of research has no more dramatic illustration than its failure to engage with social and political philosophy. One of the main themes of modern religious education is how to respond to religious and moral diversity in society and this is precisely the same theme that has been central to social and political philosophy since the 1970s (see Kymlicka 2002: 327–376). A plausible case can be made that John Rawls's *A Theory of Justice* (1971), the most influential book in political philosophy in the last 50 years, can be interpreted, in part, as an attempt as respond to the issue of diversity in society, for the point of departure for his concept of 'justice as fairness' is that the 'benefits and burdens of social cooperation' are *unevenly* distributed in societies (Rawls 1971: 5); in other words, there is diversity in their distribution. The theme of diversity became much more central in Rawls's later *Political Liberalism* (1996: 3–4), in fact it becomes *the* central issue:

> The political culture of a democratic society is always marked by a diversity of opposing and irreconcilable religious, philosophical, and moral doctrines. Some of these are perfectly reasonable, and this diversity among reasonable

doctrines political liberalism sees as the inevitable long-run result of the powers of human reason at work within the background of enduring free institutions. Thus… what are the grounds of toleration so understood and given the fact of reasonable pluralism as the inevitable outcome of free institutions?… [H]ow is it possible for there to exist over time a just and stable society of free and equal citizens, who remain profoundly divided by reasonable religious, philosophical, and moral doctrines?

In response Rawls (1996: 133–172) developed the idea of 'overlapping consensus'. In an overlapping consensus, citizens endorse a common set of laws, those central to the maintenance of a stable and just society, for different reasons: each citizen supports a political conception of justice for reasons internal to his or her own comprehensive doctrine. The challenge of how to develop the political virtue of toleration is a related theme (Rawls 1996: 58–62 and 196–200). Toleration, as conceived by Rawls, recognises the existence of irreconcilable differences in (what he calls) 'comprehensive doctrines': the challenge is how to create and maintain social institutions given profound differences between 'free and equal' citizens. This orientation is interesting because it contrasts with the orientation of much theorising by English religious educators; either as with John Hull (discussed in Chapter 8) and Geoff Teece (2005; see the reply by Barnes & Wright 2006) where religious difference is ultimately explained away as each religion secures salvation for its adherents, or as with postmodern theorists such as Robert Jackson (1997 and 2004) where religious difference becomes so personalised and individualised that toleration is reduced to accommodating differences that have become insignificant and unimportant, given that religious differences lack substantive epistemic or social form (see Barnes 2014: 126–217). Neither approach, in the last analysis, takes difference and diversity sufficiently seriously, consequently genuine toleration, that is toleration interpreted as the need to develop social strategies and personal qualities to 'accept the other' who espouses a different 'comprehensive doctrine' is not strictly required.

Any dialogue with political philosophy on issues of joint interest and concern requires both acts of interpretation and critical judgements on which position in political philosophy is best supported and best serves the interests of education. The writings and commitments of John Rawls provide an obvious resource for religious educators, even though they have been almost completely overlooked by British educators, albeit with one important exception, that of Daniel Moulin (2009), who draws on them to 'construct a just and fair pedagogy, which is truly liberal in its assumptions'. Along with James Robson, Moulin (2012) has also employed Rawls's concepts of reasonable pluralism, overlapping consensus and hypothetical contract to defend both the educational legitimacy of faith schools and the non-compulsory attendance by pupils at acts of collective worship in religiously unaffiliated schools. The general lack of interest in political philosophy, however, is not the case elsewhere. Manfred Pirner (2015a, 2015b, 2015c and 2018) has made positive and extensive use of Rawls's ideas in a series of articles and essays that address issues that are central to religious education in pluralist societies, that of how religious education can contribute to the 'common good', and of the role that should be accorded to rights in religious education. By contrast, Bernhard Grümme (2015) has entered into dialogue with the political philosophy of Jurgen Habermas (who also is a dialogue partner for Pirner 2015a and 2015c). Both Pirner and Grümme are German religious educators and both can be regarded as particularly well-informed representatives of a much broader and deeper engagement by German religious educators with political philosophy than is the case with British religious educators. It is hoped that by calling attention to the relevance of political philosophy to religious education, interest will be stimulated to interact with and appropriate some of the ideas and some of the analyses of political philosophers. (Elsewhere I have attempted to initiate such a dialogue by drawing on and interacting with the 'agonistic philosophy' of the English political philosopher, John Gray 1995 and 2000; see Barnes 2010).

Theology

Since the 1970s and the transition from confessional to non-confessional religious education in (what are now termed) community schools, the contribution of theology, in its different forms, has been neglected as an explicit theme in English religious education and as a relevant dialogue partner (though not in other national contexts; see the substantial study of Schröder 2012). For many religious educators the transition represented a welcome release from Christian confessionalism in schools, the practice of which was viewed as being grounded in conservative forms of Christian theology and the hegemony of the Christian churches over education. Multi-faith religious education self-consciously perceived itself as opposed to confessionalism and accordingly looked to the newly emerging subject of religious studies for inspiration rather than to theology. The prejudice against theology continues among many religious educators; reinforced perhaps by the fact that the majority of religious education teachers may not now identify themselves with any particular religion (see Miller & McKenna 2011: 177–178, in which they record that only three out of ten teachers in their small sample regard religion as 'important' in their lives). The problem is that theology is perceived as inherently confessional and therefore illegitimate as a dialogue partner or as having any relevance to religious education with its commitment to diversity, 'neutrality' and inclusivity (as in Alberts 2007).

One noteworthy historical exception to the marginalisation of theology in non-confessional religious education is the work of Trevor Cooling, who 'argued [originally in the 1980s] that contemporary phenomenological approaches were misrepresenting Christianity by not giving enough attention to the central place of theological beliefs in Christians' lives' (Pett & Cooling 2018: 258; also Cooling 2000). In response he developed the 'concept-cracking' approach (Cooling 1994). 'It represented an attempt to shift pedagogy towards more explicit emphasis on... religious material' (Pett and Cooling 2018: 258), by endeavouring to show the central role of beliefs and doctrines in Christianity and its practice. Accordingly, any attempt to understand Christianity in religious education, even non-confessional religious education, needs to attend to its theological beliefs and doctrines. More recently, others have returned to the challenge of developing a pedagogy that has the potential to provide a nuanced and accurate representation of Christianity in schools, this time drawing on the insights and commitments of narrative theology. This new resource which enshrines a theologically-based pedagogy is called 'Understanding Christianity' (Pett et al. 2016). It comprises 31 units of work for teachers of 4–14-year-olds, with teaching and learning strategies, classroom resources, and artwork to connect core concepts with the wider salvation narrative of Christianity, which is regarded as its defining concept. As with 'concept-cracking' this new approach aims to provide an understanding of Christianity that is equally appropriate to the aims and rationale of religious education in non-religious schools as it is appropriate to Christian schools. What is important about this resource is that it is a serious attempt to meet the criticism, expressed by Inspectors and others that too many pupils are leaving school with a very limited understanding of Christianity, particularly of its central beliefs.

Theology is relevant to religious education once the important role of beliefs and doctrines in the different religions is appreciated—Christian theology, Islamic theology, etc. Such an appreciation is consistent with the aim of providing an understanding of religions and is properly distinguished from attempts to convert or to inculcate religious faith. The final section of Chapter 3 developed this position and argues for the 'rehabilitation' of (certain aspects of) theology within non-confessional religious education.

The views of pupils

The views of pupils are notably absent in the responses to identified weakness in religious education that have been considered. Theirs is the absent voice; and while it can be acknowledged that their views ought not to determine the nature and content of religious education, for reasons discussed in Chapter 2, this does not entail that their opinions and perceptions are completely without relevance. We live in an age when market research is an essential element of business, when surveys of customer satisfaction are conducted by both public and private institutions and when focus groups are established to elicit opinions and to anticipate public responses on a range of subjects, yet not one of the responses to identified weaknesses in religious education refers to the opinion of pupils. None of the writers and researchers considered in earlier chapters consulted pupils on their proposals about the future direction of religious education and none of the writers referred to pupils' attitudes to religious education as currently practised. Not one single source interacts with the extensive quantitative and qualitative data on pupils' beliefs and their perceptions of the practice of religious education produced by the *Does Religious Education Work?* project (Conroy et al. 2013: 189–217). Its findings are completely ignored, even though they are highly pertinent to many of the issues central to the practice of religious education. Is it because the findings were not congenial to the 'preconceived' solutions to weaknesses? In almost all cases where positive social attitudes were canvassed, pupils at Catholic schools expressed the highest levels of commitment. For example, responses to the question, 'Do you believe your school has helped you to get along better with members of other religious groups?' showed that those who attended 'denominational Christian schools' were most likely to respond positively then those who attended 'diverse (community) schools' (Conroy et al. 2013: 208). Such evidence, while ignored, is surely relevant to the educational legitimacy of confessional schools and confessional religious education.

There are three distinguishable broad areas of research about pupils and young people that are relevant to religious education: their beliefs and values and the influences that have a bearing on these; their perceptions and experience of curriculum religious education—its content and pedagogy, its relevance and importance, etc.—and, finally, the form of religious education that they would like to receive—its aims, content and means of delivery, etc. The beliefs, values and commitments of young people have been extensively researched and there is a wealth of data available to religious educators, and although some reference is made to this by a number of the writers considered in earlier chapters, their interest is exclusively confined to the observation that young people are increasingly inclined to be sceptical about the claims of institutional religion and to construct their own personal set of beliefs and values. Well supported research findings that show high correlations between religious belief and positive social behaviour and attitudes in young people are not considered as relevant to the role of religion in schools and in religious education. A strong case can be made that much more research needs to be conducted on the views of pupils about the religious education they receive in schools. Equally, those who write about religious education need to interact with current and future research findings, whether they find them congenial to their preconceived beliefs and theories or not.

One of the conclusions of the *Does Religious Education Work?* project, was that 'much Religious Education failed to locate religious ideas in their historical and discursive contexts' (Conroy et al. 2013: 224). The analogous comment can be said about recent writings and research of religious educators: too little attention is given to the genealogical history of the beliefs, ideas and commitments that have shaped and moulded religious education into what it is now. The systemic weaknesses of what it is now will not be overcome without a critical, reflexive engagement with the past and the ways in which the ideas of the past shape the present. 'Those who cannot remember the past are condemned to repeat it' (Santayana 1905: 284). This judgement when applied to English religious education could read, 'Those who choose to ignore the past are condemned to live with its negative effects.'

BIBLIOGRAPHY

Advisory Group on Citizenship (1998) *Education for Citizenship and the Teaching of Democracy in Schools* (the Crick Report). London: QCA.

Alberts, W. (2007) *Integrative Religious Education in Europe.* Berlin: Walter de Gruyter.

Aldridge, D. (2015) 'The case for Humanism in religious education,' *Journal of Beliefs and Values*, 36(1): 92–103.

All Party Parliamentary Group (2013) *Religious Education.* London: APPG.

Altmeyer, S. (2010) 'Competences in inter-religious learning,' in K. Engebretson, M. de Souza, G. Durka and L. Gearon (eds) *International Handbook of Inter-religious Education.* Dordrecht: Springer.

Alves, C. (1991) 'Just a matter of words? The religious debate in the House of Lords,' *British Journal of Religious Education*, 13(3): 168–174.

American Academy of Religion (2010) *Guidelines for Teaching about Religion in K–12 Public Schools in the United States.* Available HTTP: <https://www.aarweb.org/sites/default/files/pdfs/Pub lications/epublications/AARK-12CurriculumGuidelines.pdf> (accessed 27 March 2019).

Anscombe, E. (1958) 'Modern moral philosophy,' *Philosophy*, 33 (January): 1–19.

Anttonen, V. (2000) 'Sacred,' in W. Braun and R. T. McCutcheon (eds) *Guide to the Study of Religion.* London: Cassell.

Arnal, W. and McCutcheon, R. (2012) *The Sacred Is the Profane: The political nature of 'Religion'.* New York: Oxford University Press.

Association of Muslim Social Scientists (2004) *Muslims on Education: A position paper.* Richmond: AMSS.

Astley, J. (1994) *The Philosophy of Christian Religious Education.* Birmingham, Alabama: Religious Education Press.

Astley, J. and Barnes, L. P. (2018) 'The role of language in religious education,' in L. P. Barnes (ed.) *Learning to Teach Religious Education in the Secondary School: A companion to school experience.* London: Routledge.

Barnes, L. P. (2007) 'The disputed legacy of Ninian Smart and phenomenological religious education: a critical response to Kevin O'Grady,' *British Journal of Religious Education*, 29 (2): 157–168.

Barnes, L. P. (2009) 'An honest appraisal of phenomenological religious education and a final, honest reply to Kevin O'Grady,' *British Journal of Religious Education*, 31(1): 69–72.

Barnes, L. P. (2010) 'Enlightenment's Wake: Religion and Education at the Close of the Modern Age,' in G. Durka, E. Engebretson and L. Gearon (eds) *International Handbook of Inter-Religious Education: International Handbooks of Religion and Education*, Vol. 4: Philadelphia: Springer.

Barnes, L. P. (2013) 'Muslim terror, religious violence and representations of religion in the liberal democratic state,' in C. A. Lewis, M. B. Rogers, K. M. Loewenthal, R. Amlôt, M. Cinnirella and H. Ansari (eds) *Aspects of Terrorism and Martyrdom: Dying for good, dying for God*. Lewiston: Edwin Mellen Press.

Barnes, L. P. (2014) *Education, Religion and Diversity: Developing a new model of religious education*. London: Routledge.

Barnes, L. P. (2015a) 'Human rights, religious education and the challenge of diversity: A British perspective,' in M. L. Pirner, J. Lähnemann, H. Bielefeldt (eds) *Menschenrechte und inter-religiöse Bildung: Referate und Ergebnisse des Nürnberger Forums 2013*. Berlin: EB-Verlag.

Barnes, L. P. (2015b) 'Humanism, non-religious worldviews and the future of Religious Education,' *Journal of Beliefs & Values*, 36(1): 79–91.

Barnes, L. P.(2018) 'Universal, unconditional forgiveness: a critical response to Professor Giannini', *Journal of Religious Ethics*, 46(4):784–792.

Barnes, L. P. and Wright, A. (2006) 'Romanticism, representations of religion and critical religious education,' *British Journal of Religious Education*, 28(1): 65–77

Barnes, L. P. and Felderhof, M. (2014) 'Reviewing the Religious Education Review,' *Journal of Beliefs and Values*, 35(1): 108–117.

Bates, D. (1996) 'Christianity, culture and other religions (Part 2): F H Hilliard, Ninian Smart and the 1988 Education Reform Act,' *British Journal of Religious Education*, 18(2): 85–102.

Bell, C. (1992) *Ritual Theory, Ritual Practice*. Oxford: Oxford University Press.

Bell, C. (1997) *Ritual: Perspectives and dimensions*. Oxford: Oxford University Press.

Bernard of Clairvaux (2014 [1126–1141]) *On Loving God*. West Monroe, Louisiana: Athanasius Press.

Best, R. (ed.) (1996) *Education, Spirituality and the Whole Child*. London: Cassell.

Bhikhu, P. (1982) *Marx's Theory of Ideology*. London: Croom Helm.

Bigger, S. (ed.) (1999) *Spiritual, Moral, Social, and Cultural Education: Exploring values in the curriculum*. London: David Fulton.

Blackham, H. J. (1964) 'A humanist view of religious education,' *Learning for Living*, 4(2): 19–20.

Blair, A. (1996) Leader's speech, Blackpool. Available HTTP: <http://www.britishpoliticalspeech.org/speech-archive.htm?speech=202> (accessed 12 April 2019).

Bornkamm, G. (1971) *Paul*. London: Hodder and Stoughton.

Bottomore, T. B. (1981) *Modern Interpretations of Marx*. Oxford: Blackwell.

Bowie, R. A. (2017) 'The rise and fall of human rights in English education policy? Inescapable national interests and PREVENT,' *Education, Citizenship and Social Justice*, 12(2): 111–122.

Brewer, J. D. (2011) *Religion, Civil Society, and Peace in Northern Ireland*. Oxford: Oxford University Press.

Brine, A. (no date) ALAN'S BLOG. Settlements – what's all this about settlements! – Alan Brine. Available HTTP: <http://www.reonline.org.uk/news/alans-blog-settlements-whats-all-this-about-settlements-alan-brine/> (accessed 24 January 2019).

British Humanist Society (1967) *Religion in Schools: Humanist proposals for state-aided schools in England and Wales*. London: BHA.

Brown, A. (2002) 'The statutory requirements for religious education 1988–2001: Religious, political and social influences,' in L. Broadbent and A. Brown (eds) *Issues in Religious Education*. London: Routledge.

Brown, C. G. (2009) *The Death of Christian Britain: Understanding secularisation 1800–2000*, 2nd edition. New York and London: Routledge.

Bultmann, R. (1964) 'Is exegesis with presuppositions possible?' in *Existence and Faith: Shorter writings of Rudolf Bultmann*. London: Collins, Fontana.

Burkard, T. and Rice, S. T. (2009) *School Quangos: An agenda for abolition and reform*. London: Centre for Policy Studies.

Butler-Sloss, E. (2015) *Living with Difference: Community, diversity and the common good*. Cambridge: Woolf Institute. Available HTTP: <https://corablivingwithdifference.files.wordpress.com/2015/12/living-with-difference-online.pdf> (accessed 26 March 2019).

Cairo Declaration on Human Rights in Islam (1990) Available HTTP: <http://www.fmreview.org/sites/fmr/files/FMRdownloads/en/FMRpdfs/Human-Rights/cairo.pdf> (accessed 27 March 2019).

Canning, J. (2005) *A History of Medieval Political Thought 300–1450*. London: Routledge.

Carolei, D. (2018) How is Oxfam being held accountable over the Haiti scandal? Blog entry. Available HTTP: <http://eprints.lse.ac.uk/89096/1/politicsandpolicy-how-is-oxfam-being-held-accountable-over-the-haiti.pdf> (accessed 3 November 2018).

Chater, M. (2000) 'To teach is to set free: Liberation theology and the democratisation of the citizenship agenda,' *British Journal of Religious Education*, 23(1): 5–14.

Chater, M. (2012) What's worth fighting for in RE? Available HTTP: <http://www.reonline.org.uk/news/whats-worth-fighting-for-in-re/> (accessed 1 March 2019).

Chater, M. (2014) 'The fire next time? A critical discussion of the National Curriculum Framework for RE and the policy recommendations in the Review of Religious Education in England,' *British Journal of Religious Education*, 36(3): 256–264.

Chater, M. and Erricker, C. (2013) *Does Religious Education Have a Future?* London: Routledge.

Chorley, G. (1984) 'Cowper-Temple Clause,' in J. M. Sutcliffe (ed.) *A Dictionary of Religious Education*. London: SCM Press.

Clarke, C. and Woodhead, L. (2015) *A New Settlement: Religion and belief in schools* (Westminster Faith Debates). Available HTTP: <http://faithdebates.org.uk/wp-content/uploads/2015/06/A-New-Settlement-for-Religion-and-Belief-in-schools.pdf> (accessed 26 February 2019).

Clarke, C. and Woodhead, L. (2018) *A New Settlement Revised: Religion and belief in schools* (Westminster Faith Debates). Available HTTP: <http://faithdebates.org.uk/wp-content/uploads/2018/07/Clarke-Woodhead-A-New-Settlement-Revised.pdf> (accessed 10 May 2019).

Cohen, S. (2011) *Folk Devils and Moral Panics: The creation of the Mods and Rockers*. London: Routledge.

Cohen, A. B. and. Johnson, K. A. (2011) 'Religion and Well-being,' A paper presented at the Yale Center for Faith and Culture consultation on Happiness and Human Flourishing, sponsored by the McDonald Agape Foundation. Available HTTP: <https://faith.yale.edu/sites/default/files/cohen_and_johnson_1.pdf> (accessed 02 November 2018).

Cole, W. O. (1976) 'Texts within contexts: The Birmingham Syllabus and its handbook,' *Learning for Living*, 15(4): 127–128.

Commission on Religious Education in Schools (1970) *The Fourth R: Durham Report on Religious Education*. London: SPCK Publishing.

Commission on Religious Education (2017) *Interim Report: Religious Education for All* London: Religious Education Council of England & Wales. Available HTTP: <https://www.

commissiononre.org.uk/wp-content/uploads/2017/09/Commission-on-Religious-Educa
tion-Interim-Report-2017.pdf> (accessed 27 March 2019).

Commission on Religious Education (2018) *Final Report: Religion and Worldviews: The way forward. A national plan for RE.* London: Religious Education Council of England and Wales. Available HTTP: <https://www.commissiononre.org.uk/wp-content/uploads/2018/09/Final-Report-of-the-Commission-on-RE.pdf> (accessed 25 February 2019).

Conroy, J. C., Lundie, D., Davis, R. A., Baumfield, V., Barnes, L. P., Gallagher, T., Lowden, K., Bourque, N. and Wenell, K. (2013) *Does Religious Education Work? A Multi-dimensional investigation.* London: Bloomsbury.

Cooling, T. (1994) *Concept Cracking: Exploring Christian beliefs in school.* Nottingham: Stapleford Centre.

Cooling, T. (2000) 'The Stapleford Project: Theology as the basis for religious education,' in M. Grimmitt (ed.) *Pedagogies of Religious Education.* Great Wakering: McCrimmons.

Copley, T. (2005) *Indoctrination, Education and God.* London: SPCK.

Copley, T. (2008a) *Teaching Religion: Sixty years of religious education in England and Wales.* Exeter: University of Exeter Press.

Copley, T. (2008b) 'Non-indoctrinatory religious education in secular cultures,' *Religious Education,* 103(1): 22–31.

Cruickshank, M. (1964) *Church and State in English Education: 1870 to the present day.* London: Macmillan.

Cusack, C. (2011) 'Review: The Death of Christian Britain: Understanding Secularisation 1800–2000, by Callum G. Brown,' *Journal of Religious History,* 35(2): 268–269.

Cush, D. (1999) 'The relationships between religious studies, religious education and theology: Big brother, little sister and the clerical uncle?' *British Journal of Religious Education,* 21 (3): 137–146.

Cush, D. and Robinson, C. (2014) 'Developments in religious studies: A dialogue with religious education,' *British Journal of Religious Education,* 36(1): 4–17.

Dembour, M-B. (2010) 'Critiques,' in D. Moeckli, S. Shah, S. Sivakumaran and D. Harris (eds) *International Human Rights Law.* Oxford: Oxford University Press.

Department for Children, Schools and Families (DCSF) (2009) *Religious Education in English Schools: Non-statutory guidance 2009.* Nottingham: DCSF Publications. Available HTTP: <https://webarchive.nationalarchives.gov.uk/20100209115319/http://www.qcda.gov.uk/libraryAssets/media/8222-DCSF-Religious_Ed_in_Eng-consultation-FINAL.pdf> (accessed 26 February 2019).

Department for Children, Schools and Families (DCSF) (2010) *Religious Education in English Schools: Non-statutory guidance 2010.* London: DCSF Publications. Available HTTP: <https://assets.publishing.service.gov.uk/government/uploads/system/uploads/attachment_data/file/190260/DCSF-00114-2010.pdf> (accessed 27 February 2019).

Department of Education (DoE) (2013) *Improving the Spiritual, Moral, Social and Cultural (SMSC) Development of Pupils: Departmental advice for independent schools, academies and free schools.* London: DoE.

Department of Education (DoENI) (2007) *Core Syllabus for Religious Education.* Available HTTP: <https://www.education-ni.gov.uk/sites/default/files/publications/de/religious-education-core-syllabus-english-version.pdf> (accessed 25 March 2019).

Diener, E., Suh, E., Lucas, R., and Smith, H. (1999) 'Subjective well-being: Three decades of progress,' *Psychological Bulletin,* 125(2): 276–302.

Dinham, A. and Shaw, M. (2015) *RE for Real: The future of teaching and learning about religion and belief.* Available HTTP: <https://www.gold.ac.uk/media/documents-by-section/departments/research-centres-and-units/research-units/faiths-and-civil-society/REforREaveb-b.pdf> (accessed 27 February 2019).

Eagleton, T. (2007) *Ideology: An introduction*, Updated edition. London: Verso.

Education Act (1944) London: HMSO.

Education (National Curriculum) (England) Order (2000) London: HMSO.

Education Reform Act (1988) London: HMSO.

Eliade, M. (1958) *Patterns in Comparative Religion*. London: Sheed and Ward.

Eliade, M. (1959) *The Sacred and the Profane*. New York: Harcourt, Brace & Jovanovich.

Felderhof, M. (2012) 'Secular Humanism,' in L. P. Barnes (ed.) *Debates in Religious Education*. London: Routledge.

Felderhof, M. and Thompson, P. (eds) (2014) *Teaching Virtue: The contribution of Religious Education*. London: Bloomsbury.

Ferguson, N. (2014) *The Great Degeneration: How institutions decay and economies die*. London: Penguin Books.

Field, C. D. (2017) *Secularization in the Long 1960s: Numerating religion in Britain*. Oxford: Oxford University Press.

Fitzgerald, T. (2000) *The Ideology of Religious Studies*. New York: Oxford University Press.

Foucault, M. (1991) *Discipline and Punish: The birth of the prison*. Harmondsworth: Penguin Books.

Francis, L. J. (2010) 'Religion and happiness: Perspectives from the psychology of religion, positive psychology and empirical theology,' in I. Steedman, J. R. Atherton, E. Graham (eds) *The Practices of Happiness: Political economy, religion and wellbeing*. London: Routledge.

Freathy, R. J. K. and Parker, S. G. (2013) 'Secularists, Humanists and religious education: Religious crisis and curriculum change in England, 1963–1975,' *History of Education*, 42 (2): 222–256.

Freathy, R. J. K. and Parker, S. G. (2015) 'Prospects and problems for Religious Education in England, 1967–1970: Curriculum reform in political context,' *Journal of Beliefs & Values*, 36(1): 5–30.

Freeden, M. (2003) *Ideology: A very short introduction*. Oxford: Oxford University Press.

Freud, S. (1957) *Complete Psychological Works of Sigmund Freud, vol. XI: 'Five lectures on psychoanalysis. Leonardo da Vinci. Other works'*. London: Hogarth Press.

Freud, S. (1961) *Complete Psychological Works of Sigmund Freud, vol. XXI: 'The future of an illusion. Civilization and its discontents. Other works'*. London: Hogarth Press.

Gadamer, H-G. (1975) *Truth and Method*. London: Sheed and Ward.

Gallagher, E. and Worrall, S. (1982) *Christians in Ulster, 1968–80*. Oxford: Oxford University Press.

Gaskin, J. C. A. (1984) *The Quest for Eternity: An outline of the philosophy of religion*. Harmondsworth: Penguin Books.

Gaskin, J. C. A. (1987) *Hume's Philosophy of Religion*. London: Macmillan.

Gearon, L. (2012) 'European religious education and European civil religion,' *British Journal of Educational Studies*, 60(2): 151–169.

Gearon, L. (2014) *On Holy Ground: The theory and practice of religious education*. London: Routledge.

Gearon, L. (2015) 'Education, security and intelligence studies,' *British Journal of Educational Studies*, 63(3): 263–279.

Gillborn, D. (2008) 'Tony Blair and the politics of race in education: Whiteness, doublethink and New Labour,' *Oxford Review of Education*, 34(6): 713–725.

Gravel, S. and Lefebvre, S. (2012) 'Impartialité et neutralité autour du programme Québécois Ethique et culture religieuse,' in M. Estivalèzes and S. Lefebvre (eds) *Le Programme d'Ethique et Culture Religieuse. De l'exigeante conciliation entre le soi, l'autre et le nous*. Ville De Québec: Presses de l'Université Laval.

Gray, J. (1995) *Enlightenment's Wake: Politics and culture at the close of the Modern Age*. London: Routledge.

Gray, J. (2000) *Two Faces of Liberalism*. New York: The New Press.

Gray, J. (2004) *Heresies: Against progress and other illusions*. London: Granta Books.

Gray, J. (2008) *Black Mass: Apocalyptic religion and the death of Utopia*. London: Penguin Books.

Gray, J. 'Critiques of Utopia and Apocalypse.' Available HTTP: <http://fivebooks.com/interview/john-gray-on-critiques-of-utopia-and-apocalypse/> (accessed 21 March 2019).

Green, M. and Elliot, M. (2010) 'Religion, health, and psychological well-being,' *Journal of Religion and Health*, 49(2): 149–163.

Griffiths, P. (1999) *Religious Reading: The place of reading in the practice of religion*. New York: Oxford University Press.

Grimmitt, M. (1973/1978, 2nd edition) *What can I do in RE?* Great Wakering: Mayhew-McCrimmon.

Grümme, B. (2015) *Öffentliche Religionspädagogik: Religiöse Bildung in pluralen Lebenswelten*. Stuttgart: W. Kohlhammer.

Halstead, J. M. and Taylor, M. J. (eds) (1996) *Values in Education and Education in Values*. London: Routledge Falmer.

Hand, M. 'Why "Religion and Worldviews" is a non-starter.' Available HTTP: <https://blog.bham.ac.uk/socialsciencesbirmingham/2018/10/10/religion-and-world-views/> (accessed 20 February 2019).

Hanf, T. and El Mufti, K. (eds) (2015) *Policies and Politics in Teaching Religion*. London: Nomos/Bloomsbury.

Hannam, P. and Biesta, G. (2019) 'Religious education, a matter of understanding? Reflections on the final report of the Commission on Religious Education,' *Journal of Beliefs & Values*, 40(1): 55–63.

Hayward, J. (1996) *Elitism, Populism, and European Politics*. Oxford: Oxford University Press.

Heiler, F. (1961) *Erscheinungsformen und Wesen der Religion*. Stuttgart: Kohlhammer.

Helmer, C. (2011) 'Theology and the study of religion: A relationship,' in T. Lewis (ed) *The Cambridge Companion to Religious Studies*. Cambridge: Cambridge University Press.

Hervieu-Léger, D. (1999) *Le Pèlerin et le converti. La religion en movement*. Paris: Flammarion.

Hick, J. (1989) *An Interpretation of Religion: Human responses to the transcendent*. London: Macmillan.

Hinnells, J. R. (ed.) (1970) *Comparative Religion in Education*. Newcastle: Oriel Press.

Hirsch, E. D. (1967) 'Gadamer's theory of interpretation,' in E. D. Hirsch *Validity in Interpretation*. New Haven: Yale University Press.

Hirst, P. (1965) 'Liberal education and the nature of knowledge,' in R. D. Archambault (ed.) *Philosophical Analysis and Education*. London: Routledge & Kegan Paul.

Hirst, P. (1966) 'Educational Theory,' in J. W. Tibble (ed.) *The Study of Education*. London: Routledge & Kegan Paul.

Hirst, P. (1972) 'Christian education – A contradiction in terms,' *Learning for Living*, 11(4): 6–11.

Hirst, P. and Peters, R. (1970) *The Logic of Education*. London: Routledge & Kegan Paul.

Hollenbach, D. (2008) *The Common Good and Christian Ethics*. Cambridge: Cambridge University Press.

Hull, J. M. (1984) *Studies in Religion and Education*. Lewes, UK: The Falmer Press.

Hull, J. M. (1989) 'The content of religious education and the 1988 Education Reform Bill,' *British Journal of Religious Education*, 11(2): 59–61, and 91.

Hull, J. M. (1992) 'The transmission of religious prejudice,' *British Journal of Religious Education*, 14(2): 69–72.

Hull, J. M. (2000) 'Religionism and Religious Education,' in M. Leicester and S. Modgil (eds) *Spiritual and Religious Education*. London: Falmer Press.

Hume, D. (2000 [1738]) *A Treatise of Human Nature*. Oxford: Clarendon Press.

Jackson, R. (1990) 'Religious studies and developments in religious education in England and Wales,' in U. King (ed.) *Turning Points in Religious Studies*. Edinburgh: T & T Clark.

Jackson, R. (1995) 'Religious education's representation of "religions" and "cultures",' *British Journal of Educational Studies*, 43(3): 272–289.

Jackson, R. (1997) *Religious Education: An interpretive approach*. London: Hodder and Stoughton.

Jackson, R. (2004) *Rethinking Religious Education and Plurality: Issues in diversity and pedagogy*. London: Routledge Falmer.

Jackson, R. (2013) 'Religious education and human rights.' Available HTTP: <http://faith debates.org.uk/wp-content/uploads/2013/09/1330520267_Robert-Jackson-final-text-a s-delivered.pdf> (accessed 27 March 2019).

Jackson, R. (2015a) 'Misrepresenting religious education's past and present in looking forward: Gearon using Kuhn's concepts of paradigm, paradigm shift and incommensurability,' *Journal of Beliefs & Values*, 36(1): 64–78.

Jackson, R. (2015b) 'The politicisation and securitisation of religious education? A rejoinder,' *British Journal of Educational Studies*, 63(3): 345–366.

Jackson, R. and Everington, J. (2017) 'Teaching inclusive religious education impartially: An English perspective,' *British Journal of Religious Education*, 39(1): 7–24.

Jakobsen, J. R. (1996) 'Ideology,' in L. M. Russell and J. S. Clarkson (eds) *Dictionary of Feminist Theologies*. London: Mowbray.

Johnston, D. and Sampson, C. (1995) *Religion: The missing dimension of Statecraft*. New York: Oxford University Press.

Jüngel, E. (1992) *Christ, Justice and Peace*. Edinburgh: T & T Clark.

Kant, I. (1987 [1790]) *Critique of Judgment: Including the First Introduction*, trans. and intro. Werner S. Pluhar, with a foreword by Mary J. Gregor. Indianapolis: Hackett Publishing Company.

Kant, I. (1999 [1784]) *Practical Philosophy*. Cambridge: Cambridge University Press.

Kiwan, D. (2008) 'Citizenship education in England at the cross-roads? Four models of citizenship and their implications for ethnic and religious diversity,' *Oxford Review of Education*, 34(1): 39–58.

Kristensen, W. B. (1960) *The Meaning of Religion*. The Hague: Nijhoff.

Kuhn, T. S. (1970) *The Structure of Scientific Revolutions*, 2nd edition. Chicago: University of Chicago Press.

Kymlicka, W. (2002) *Contemporary Political Philosophy: An Introduction*, 2nd edition. New York: Oxford University Press.

Kymlicka, W. and Norman, W. (1994) 'Return of the citizen: A survey of recent work on citizenship theory,' *Ethics*, 104(2): 352–381.

Leeuw, G. van der. (1964) *Religion in Manifestation and Essence: A Study in Phenomenology*. London: Allen and Unwin.

Levine, A. (2007) *Political Keywords: A guide for students, activists and everyone else*. Malden, MA: Blackwell Publishing.

Lewis, T. (2011) 'On the role of normativity in religious studies,' in R. A. Orsi (ed.) *The Cambridge Companion to Religious Studies*. Cambridge: Cambridge University Press.

Locke, J. (2016 [1689]) *Second Treatise of Government and A Letter Concerning Toleration*. Oxford: Oxford University Press.

Long, R. (2016) *Religious Education in Schools (England): Briefing Paper Number 07167*, 7 July 2016. London: House of Commons.

Loosemore, A. (1993) 'Agreed Syllabuses of Religious Education: Past and present in England,' *Panorama. International Journal of Comparative Religious Education and Values*, 5: 79–95.

Louden, L. (2003) *The Conscience Clause in Religious Education and Collective Worship: Conscientious objection or curriculum choice?*Oxford: Culham Institute.

Louden, L. (2004) 'The conscience clause in religious education and collective worship: Conscientious objection or curriculum choice?' *British Journal of Religious Education*, 26(3): 273–284.

Lundie, D. (2018) *Religious Education and the Right of Withdrawal*. Liverpool: Liverpool Hope University. Available HTTP: <https://davidlundie.files.wordpress.com/2018/04/report-on-re-opt-out-wcover.pdf> (accessed 27 March 2019).

MacIntyre, A. (1985) *After Virtue: A study in moral theory*, 2nd edition. London: Duckworth.

MacIntyre, A. (1988) *Whose Justice? Which rationality?*London: Duckworth.

Malone, P. (1998) 'Religious education and prejudice among students taking the course studies in religion,' *British Journal of Religious Education*, 21(1): 7–19.

Martin, D. (2017) 'Book review: *Crossings and crosses: Borders, educations, and religions in Northern Europe*,' *Journal of Contemporary Religion*, 32(1): 169–170.

Marvell, J. (1976) 'Phenomenology and the future of religious education,' *Learning for Living*, 16(1): 4–8.

Marx, K. and Engels, F. (1965 [1845]) *The German Ideology*. London: Lawrence & Wishart.

McBride, M. (2015) *What Works to Reduce Prejudice and Discrimination? A review of the evidence.* Edinburgh: Scottish Government.

McCutcheon, R. (1997) *Manufacturing Religion: The discourse of sui generis religion and the politics of nostalgia.* New York: Oxford University Press.

McCutcheon, R. (2001) *Critics Not Caretakers: Redescribing the public study of religion.* New York: State University of New York Press.

McGrady, A. (2006) 'Religious education, citizenship and human rights: Perspectives from the United Nations and the Council of Europe,' in M. de Souza, G. Durka, K. Engebretson, R. Jackson and A. McGrady (eds) *International Handbook of the Religious, Moral and Spiritual Dimensions in Education*. Dordrecht: Springer.

McLaughlin, T. H. (2000) 'Philosophy and educational policy: Possibilities, tensions and tasks,' *Journal of Education Policy*, 15(4): 441–457.

McLellan, D. (1973) *Karl Marx: His Life and Thought*. London: Macmillan.

McLeod, H. (2005) 'Religion in the 20th Century,' *Journal of Modern European History*, 3(2): 205–230.

Meyer, K. (2001) 'The use of religious material in teaching "World Religions" in German and English schools,' *Panorama. International Journal of Comparative Religious Education and Values*, 13(2): 49–63.

Miethke, J. (2000) *De potestate papae: Die päpstliche Amtskompetenz im Widerstreit der politischen Theorie von Thomas von Aquin bis Wilhelm von Ockham*. Tübingen: Mohr Siebeck.

Mill, J. S. (1974 [1859]) *On Liberty*. Harmondsworth: Penguin Books.

Miller, J. (2009) 'So, what do the Toledo Guiding Principles have to do with me?', *Resource* 31(2): 6–9.

Miller, J. and McKenna, U. (2011) 'Religion and religious education: Comparing and contrasting pupils' and teachers' views in an English school,' *British Journal of Religious Education*, 33(2): 173–187.

Minney, R. (1975) *Of Many Mouths and Eyes*. London: Hodder & Stoughton.

Moffitt, B. (2017) *The Global Rise of Populism: Performance, political style, and representation.* Stanford, CA: Stanford University Press.

Morris, A. B. (2005) 'Academic standards in Catholic schools in England: Indications of causality,' *London Review of Education*, 3(1): 81–99.

Moulin, D. (2009) 'A too liberal religious education? A thought experiment for teachers and theorists,' *British Journal of Religious Education*, 31(2): 153–165.

Moulin, D. (2011) 'Giving voice to "the silent minority": The experience of religious students in secondary school religious education lessons,' *British Journal of Religious Education*, 33(3): 313–326.

Moulin, D. (2015a) 'Religious identity choices in English secondary schools,' *British Educational Research Journal*, 41(3): 489–504.

Moulin, D. (2015b) 'Doubts about religious education in public schooling,' *International Journal of Christianity & Education*, 19(2): 135–148.

Moulin, D. (2016a) 'Reported schooling experiences of adolescent Jews attending non-Jewish secondary schools in England,' *Race, Ethnicity and Education*, 19(4): 683–705.

Moulin, D. (2016b) 'Reported experiences of anti-Christian prejudice among Christian adolescents in England,' *Journal of Contemporary Religion*, 31(2): 223–238.

Moulin, D. and Robson, J. (2012) 'Doing God in a liberal democracy,' *Oxford Review of Education*, 38(5): 539–550.

Mudde, C. and Kaltwasser, C. R. (2017) *Populism: A very short introduction*. New York: Oxford University Press.

Murphy, N. (2018) *A Philosophy of the Christian Religion*. London: SPCK.

Nagle, T. (2012) *Mind and Cosmos: Why the materialist neo-Darwinian conception of nature is entirely false*. New York: Oxford University Press.

National Curriculum Council (1993) *Moral and Spiritual Education*. York: NCC.

National Association of Teachers of Religious Education (NATRE) (2017) *The State of the Nation: A report on Religious Education provision within secondary schools in England*. Available HTTP: <https://www.natre.org.uk/uploads/Free%20Resources/SOTN%202017%20Report%20web%20version%20FINAL.pdf> (accessed 16 May 2019).

Naugle, D. K. (2002) *Worldview: The history of a concept*. Grand Rapids, UK: Eerdmans.

Netto, B. (1989) 'On removing theology from religious education,' *British Journal of Religious Education*, 11(3): 163–168.

Niebuhr, H. R. (1951) *Christ and Culture*. New York: Harper & Row.

Nowell-Smith, P. H. (1954) *Ethics*. Harmondsworth: Penguin Books.

Nozick, R. (2001 [1974]) *Anarchy, State and Utopia*. Oxford: Blackwell.

ODIHR Advisory Council of Experts on Freedom of Religion or Belief (2007) *Toledo Guiding Principles on Teaching about Religions and Beliefs in Public Schools*. Warsaw: OSCE Office for Democratic Institutions and Human Rights (ODIHR).

Ofqual (2018) *Change in GCSE entries for EBacc subjects*. Available HTTP: <https://assets.publishing.service.gov.uk/government/uploads/system/uploads/attachment_data/file/712450/Report_-_summer_2018_exam_entries_GCSEs_Level_1_2_AS_and_A_levels.pdf> (accessed 21 March 2019).

Ofsted (2007) *Making Sense of Religion: A report on religious education in schools and the impact of locally agreed syllabuses*. Manchester: Ofsted.

Ofsted (2010) *Transforming Religious Education*. Manchester: Ofsted.

Ofsted (2013) *Religious Education: Realising the potential*. Manchester: Ofsted.

O'Grady, K. (2005) 'Professor Ninian Smart, phenomenology and religious education,' *British Journal of Religious Education*, 27(3): 227–237.

O'Grady, K. (2009) 'Honesty in religious education: Some further remarks on the legacy of Ninian Smart and related issues, in reply to L. Philip Barnes,' *British Journal of Religious Education*, 31(1): 63–66.

Orchard, S. (1991) 'What was wrong with religious education? An analysis of HMI reports 1985–1988,' *British Journal of Religious Education*, 14(1): 15–21.

Orchard, S. (1993) 'A further analysis of HMI reports on religious education: 1989–91,' *British Journal of Religious Education*, 16(1): 21–27.

Osborne, G. R. (2006) *The Hermeneutical Spiral*. Downers Grove: IVP.

Otto, R. (1958) *The Idea of the Holy: An enquiry into the non-rational factor of the idea of the divine and its relation to the rational*. London: Oxford University Press.

Pals, D. L. (2014) *Nine Theories of Religion*. New York: Oxford University Press.

Paluck, E. L. and Green, D. P. (2009) 'Prejudice Reduction: What do we know? A critical look at evidence from the field and the laboratory, *Annual Review of Psychology*, 60: 339–367.

Parker, S. G. (2018) 'Editorial: "Conscience", the right of withdrawal, and religious education,' *Journal of Beliefs & Values*, 39(3): 255–257.

Parker, S. G. and Freathy, R. J. K. (2011) 'Context, complexity and contestation: Birmingham's agreed syllabuses for religious education since the 1970s,' *Journal of Beliefs & Values*, 32(2): 247–263.

Parker, S. G.Freathy, R. J. K. and Aldridge, D. (2015) 'The future of religious education: Crisis, reform and iconoclasm,' *Journal of Beliefs & Values*, 36(1): 1–4.

Parsons, G. (1994) 'There and back again? Religion and the 1944 and 1988 Education Acts,' in G. Parsons (ed.) *The Growth of Religious Diversity*, vol. 2. London: Routledge.

Penner, H. H. (2000) 'Interpretation,' in W. Braun and R. T. McCutcheon (eds), *Guide to the Study of Religion*. London: Cassell.

Pépin, L. (2009) *Teaching about Religions in European School Systems: Policy issues and trends*. London: Alliance Publishing Trust.

Peters, R. S. (1970) 'Education and the educated man,' *Journal of Philosophy of Education*, 4 (1): 5–20.

Pett, S. (2017) 'Making a difference? Developing "understanding Christianity",' *Professional Reflection*, 34(2): 60–63.

Pett, S. and Cooling, T. (2018) 'Understanding Christianity: Exploring a hermeneutical pedagogy for teaching Christianity,' *British Journal of Religious Education*, 40(3): 257–267.

Pett, S., Blaylock, L., Christopher, K., Diamond-Conway, J., Matter, H. and Moss, F. (2016) *Understanding Christianity: Text impact connections – The Teacher's Handbook*. Birmingham: RE Today.

Pettman, J. (1992) *Living in the Margins: Racism, sexism and feminism in Australia*. St Leonards, NSW: Allen and Unwin.

Pew Research Center's Forum on Religion & Public Life (2012) *The World's Muslims: Unity and diversity*. Washington, DC: Pew Research Center.

Pirner, M. L. (2015a) 'Religion und öffentliche Vernunft. Impulse aus der Diskussion um die Grundlagen liberaler Gesellschaften für eine Öffentliche Religionspädagogik,' *Zeitschrift für Pädagogik und Theologie*, 67(4): 310–318.

Pirner, M. L. (2015b) 'Inclusive education – a Christian perspective to an "overlapping consensus",' *Journal of Christian Education*, 19(3): 229–239.

Pirner, M. L. (2015c) 'Re-präsentation und Übersetzung als zentrale Aufgaben einer Öffentlichen Theologie und Religionspädagogik,' *Evangelische Theologie*, 75(6): 446–458.

Pirner, M. L. (2016) 'Human rights, religions, and education. A theoretical framework,' in M. L. Pirner, J. Lähnemann and H. Bielefeldtd (eds) *Human Rights and Religion in Educational Contexts*. Dordrecht: Springer.

Pirner, M. L. (2018) 'The contribution of religions to the common good: Philosophical perspectives,' in M. L. Pirner, J. Lähnemann, W. Haussmann, and S. Schwarz (eds) *Public Theology, Religious Diversity and Interreligious Learning*. London: Routledge.

Pizza, M. and Lewis, J. R. (eds) (2009) *Handbook of Contemporary Paganism. Brill Handbook on Contemporary Religion 2*. Leiden and Boston: Brill.

Plantinga, A. (2000) *Warranted Christian Belief.* New York: Oxford University Press.

Plantinga, A. and Wolterstorff, N. (eds) (1984) *Faith and Rationality.* Notre Dame: University of Notre Dame.

Priestley, J. G. (2006) 'Agreed syllabuses: Their history and development in England and Wales 1944–2004,' in M. de Souza, K. Engebretson, G. Durka, R. Jackson, and A. McGrady (eds) *International Handbook of the Religious, Moral and Spiritual Dimensions in Education: Part 2.* Dordrecht: Springer.

Putnam, R. D. (2000) *Bowling Alone: The collapse and revival of American community.* New York: Simon & Schuster Publications.

Qualifications and Curriculum Authority (2004) *Religious Education: The non-statutory national framework.* London: QCA.

Rawls, J. (1971) *A Theory of Justice.* Cambridge, MA: Harvard University Press.

Rawls, J. (1996) *Political Liberalism.* New York: Columbia University Press.

Religious Education Council of England and Wales (RECEW) (2013) *A Review of Religious Education in England.* London: Religious Education Council of England and Wales. Available HTTP: <http://resubjectreview.recouncil.org.uk/media/file/RE_Review.pdf> (accessed 25 February 2019).

Religious Education Council of England and Wales (RECEW) (2018) *Falling numbers of Religious Studies GCSE entries suggests schools struggling to meet legal obligations.* Available HTTP: <https://www.religiouseducationcouncil.org.uk/news/falling-numbers-of-religious-studies-gcse-entries-suggests-schools-struggling-to-meet-legal-obligations/> (accessed 21 March 2019).

Rabinow, P. (ed.) (1991) *The Foucault Reader.* New York: Pantheon Books.

RE Today Services (no date) *Highest Number of Entries for Full Course GCSE in Religious Studies since 2002.* Available HTTP: <https://www.religiouseducationcouncil.org.uk/news/falling-numbers-of-religious-studies-gcse-entries-suggests-schools-struggling-to-meet-legal-obligations/> (accessed 21 March 2019).

Riley, J. (2015) *The Routledge Philosophy Guidebook to Mill's On Liberty,* 2nd edition. New York: Routledge.

Robson, G. (1996) 'Religious education, government policy and professional practice 1985–1995,' *British Journal of Religious Education,* 19(1):13–23.

Roebben, B. (2016) *Theology Made in Dignity: On the precarious role of theology in religious education.* Leuven, Belgium: Peeters.

Rose, D. (2003) 'The voice of the cultural restorationists: Recent trends in RE policy-making,' *The Curriculum Journal,* 14(3): 305–326.

Rousseau, J-J. (1997 [1762]) *Rousseau: The Social Contract and other later political writings,* edited by Victor Gourevitch. Cambridge: Cambridge University Press.

Santayana, G. (1905) *The Life of Reason: Reason in common sense.* New York: Charles Scribner's Sons.

Schaper, J. (ed.) (2009) *Die Textualisierung der Religion.* Tübingen: Mohr Siebeck.

Schlamm, L. (1992) 'Numinous experience and religious language,' *Religious Studies,* 28(4): 533–551.

Schleiermacher, F. (1928) *The Christian Faith.* Edinburgh: T & T Clark.

Schleiermacher, F. (1958) *On Religion: Speeches to its cultural despisers.* New York: Harper & Row.

School Curriculum and Assessment Authority (SCAA) (1996a) *Education for Adult Life: The spiritual and moral development of young people.* London: SCAA.

School Curriculum and Assessment Authority (SCAA) (1996b) *The National Forum for Values in Education and the Community: Consultation on values in education and the community, COM/96/608.* London: SCAA.

School Curriculum and Assessment Authority (SCAA) (1996c) *The National Forum for Values in Education and the Community: Final report and recommendations, SCAA 96/43*. London: SCAA.

Schools Council (1971) *Working Paper 36: Religious Education in Secondary Schools*. London: Evans/Methuen.

Schreiner, P. (2017) 'Different approaches—common aims: Current developments in religious education in Europe,' in J. Arthur and L. P. Barnes (eds) *Education and Religion: Major themes in education, Vol. 1*. Abingdon: Routledge.

Schröder, B. (2012) *Religionspädagogik*. Tübingen: Mohr Siebeck.

Schweitzer, F. (2018) 'Sacrificing Cinderella: Will giving up religious education help to establish a more promising successor?' *Journal of Beliefs & Values*, 39(4): 516–522.

Schweitzer, F. and Schreiner, P. (2019) *International Knowledge Transfer in Religious Education – A Manifesto for Discussion*. Available HTTP: <https://comenius.de/themen/Evangelische-Bildungsverantwortung-in-Europa/2019-Manifesto_on-International-Knowledge-Transfer-in-Religious-Education.pdf?m=1552893898> (accessed 15 May 2019).

Sire, J. (2009) *The Universe Next Door*. Downers Grove, IL: IVP Academic.

Sire, J. (2017) *Naming the Elephant: Worldview as a concept*. Downers Grove: IVP Press.

Sharpe, E. F. (1975) 'The phenomenology of religion,' *Learning for Living*, 15(1): 4–9.

Slotte, P. (2011) 'Securing freedom whilst enhancing competence: The "Knowledge about Christianity, Religions and Life Stances" subject and the judgment of the European Court of Human Rights,' *Religion and Human Rights*, 6(1): 41–73.

Smart, N. (1968) *Secular Education and the Logic of Religion*. London: Faber.

Smart, N. (1971) *The Religious Experience of Mankind*. London: Collins.

Smart, N. (1999) *World Philosophies*. London: Routledge.

Smidt, C. E. (2003) *Religion as Social Capital: Producing the common good*. Waco, TX: Baylor University Press.

Smith, J. W. D. (1969) *Religious Education in a Secular Setting*. London: SCM Press.

Stackhouse, Jr. J. G. (2014) *Need to Know: Vocation as the heart of Christian epistemology*. Oxford: Oxford University Press.

Stopes-Roe, H. V. (1976) 'The concept of a "life stance" in education,' *Learning for Living*, 16(1): 25–28.

Swindal, J. (2019) 'Faith and Reason,' in *The Internet Encyclopedia of Philosophy*. Available HTTP: <https://www.iep.utm.edu/faith-re/> (accessed 14 April 2019).

Taylor, C. (1989) *Sources of the Self*. Cambridge: Cambridge University Press.

Taylor, M. (1998) *Values Education and Values in Education: A guide to the issues commissioned by ATL*. London: Association of Teachers and Lecturers.

Teece, G. (2005) 'Traversing the gap: Andrew Wright, John Hick and critical religious education,' *British Journal of Religious Education*, 27(1): 29–40.

Teece, G. (2014) 'Review: Does religious education have a future? Pedagogical and policy prospects, by Mark Chater and Clive Erricker,' *British Journal of Religious Education*, 36(1): 108–112.

The Danish Institute for Human Rights (2013) *The Human Rights Education Toolbox*. Copenhagen: The Danish Institute for Human Rights.

The Education (National Curriculum) (England) Order 2000. London: HMSO.

Thielicke, H. (1990) *Modern Faith and Thought*. Grand Rapids, Michigan: Eerdmans.

Thiessen, E. J. (2011) *The Ethics of Evangelism: A philosophical defense of ethical proselytizing and persuasion*. Downers Grove, IL: IVP Academic.

Thiessen, E. J. (2018) *The Scandal of Evangelism: A biblical study of the ethics of evangelism*. Eugene, OR: Cascade Books.

Thompson, J. B. (1984) *Studies in the Theory of Ideology*. Cambridge: Cambridge University Press.

Thompson, P. (2004) *Whatever Happened to Religious Education?*London: Lutterworth Press.

Ubani, M. (2013) 'Threats and Solutions: multiculturalism, religion and educational policy,' *Intercultural Education*, 24(3): 195–210.

United Nations (1948) *Universal Declaration of Human Rights*. Available HTTP: <http://www.un.org/en/universal-declaration-human-rights> (accessed 27 March 2019).

United Nations (1981) *Declaration on the Elimination of All Forms of Intolerance and of Discrimination Based on Religion or Belief*. Available HTTP: <http://www.un.org/documents/ga/res/36/a36r055.htm> (accessed 27 March 2019).

van der Kooij, J. C., de Ruyter, D. J. and Miedema, S. (2013) '"Worldview": The meaning of the concept and the impact on religious education,' *Religious Education*, 108(2): 210–228.

van der Leeuw, G. (1964) *Religion in Manifestation and Essence: A study in phenomenology*. London: Allen and Unwin.

Wainwright, W. J. (1981) *Mysticism; A study of its nature, cognitive value and moral implications*. Brighton: Harvester Press.

Weber, M. (2001 [1904–1905]) *The Protestant Ethic and the Spirit of Capitalism*. London: Routledge.

Wiebe, D. (1999) *The Politics of Religious Studies*. New York: Palgrave.

Wilken R. L. (2019) *Liberty in the Things of God: The Christian origins of religious freedom*. New Haven: Yale University Press.

Wintersgill, C. B. and Brine, I. (2016) 'Government national agencies for inspection and curriculum development in RE,' in B. Gates (ed.) *Religion and Nationhood: Insider and outsider perspectives on religious education in England*. Tübingen: Mohr Siebeck.

Wittgenstein, L. (1958) *Philosophical Investigations*. Oxford: Basil Blackwell.

Wolterstorff, N. (2010) *Justice: Rights and Wrongs*. Princeton: Princeton University Press.

Wright, A. (1994) *Religious Education in the Secondary School: Prospects for religious literacy*. London: David Fulton.

Wright, A. (2000) *Spirituality and Education*. London: Routledge.

Wright, A. (2004) *Religion, Education and Post-Modernity*. London: Routledge Falmer.

Wright, A. (2007) *Critical Religious Education, Multiculturalism and the Pursuit of Truth*. Cardiff: University of Wales Press.

INDEX